Advance Praise for *The Coming American Renaissance*

"This book is a major contribution to our national economic debate. It is very convincing in arguing the thesis that America's best days lie ahead of us. Drawing together the threads of economic change, Moynihan also shows how average Americans can take advantage of them."

> Lawrence H. Summers
> Former Nathaniel Ropes Professor of Political Economy
> Harvard University

"Michael Moynihan has produced a well-researched, lively written rebuttal to the premise that the United States is on the decline. He argues eloquently that the next two decades will be marked by an American renaissance. I highly recommend it for anyone who cares about our future."

> Paul A. Allaire
> Chairman and CEO
> Xerox Corporation

"Amidst the election year rhetoric of doom and gloom, Michael Moynihan's *The Coming American Renaissance* refocuses us on the greatest insurance of U.S. competitiveness, technological leadership, and creativity—the American people themselves."

> George M. C. Fisher
> Chairman, President and Chief Executive Officer
> Eastman Kodak Company

"My reaction to Michael Moynihan's book is to wish I had written it. It expresses so well my thoughts after fifty years of competing with the world. The competition got a lot tougher but we learned to adjust. We are still the dominant economic world power and the coming American renaissance will make us still greater."

> Edmund T. Pratt, Jr.
> Former Chairman and CEO, Pfizer
> Former Chairman, The Business Roundtable

"For those who want evidence that America's future is bright and want a piece of the action, here's an information-packed guide to where it will happen, what businesses will thrive and why an open global economy, with highly mobile capital, technology, and talent, will work to the advantage of Americans. Pack up your computer, move to the exurbs and don't look back."

> Lewis M. Branscomb
> Director, Science, Technology and Public Policy
> John F. Kennedy School of Government,
>   Harvard University

"In this book, Michael Moynihan shows us the road signs and charts the course for America to move into a future of better times. His contribution is in using real evidence and events to urge optimism on the country's leaders and citizenry. It is a positive message we need to hear, and a stimulating book of ideas that we can apply to reach brighter economic, social, and personal destinations."

> Hon. John D. Rockefeller IV
> United States Senator, West Virginia

"This insightful book explains the complicated changes our economy is experiencing in straightforward practical terms. It is a serious work that should provoke a much-needed debate about our economic future."

> Hon. Ernest F. Hollings
> United States Senator, South Carolina

The Coming American Renaissance

HOW TO BENEFIT FROM AMERICA'S ECONOMIC RESURGENCE

Michael Moynihan

Simon & Schuster

FOR MY PARENTS

SIMON & SCHUSTER
Rockefeller Center
1230 Avenue of the Americas
New York, NY 10020

SIMON & SCHUSTER and colophon are registered trademarks
of Simon & Schuster Inc.

Designed by Elina D. Nudelman

Manufactured in the United States of America

1   3   5   7   9   10   8   6   4   2

Library of Congress Cataloging-in-Publication Data

Moynihan, Michael, date
    The coming American renaissance : how to benefit from America's
economic resurgence / Michael Moynihan.
        p.   cm.
    Includes bibliographical references and index.
        1. United States—Economic conditions—1945–   2. Economic
forecasting—United States.   I. Title.
    HC106.5.M69   1996
    330.973'001'12—dc20   96-19657
                                                                      CIP

ISBN 0-684-81207-X

Contents

Acknowledgments

This book reflects the aid and advice of many people, but one, my father, also Michael Moynihan, stands out so much that the name of the author might stand for two people. Early on, it occurred to me that this book would benefit from a multigenerational perspective. Beyond my own knowledge about America's and the world's recent history, I was able to draw on his firsthand knowledge of the middle of the century as well as his encyclopedic knowledge of world history. As someone who served in the Kennedy administration and spent many years working in France, he furnished unique insights into America's ascendancy in the postwar years and America in relation to Europe and Japan. He contributed a wealth of information on trade, economics, and other topics, drafted some sections, and meticulously reviewed the manuscript at every stage.

I would also like to thank my mother, Helena Smith Moynihan, for reviewing the manuscript with a literary eye. My brother, Eamon Moynihan, pored over the manuscript, finding numerous ways to improve it, and with his wife, Lene Skou-Moynihan, provided critical last-minute help with research. My sister, Molly Moynihan, read the book while taking care of a newborn baby.

Lorraine Negley had the difficult challenge of putting up with me during this period and provided a continuous stream of support, advice, and comments about the manuscript.

Dean Peterson, formerly chief economist for RJR Nabisco Inc., now with the U.S. delegation to the European Bank for Reconstruction and Development, provided key statistics, proved a sounding board for ideas, and shared with me his exhaustive knowledge of and unique insights into global trade.

I would like to thank Professor Lewis M. Branscomb of the Kennedy School at Harvard for making me at home in the world of technology policy *and for his prescient insights into the sources of competitive advantage. Other professors at the Kennedy School also shaped my thinking and the direction of this book. Professor John D. Montgomery shared with me his insights into the challenge of development. Professor Roger Porter, formerly chief domestic policy adviser to President Bush, provided me, as he does all his students, with a clear framework for looking at America's role in the world. Professor Robert Glauber, formerly undersecretary of the Treasury for Finance, pointed me in key directions early on in the course of my research.*

Countless business and government leaders were generous with their insights and time, including George M.C. Fisher, CEO of Eastman Kodak; Edward R. McCracken, CEO of Silicon Graphics; Dr. Mary Good, undersecretary of commerce for technology (who later became my boss); and my uncle, Senator Daniel P. Moynihan.

For my introduction to the world of business, I would like to thank A. Joseph Debe, the inventor of derivative securities, a true financial innovator and one of the smartest people ever to work on Wall Street. I could have had no better teacher in economics.

My editor, Fred Hills of Simon & Schuster, is the best in the business. He believed in the idea from the beginning, shepherded the book through the production process, and improved it at every stage. Burton Beals did an exceptional job line editing the book, proving that this art has not been lost in the age of the conglomerate. Hilary Black worked extra hours to bring the book out on time.

My agent, Sally Wofford Girand, was present at the creation and helped shape the proposal and book as it evolved, believing in it from start to finish.

I would also like to thank Rick MacArthur of Harper's *magazine for his insights into the publishing process and friendship.*

In addition, I would like to thank Dorothy Robyn of the National Economic Council, Pat Windham of the staff of the Senate commerce committee, Jeff Minich of Chemical Bank, Danny Lam, an authority on the computer industry at Auburn University, and others who read the manuscript. Alicia Hetzner of the World Bank and Shirley Dreifus, formerly of the Economist Intelligence Unit and now of Strategic Communications Group, hired me to work on many of these issues in other contexts.

Countless others provided data and insights, including Tom Ehrbar of the Economist Intelligence Unit and Joseph Neu of International Treasurer. *For their support and inspiration, I would like to thank my friends and classmates from the Kennedy School. Finally, I wish to thank all those people whose contribution is not diminished by my failure to mention them here.*

Writing this book was a challenge, but one that I always enjoyed. It is a wonderful thing to write about the future, particularly America's, which I believe will be bright. The world is interdependent, and history has shown that the good fortune of this country has boded well for the rest of the world. And so there is reason to be optimistic at the approach of the millennium.

Michael Moynihan

Washington, D.C.
May 1996

Introduction

On the eve of the next millennium, America has become a nation of Eeyores. Like Winnie the Pooh's pessimistic companion, we view every cloud as a sign of rain and every pot of honey as beyond our reach. For several years, a strange unease has afflicted the country. At times, it has simmered below the surface; at other times, it has erupted in rage. Every election turns on themes like anger against Washington, anxiety about the future, and the supposed need for radical change. But it is not just politicians, journalists, and religious fundamentalists who are fanning the flames of a perceived apocalypse. Since the 1980s, a variety of economists have argued that America is in decline. On the left, they focus on stagnant wages and the gap between rich and poor. On the right, they see America as crumbling beneath the weight of taxes. Both left and right find common ground in decrying the knowledge-based society. They proclaim that people without skills—the disadvantaged, according to Labor Secretary Robert Reich (who says they can be trained), the unintelligent, according to author Charles Murray (who says they cannot)—will not survive in the new economy.

Our national obsession with decline and disaster began in the 1980s. Historian Paul Kennedy, in *The Rise and Fall of the Great Powers*, argued that U.S. military overextension would vitiate America's economic power—a reference to the Reagan military buildup. A few years later, in *Preparing for the Twenty-first Century*, he predicted a growing gap between rich and poor, social upheaval, and the triumph of Asia. Lester Thurow, in *Head to Head*, projected that a unified Europe would soon wrest dominance of the world economy from the United States. Clyde Prestowitz, in *Trading Places: How We Allowed Japan to Take the Lead,* suggested that Japan had already displaced America at the top. The cry was taken up abroad. Former Japanese Diet member Shintaro Ishihara and Sony founder Akio Morita, in *The Japan That Can Say No: Why Japan Will Be First Among Equals,* claimed that Japan would soon inherit the earth.

Concern over America's economic future helped to defeat George Bush and make Bill Clinton president. But with the election of Clinton, a strange thing happened. Republicans, hitherto America's defenders, joined the chorus bewailing its future. To the din of intellectuals from the left and center who had been writing about American decline were now added new, louder voices from the right. In *Facing Up: How to Rescue the Economy from Crushing Debt and Restore the American Dream,* former Nixon adviser Pete Peterson argued that the deficit would destroy the country. Rush Limbaugh asked questions like "When you have an eight-year-old asking for a free lunch, isn't it safe to say the country's finished?"[1] Bob Livingston, a Republican congressman from Louisiana, warned that without a balanced budget amendment "There'll be joblessness, there'll be rampant disorder in the streets, and we simply won't be able to cope with that sort of misery."[2] Ross Perot, from the middle, raised the specter of disaster over issues such as NAFTA and the deficit.

In this cacophony of doom and gloom, it has become increasingly difficult to recognize the country we actually live in.

The America that actually exists, the one described by objective statistics and that you see when you walk out the door, is not in decline or on the verge of catastrophe. By any objective measure, the U.S. economy is thriving. Economic performance in recent years has not just been good, it has been better than in any comparable period of the postwar era. The overwhelming evidence suggests that America is not in decline at all but in the midst of an economic revival. Europe and Japan, meanwhile, and now China and Korea are languishing or facing major problems. The arguments of those who deny America a central role in the future require one to say either that the numbers are wrong or that they don't matter. They require nothing less than the suspension of reason or Eeyore's unflappable pessimism.

The American economic revival is broad-based, affecting manufacturing as well as services and lifting East and West, North and South. Examples of resurgence abound. In Utah, an explosion of software companies has created a new Silicon Valley. In Detroit, labor is in short supply as the U.S. auto business hums. From California to New Jersey, cable and telephone companies are competing to build the information highway. The numbers tell a singular story: gross domestic product growth, jobs, trade, output, productivity, and purchasing power all show the United States in the midst of a robust expansion.

But the current cyclical recovery is only a part of a larger story, the one I intend to tell in this book. For behind the current recovery lies a far greater phenomenon, that of America's long-term economic resurgence. From out of the turmoil of the 1980s and the crucible of the last recession, America has reinvented its economy. While the recovery has gotten little respect at home, it has taken the world by storm. Called Rising Sam in Japan, America is commanding new respect. What has changed about the U.S. economy in the last few years? New technologies, the end of the Cold War, and demographic changes, combined with uncommon natural advantages have put the United States back in the driver's seat. The story of this resurgence is one of enormous economic opportunity for individual Americans. Yet up to now it has remained untold.

How to reconcile such buoyant economic news with the preachings of gloom and doom? In part, the gloom reflects the Clinton administration's inclination in its early years to focus on problems, to create an environment for activism. Contrast that with the attitude of Ronald Reagan, a relentless optimist. At the same time, the current malaise derives most of its force from the series of unprecedented events that occurred in the 1980s and shook the nation's economic foundations. Ballooning trade deficits, the overnight disappearance of industries like consumer electronics, and the purchase by Japanese investors of American icons like Rockefeller

Center filled the headlines. Banks failed, crime rose, and speculators grew rich while deficits soared. It is the hangover from this period that informs even conservative critiques of the economy today.

But now enough time has elapsed for us to assess the real condition in which the United States emerged from the last business cycle and the end of the Cold War. Clearly the United States is stronger than ever. The end of the Cold War demilitarized the American economy. In the last five years, U.S. firms have re-engineered themselves with a vengeance, going well beyond competitors in other countries. A cheaper dollar has enhanced the competitiveness of American goods.

America's comparative position has also received help from problems abroad. Thurow failed to see the nationalism that would block European unity. Ishihara failed to predict the collapse of the Japanese bubble economy. Peterson ignored a steady decline in the federal deficit. The surge of new workers—baby boomers, immigrants, and women—that suppressed wages and productivity in the 1970s and 1980s has finally run its course. Moreover, few people foresaw the development of what promises to be the single greatest driver of growth and creator of wealth over the next two decades: the information superhighway, where America has a commanding lead.

The wisdom of a few years ago, that the United States was on its way out, has been overtaken by events that prove the contrary.

The next few decades will be decades of American economic revival and growth. But while a rising tide lifts all ships, some will go farther than others. Accordingly, this book also looks at how, why, and where the revival and growth will occur and what forms they will take.

A central tenet of this book is that Americans should build their future around industries in which the United States will prosper, work in ways that the economy will reward, and locate in regions of the country that will boom.

While no one can predict the details, the broad patterns of economic growth are clear from industry trends, census data about internal migration and rising incomes, demographics, and an analysis of what farsighted people are doing today.

The future will not reward those who resist change. Rather it will reward those who adapt most rapidly, whether they are countries, companies, or people. The years ahead will not be calm or devoid of crisis. The Italian Renaissance was a period of excitement and turmoil, too. It was a time that witnessed great art and architecture, important scientific discoveries, the first trips to America and Asia, and an explosion of trade, but it was also a time of war, political upheaval, social dislocation, and occasional calamities. It was not Utopian. Nevertheless, it was a period of rapid advancement for humanity. By comparison, the pace of political change over the next quarter century will be slow, but intellectual, scientific, and organizational change will occur rapidly.

In the pages that follow, I will examine in detail the human, natural, and technological resources that will enable the United States to thrive and prosper over the next quarter century, a period that will become, doomsayers to the contrary, an American Renaissance.

Behold America! . . .
See the steamers coming and going, steaming in or out of port
See, dusky and undulating, the long pennants of smoke . . .
Mark the spirit of invention everywhere, thy rapid patents
Thy continual workshops, foundries, risen or rising,
See from their chimneys how the tall flame-fires stream . . .
Think not our chant, our show, merely for products gross or
lucre—it is for thee, the soul in thee, electric spiritual!

—Walt Whitman
Song of the Exposition, LEAVES OF GRASS

Chapter 1

From Prosperity
to Prophecies of Doom
in Postwar America

In 1941, Henry Luce chose his photo magazine, *Life,* not his
newsmagazine, *Time,* or his business journal, *Fortune,* to publish an article that would become famous. Its title: "The American Century." Read one way, Luce's article was just another
editorial in support of joining the war in Europe, one of hundreds
to appear at the time. But read another way, Luce asked something
more of Americans, something that captured the public imagination. He summoned all Americans, those who liked pictures as well
as business, to join in an "American Century."

In 1941, this was a bold call to arms. The United States was still
escaping the Great Depression, and one in ten workers remained
unemployed. The birthrate was stagnant, having dropped to 19.4
per 1,000 in 1940 from a high of 28.1 in 1921. Abroad, Hitler,
Stalin, Mussolini, Franco, and the Japanese warlords had banished
democracy in vast stretches of Europe and Asia. These huge, foreboding problems were not lost on Americans. "We Americans are
unhappy," Luce wrote in his introduction. "We are not happy
about America. We are not happy about ourselves in relation to

America. We are nervous—or gloomy—or apathetic. As we look toward the future—our own future and the future of other nations—we are filled with foreboding." Luce's article anticipated sentiments heard today. But he went on to argue that the twentieth century belonged to America. And he proved to be right. Luce saw the strengths—in industry, size, and resolve—that would propel America into a role of leadership. At that point, the century had been a series of ups and downs. The 1920s had witnessed a boom and seen American products from jazz to typewriters grow famous abroad. But the century had begun with the era of big trusts, financial panics, and World War I, and the 1920s had ended with the stock market crash and the Depression, which threw millions out of work. America's golden age did not begin until World War II ended. We entered the war—as Luce had wanted—and won. And in 1945, America found itself the heir to Western civilization.

The Postwar Golden Era: 1945 to 1973

What is now called America's golden age actually began with the recession of 1945 and 1946 when the economy shrank by a quarter. The downturn was intensified by a huge war debt and a federal deficit of 35 percent of GDP, eighteen times that of today. Lest anyone romanticize this period, after the recession shortages of goods persisted, aggravated by a wave of strikes. Pent-up demand following years of self-deprivation enabled U.S. manufacturers to sell anything they could make at first. But as foreign producers recovered, they challenged American industries. When Swiss watches flooded the U.S. market, the American watch industry hired General Omar Bradley to argue that without workers able to assemble watches, America would lose its ability to make proximity fuzes for bombs. No sooner had America emerged from one war than it fought another, with an unsatisfactory conclusion, in Korea. The 1948 economic slowdown almost toppled President Harry Truman, the 1954 recession deprived President Dwight D. Eisenhower of a Republican Congress, and the 1960 recession tipped the scales for John F. Kennedy. The golden years were not always golden.

Moreover, to the extent the period was good for the United States, it was also good for the rest of the world. The American economy grew at an average annual rate of 3.66 percent—well above that of any comparable period before or since (although about equal to growth during the Clinton years). But some other countries grew faster,[1] including Germany and Japan at rates of 5.29 percent and 9.29 percent, respectively.[2] The USSR also grew rapidly and beat America into space with *Sputnik*.

What now seems to have been a golden age and the apotheosis of the American Century, the decades of the 1950s and 1960s, was far from perfect.

Yet, while anxiety levels ran high, there is no denying that these were, by and large, good years for the country. The G.I. Bill opened advanced education to the working classes, promoting a giant step into the middle class. Jackie Robinson joined the Brooklyn Dodgers in 1947, breaking the race barrier in professional baseball. By 1950, the U.S. birthrate had jumped to 25 per 1,000 and the baby boom was on. President Eisenhower's highway system, justi-fied as a national security measure, fueled expansion, the growth of the suburbs, and the triumph of the nuclear family. The middle class grew and prospered. American cars ruled the roads. Both literally and figuratively, America was in the driver's seat.

But as Europe began to recover, Italy, following Switzerland's trick with watches, made inroads into the U.S. shoe industry. Japan made inroads into steel, cameras, and textiles. By the 1960s, Japa-nese transistor radios dominated the world market. Still, the more advanced technological industries—the manufacture of television sets, copying machines, aircraft, and, most importantly, cars—remained American preserves. Clever new inventions in the 1960s such as the Polaroid Land camera for adults and the Whamm-o superball for children were American. After *Sputnik*, America's space program soon caught up to and passed the Soviets'. Apart from managing the business cycle, our principal challenge during the third quarter of the century was to stay ahead of the Soviet Union militarily and to contain Communist expansion. In Korea, Greece, Turkey, the Congo, and eventually Vietnam, the U.S. accepted the role of world's policeman. The country was so rich that, in 1965, President Lyndon Johnson set out to fight a war on poverty at the same time that the country was fighting a shooting war in Vietnam, his famous guns *and* butter. Still, these were the golden years—marked by war, assassinations, racial strife, and domestic upheaval, but nevertheless a period of economic security and rising wages, compared to which the present is so often found to fall short.

The End of Bretton Woods and American Hegemony

Every treasury has its limit, however, and in the early 1970s America reached its. Primarily as a result of fighting two wars at once, the United States experienced international cash flow problems. Under the Bretton Woods system of international currencies set up in 1944, the United States was obligated to buy back dollars for gold. But by the early 1970s, the dollars held by foreigners relative to the nation's reserves of gold at Fort Knox had risen to dangerous levels. In 1973, in the midst of wage and price controls that were intended to halt inflation, President Richard Nixon took the United States out of the system and off the gold standard. The end of the link between gold and the dollar cut the cord between money and goods, and allowed a surge of inflation. That same year, other engines of postwar prosperity were also losing steam.

The Productivity Slowdown

Nineteen seventy-three was a watershed year for other reasons as well. Throughout the postwar period, a "green revolution" in agriculture not only in the United States but worldwide had improved farm productivity, freeing up workers for other jobs. Farmhands and their families moved to cities and took jobs in industry. Between 1950 and 1970, no fewer than 4 million Americans left the farm, a disproportionate number of them black. (Thereafter, farm employment stabilized.)[3] The downsizing of American agriculture, far more than the downsizing we see today, created social problems that drove initiatives such as the Great Society. At the same time, however, the downsizing of agriculture around the world led to a more rational system of production and a great leap forward in productivity.

In the manufacturing sector in the 1960s, productivity growth was particularly sharp. Expanding world trade provided limitless markets for American goods, thanks largely to U.S. prosecution of free-trade policies. A sign visible from the railroad tracks in Trenton, New Jersey, now the worse for wear, reads TRENTON MAKES, THE WORLD TAKES, and so it did in the 1950s and 1960s. General Electric found ready markets abroad for its televisions and toasters. IBM sold electric typewriters and then computers. Coca-Cola took the world by storm. New technologies created new products whose manufacture and management engaged workers in more sophisticated chores, steadily improving their productivity. But then, in the early 1970s, productivity growth began to slump. This was not an exclusively American phenomenon but affected almost all of the industrial countries, even Japan.

Why did productivity slow after 1973? First, the round of inflation set off by the scrapping of the Bretton Woods agreement raised prices to consumers, depressing demand and therefore production. Second, the "green revolution," which began in Los Baños, the Philippines, took hold in India and then swept across the developing world, came to an end. Third, technology itself seemed to punk out in the early 1970s. The Austrian-born economist Joseph Schumpeter argued that growth requires transforming technologies—something like cars, personal computers, or the information highway—to ignite an economy. Between Tang, the powdered drink developed for astronauts, and the personal computer, technology hit a lull. Fourth, the oil shocks of 1973 and 1979 led companies to invest in ways to save energy instead of in new equipment.[4]

But I would argue that another factor played the largest role in the U.S. productivity slowdown: demographics. The movement of

workers from farms to factories, a form of internal migration that
expanded the pool of industrial labor, was a development that
initially helped productivity. However, in 1965, America opened its
borders to external immigrants after forty years of keeping them
closed. In other demographic developments, the first baby
boomers graduated from college in the 1970s and women began to
go to work in larger numbers. For the next decade and a half, these
three groups (which, of course, overlap) would dramatically swell
the bottom ranks of the American workforce. Beginning in the late
1960s, three pigs entered the mouth of the python, all competing
for similar jobs. They were too much for the python to easily
swallow.

A surplus of any commodity decreases its price. Not surprisingly,
real wage growth in the United States began to ebb and 1973 was
the turning point.

**Before 1973, productivity and wages in the United States rose
rapidly in tandem. Since then, they have continued to rise, but
only slowly.**

The increase in the labor supply was not enough to end the movement of textile jobs to countries with dirt-cheap wages. In unionized industries, the increase did not cause a decrease in wages. It
did, however, increase hiring, decrease investment in laborsaving
plant and machinery, spur the creation of low-wage non-union
service businesses such as fast-food restaurants (which benefited
from women leaving the home), and thus slow the growth of wages
and productivity.

In Europe and Japan, where the baby boom was less pronounced, wages continued to rise. While Europe's "guest workers"
performed some of the same jobs as the U.S. immigrants of the
1960s, most were temporary. Japan, on the other hand, never let
foreigners in; its guest workers were robots. Strong European
unions fought immigration and work by women, while the percentage of working women in Japan actually fell. Thus, a flood of new
workers in the United States caused the American economy to
diverge from those of Europe and Japan in the early 1970s, toward

services built on low-wage, low-skilled labor and insulated from exports and away from higher-skilled unionized heavy production.

Meanwhile, the 1973 oil shock, with its fourfold rise in the price of oil, compounded the problems of the West. Some economists calculate that the oil shock cost the average family about $2,000 in 1973 dollars. Inflation shot up, leading President Gerald Ford to jawbone Americans to "whip inflation now" (WIN). In 1974, depressed demand spurred a recession, and in 1976 the Ford administration ran a deficit of 4.4 percent of GDP, more than twice the size of the deficit today. The economy had barely recovered from the 1973 oil shock when it got hit with the 1979 shock, which resulted in galloping inflation and sky-high interest rates.

Stagflation—inflation coupled with stagnant growth—characterized the decade in Europe as well as in the United States.[5] Small wonder that neither Presidents Ford nor Jimmy Carter won reelection. A few years later, economies all over Latin America collapsed when an increase in the value of the dollar made petro-dollar loans impossible to pay down, causing an international banking crisis. In the late 1970s and early 1980s, commodity shortages appeared in everything from coffee to tin, as if to prove the forecasts of the Club of Rome in its influential 1972 booklet, *The Limits to Growth*.[6] This booklet presented the lily pad hypothesis, which states that, in a lily pond, a few lilies doubling daily soon cover the entire surface of the pond—the last open half of the pond in only one day. Although it proved to be wrong on almost every count, the work won a place in history as the bible of a generation of pessimists.

The Rise of Asian Competition

While most countries, including the United States and Japan (which still imports all its oil), took the oil shocks hard, others fared better. The Arab states, for example, won big in the 1970s. Also emerging strong from the 1973 watershed were the "four tigers," the newly industrializing countries in Asia: Taiwan, Hong Kong, Korea, and Singapore. All were inspired, if not guided, by the

Japanese model of export-led growth. Exports proved an excellent mechanism for industrialization as the system of open world trade held firm. And as these agricultural and mining economies industrialized, they experienced the same wondrous increases in productivity others had before them.

Moreover, the process was telescoped. It took England fifty-eight years, from 1780 to 1838, to double its income. It took the United States forty-five years, from 1839 to 1886, to accomplish that feat. It took Japan thirty-four years, during the Meiji Restoration from 1885 during the Matsukata stabilization to 1919, to industrialize. It took Brazil only eighteen years (1961 to 1979) and, more recently, Korea eleven years (1966 to 1977) and China ten years (1977 to 1987).[7]

Industrialization occurs more rapidly today because of faster and easier ways to transfer capital, institutions, and technology, as well as the mushrooming of world trade, which has created vast markets for manufactured goods.

Exports from Asia began to pour into the United States during the 1970s, some bearing American labels as American companies shifted production abroad. Imports from Japan grew, in particular. Yet, while these were not good years for the United States, they were not especially good for Europe or Japan either. (Japanese inflation hit 23 percent in 1974.) At the beginning of the 1980s, the United States was still widely considered the unquestioned economic leader of the world. America dominated computers, cars, televisions, airplanes, heavy equipment, and most other industries. When Ronald Reagan took office in 1981, he inherited a trade surplus and a budget that was almost balanced.

The 1980s

In the 1980s, America was ready for a man like Ronald Reagan. After the trials of the 1970s, voters wanted a president who would make them feel good. Reagan himself was an eternal optimist, and he had the good fortune to have a recession in the middle of his first term. In 1983, as the economy recovered, his popularity rose sharply.

In the 1980s, however, a complex set of factors converged to challenge America's economic performance. Whereas the United States entered the 1980s as the world's undisputed superpower, by the end of the decade many people were saying that it had lost its economic leadership. America's lingering gloom and self-doubt date from the 1980s. Three developments fueled this pessimism:

- The military buildup created a huge federal debt and debt service bill that linger to this day and continue to dampen people's spirits and consume their taxes.

- An exchange rate flip-flop boosted imports and eviscerated America's export sector, creating a series of trade deficits. This same flip-flop then enabled foreign investors to buy up significant portions of the U.S. economy.

- Competition from Japan and Asia caught American industry by surprise.

The economic competitiveness problems of the 1980s were onetime events that resulted from specific policies and historical circumstances.

The defining feature of the Reagan years were huge budget deficits that pumped billions of dollars into the economy and people's pockets. The deficits followed directly from a tax cut combined with a failure to cut spending and a full-blown military buildup.[8] After the 1981 tax cut, Reagan raised taxes, but not enough to cover the mounting cost of military spending. A series of budget deficits led to a mounting national debt, and soon huge amounts of interest had to be paid to the holders of that debt, many of whom were foreign. In a few short years, the sums involved grew staggering, and America became the largest debtor nation on earth. An administration that had said it would make America strong and independent had in fact bound it over to foreign moneylenders. Investors as well as pundits began to worry about the consequences if foreign investors stopped buying U.S. notes. Americans' anxiety level began to rise.

The Reagan deficits were the result of policies that, except for a few details, Republicans preferred to ascribe to Democrats. Instead of "tax and spend," Reagan practiced "borrow and spend." He professed to admire Roosevelt (the theme song of the 1984 convention was "Happy Days Are Here Again"), and their fiscal policies bore marked similarities. But borrowings of over a trillion dollars in the 1980s far exceeded borrowings by Roosevelt during the 1930s.

Looked at squarely, the Reagan years were the largest Keynesian experiment in history.

They also saw a shift of wealth from the poor and the middle class to the rich, worsening the plight of those at the bottom.[9] Conservative theorists argued that pain on the part of the poor was good because it would prompt them to work harder. Whatever one thinks of Reaganomics, there is no question that the deficits strongly stimulated the economy. Deficit spending helped create millions of new jobs. The 1980s boom was on.

The Reagan-Era Military Buildup

Between 1981 and 1986, U.S. military spending rose from 23 percent to 28 percent of the annual federal budget, or 7 percent of GDP. (Japan, by contrast, spends about 1 percent of GDP on its military.) Between 1980 and 1987, military spending rose by an average of about $50 billion a year. Since spending did not return to 23 percent until after 1990, the buildup cost the United States about half a trillion dollars in direct appropriations. But since the buildup was financed with debt that no one wanted to pay, it increased further through reverse amortization, which is what happens when you pay off less than the interest on a loan. Today, interest on the national debt costs taxpayers over $200 billion a year in interest alone, and the buildup cost a good deal more when one considers its effects on the private economy.

The buildup probably hastened the collapse of the Soviet Union by forcing it to try to match this spending blitz.[10] But in exchange, beyond fueling the deficit, it exacted a huge toll on the American economy:

- It starved spending on infrastructure. Spending on public housing, roads, airports—the traditional work of government—slowed to a trickle during the 1980s.[11]

- It raised interest rates, not only by competing for money but by adding an inflation premium to rates as financial markets began to worry that lawmakers would simply inflate their way out of the debt.

- It transformed a peacetime economy into a partially military one, enticing *Fortune* 500 companies to seek their share of the government largesse.

The intensification of the Cold War in the 1980s encouraged many firms to exchange consumer for government markets.

At the very moment foreign competition had begun to look frightening, a new market suddenly appeared that was free of foreign competition. Not surprisingly, many U.S. firms said good-bye to consumer markets and hello to the military paymaster. Like hardworking people offered a government welfare check, they quit their regular jobs. This realignment of investment created 2.1 million military-related jobs in the 1980s but destroyed many jobs in consumer manufacturing.

U.S. electronic firms, in particular, embraced military contracts. George Fisher, CEO of Eastman Kodak and formerly CEO of Motorola, observed, "Faced with Asian competition, many companies chose to enter commercial or military markets and abandon the mass market. They saw higher margins and less competition. In my view, the U.S. should have said we're going to hold on to the consumer electronics business no matter what. We didn't." While servicing the military, Motorola did manage to hold on to a consumer business in wireless phones and pagers. RCA and GE, on the other hand, sold out entirely (to the French company Thomson).

The Japanese, with their ready access to less expensive private capital, gladly picked up the pieces. In a few short years, most U.S. companies were out of the consumer electronics market.

At first, Americans paid little attention to this shift. If they thought about it at all, they consoled themselves with the reflection that the markets the Japanese were taking involved older technology.[12] Popular anxiety remained focused on the Soviet Union. And notwithstanding the vaunted Japanese management system, a high percentage of early Japanese successes involved little more than reverse engineering Western goods, changing or adding a feature or two, and manufacturing them more efficiently.[13]

Enter the videocassette recorder. In 1984, the VCR cracked the mass-market price barrier, and millions of Americans went out to buy one. *Time* magazine put the VCR on its cover. The scary thing about the VCR was that no U.S. firm actually made one (although Ampex, a U.S. firm, had invented the technology). In 1979, Sony had introduced the Walkman. In 1984, Philips, a Dutch corporation, and Sony introduced the compact disk player. Following on the heels of these other products, the VCR underlined the United States' impotence in this important sector. By the mid-1980s, it became almost impossible to buy an up-to-date camera, stereo, VCR, or other consumer electronic device that was made in the United States. Foreign producers seemed more efficient, more enterprising.

Foreign imports seemed omnipresent, while our own industries had retooled to make military hardware that was off limits to American consumers.

Ironically, the country got its first view of the military's top-secret stealth bomber in a television ad for a new Japanese luxury car from Nissan, launched in 1989. The ad used surprisingly accurate images of the still classified aircraft to help sell the car. Japan's triumph in consumer electronics and its success with cars emboldened some Japanese to write about their nation as a possible arbiter in the Cold War. Americans' anxiety level increased another tick.

The Reagan/Regan Exchange-Rate Flip-flop

The federal deficits that began to explode during the Reagan years had other negative consequences, notably high interest rates, which, in turn, drove up the dollar. After the second oil shock in 1979 triggered inflation,[14] Federal Reserve Board Chairman Paul Volcker, at the urging of the so-called monetarists, had raised rates to unheard-of levels. In 1980, the federal discount rate hit 13 percent, and in 1981 the fed funds rate rose to 17 percent. By reducing the growth in the money supply, this strategy worked. By the end of 1981, inflation had fallen to 6 percent. When Reagan entered office, the U.S. rates were still high but inflation had already tumbled. The Reagan deficits kept interest rates high even as inflation continued to fall, thus driving up real rates, or interest rates minus inflation.

As real interest rates climbed, dollars grew more attractive to foreigners. Lest that alone not raise the dollar, the Reagan administration made a high dollar a policy goal and the Treasury defended it in currency markets. "Strong dollar, strong country," as Treasury Secretary Donald Regan put it. Within a year or two, the dollar had become all powerful. By 1983, U.S. goods were expensive and foreign goods dirt cheap. America bought more than it sold, and the U.S. trade deficit was born.

Pessimists looking back on the early 1980s, as well as many observers at the time, saw the huge trade deficits that followed as evidence that American goods were no longer competitive. However, a closer examination reveals a different cause.

With the rise of the dollar after 1983, American exports declined across the board in virtually every industry—not only those in which foreigners were more productive or had real advantages—and against every other country.

The reason is simple: exchange rates. Blame for the evisceration of the American export sector falls squarely at the doorstep of the sky-high dollar and those in the Reagan administration who urged it higher. The sky-high dollar made foreign goods irresistibly attractive. In 1984, the United States began a recovery from the 1983 recession and experienced slingshot growth of 6 percent, led by consumer spending. Traditionally, when a country comes out of a recession, consumers load up on domestic products. In this case they loaded up on imports, which shot up $77 billion in a single year. Imports flooded into the country, accompanied by the giant sucking sound of dollars flooding out. Normally, as a country's recovery progresses, there is a natural tendency for its currency to strengthen, since demand for credit raises interest rates. Thus, the already strong dollar became even stronger and American consumers continued to load up on imports while American manufacturers took it on the chin.

While all U.S. manufacturers suffered, those that were most dependent on exports suffered most. Companies that sold primarily to the domestic market—such as Chrysler and U.S. Steel—could beg Washington for protection and get it (through import tariffs, voluntary quotas, and the like). Consequently, auto, steel, and textile companies, though they struggled during the mid-1980s, stayed in the ball game. But exporters dependent on overseas markets had no such card to play.

In the early 1980s, the single largest exporter in the United States, bigger than Boeing or any other company, was the tractor maker Caterpillar. The high dollar sent Cat sprawling and bleeding red ink as its exports dropped.

All U.S. manufacturers were hurt by the high dollar. The export sector was annihilated. Why did the Reagan people try to drive the dollar up? Because they put ideology ahead of economics. Like prideful potentates throughout history, they viewed a strong dollar as a symbol of a strong country. Accordingly, they did their best to keep it up. In addition, they supported high real interest rates (rates minus inflation)—a cause of the high dollar—since high rates let those who have money make more money by lending it out. Rentiers—people who make money on money—had suffered during inflation, and the administration was intent on refilling their coffers. The policy, however, proved brutal for U.S. manufacturers. (The high dollar also precipitated the Latin American and Eastern European debt crises; oddly, the Reagan administration escaped blame for this effect.) During the early and middle 1980s, U.S. exporters clamored for a lower exchange rate. Their cries were ignored for several years and then heard at precisely the wrong time. In 1986, the Reagan administration agreed with Germany, Japan, and its principal trading partners to lower the value of the dollar. This decision, reached at the Plaza Hotel in New York City and known as the "Plaza Accord," triggered the beginning of the bubble economy in Japan.[15]

Over the long term, a falling dollar should slow imports and boost exports, improving the balance of trade.[16] But in the short term, it forces consumers to pay more for imports they are already buying, which can increase the size of a trade deficit. That's exactly what happened after 1986. Equipped with credit cards, which underwent explosive growth in the mid-1980s, American consumers continued to buy imports that were rising in price, sending the trade deficit ever upward. Indeed, credit-happy American consumers remained hooked on imports for several more years, running their cards up to the limit. By this point, Japanese firms had virtually eliminated U.S. competition in a number of industries, such as consumer electronics, leaving consumers no choice but to buy foreign goods. Over the previous few years, foreign makers had established excellent distribution networks in the United States. American exporters had lost them overseas.

To cope with the rising yen, some Japanese producers, such as Sony, opened factories in the United States. Most, however, continued to sell goods made in Japan; the first Japanese auto plants in America imported almost all their components from Japanese suppliers. Thus, as the dollar fell, dollars began to leave the United States to pay for imports at an even faster rate than before. The question for Japanese firms was what to do with them.

They hit on the idea of investing them where they had found them: in the United States.[17] As the dollar dropped and the yen strengthened, American assets from real estate to blue-chip corporations to bonds grew ever cheaper for the Japanese. They responded by buying up assets such as Rockefeller Center (1985), Firestone Tire (1988), Inter-Continental Hotels (1988), CBS Records (1988), MCA (1990), and New York's AT&T building (1992). In a few cases, purchases of high-tech companies were blocked by the government. Even so, Japanese firms bought up a large portfolio of prime assets during the 1980s. Besides using their supply of dollars, Japanese firms could borrow cheaply in the Japanese capital market, which remained largely closed to foreigners. This let them bid more than Americans for any given asset. And while many of these purchases would later prove disastrous for the Japanese, Americans' anxiety levels rose another tick.

As the dollar fell, companies based in other countries also bought up many assets. The Canadian firm Seagram bought a 25 percent stake in Du Pont, British-American Tobacco bought American Brands, and Hoechst, the German chemical giant, bought Celanese in 1987. During the 1980s, English companies actually acquired more American assets than Japanese companies did. But few Americans noticed or cared about the British invasion. The Japanese purchases were frightening to Americans because the extent of Japan's future successes remained unknown and the memory of the war with Japan was still strong.

The Rise of Global Competition

Something else was happening: the rise of global competition. During the 1980s, global competition crept up slowly on the United States. It had three phases. At first, it appeared as imports. The Reagan administration's sky-high dollar of 1982 through 1985 opened a warehouse door through which imports flooded the country. In 1986, competition took on another guise as foreign companies began to buy up American assets. Suddenly, the global economy was setting up shop inside America's borders. Finally, at the end of the decade, global competition changed again, this time assuming the mask of restructuring. When the 1991 recession hit, corporate takeovers and restructuring—previously domestic phenomena—became linked with the global economy. The companies attributed the need to lay off tens or even hundreds of thousands of people to the need to cut costs to compete with foreign producers. To many from both the left and right, globalization began to look menacing.

THE JAPANESE MANAGEMENT CHALLENGE

By the beginning of the 1980s, the strength of the Japanese business challenge was already clear. William Ouchi published a book entitled *Theory Z: How American Companies Can Meet the Japanese Challenge* in 1981. Throughout the postwar era, Japanese delegations had been frequent visitors to U.S. plants. Now American firms became interested in Japan. A large number of gray-suited executives began hurtling toward the Land of the Rising Sun. What American managers found took them by surprise. American-style mass production had changed little from the 1920s, when Frederick Taylor had developed it using time-and-motion studies and other elements of scientific management.[18] Japanese firms had long since mastered the basic elements of American-style mass production, and for a number of years had been experimenting with new management ideas.

The single largest improvement Japan had discovered was a technique known as total quality control (TQC), later expanded into total quality management (TQM). Originally a statistical method for improving quality invented by American engineers at Western Union including Joseph Juran and W. Edwards Deming, refined during World War II, and then promptly forgotten in the United States, TQC had become gospel throughout corporate Japan. Deming, whom American industry had utterly dismissed, was a hero in Japan. An award named after him was the most sought-after honor in Japanese industry.

Since the 1950s, Japanese firms had been refining total quality control methods, and by 1980 they had a thirty-year head start on American firms. Whereas Japanese firms had shrunk manufacturing defects to practically nil through better design and statistical procedures, their American counterparts were still junking a hefty percentage of what came off the line or else sending it back for rework. Quality control in the United States typically consisted of a few inspectors catching some problems and letting others go. But TQC was only one Japanese innovation. In 1952, a Toyota engineer by the name of Taiichi Ohno had developed a concept called just-in-time (JIT) delivery to reconfigure factories in order to slash levels of inventory. Under the American system, suppliers typically delivered materials once a quarter, once a month, or once a week. Ample supplies were needed to ensure that mass production never stopped. Most assembly lines started up in the morning and ran until a bell went off at night. If a glitch occurred, somewhere on the line, the rest of the factory kept running and stock piled up in the aisles. American factories were typically messy and filled with excess stock or defective pieces destined for rework.

Under the Toyota system, parts were delivered "just in time" for use in the plant, several times a day. Total quality control carried out by its suppliers meant that Toyota did not have to worry about defective parts. Instead of running mindlessly, each portion of the assembly process ran only when prompted by the step ahead through a demand-pull system known as *kanban* that at first used simple hand-painted signs and later bar codes or wireless signals. If a glitch occurred, it stopped everything before it. This demand-pull, or "customer-driven," system enabled the Japanese to make small lots of a variety of products instead of large runs of one basic product. It gave customers the chance to buy products in all sorts of different colors with different "bells and whistles." Particularly in consumer electronics, this capability helped crush U.S. competition.

Japanese engineers had also long since abandoned the linear product development model—by which scientists invented something, then tossed it over the transom to engineers, who tossed it over the transom to manufacturing—in favor of an integrated team approach. (A shortage of technology and funds in the 1950s and 1960s had forced Japanese engineers to work together.) Japanese manufacturers believed in a concept called *kaizen,* or continuous improvement. Through mechanisms such as quality circles, they constantly tried to improve, or "tweak," processes to make them run better. Some of Japan's methods stemmed from traditional Japanese customs. During the Allied occupation of Japan after World War II, General Douglas MacArthur outlawed the prewar *zaibatsu* industrial groupings. In their stead, Japanese firms developed groups called *keiretsu* that permitted different companies to work together.

Besides horizontal *keiretsu*, which teamed manufacturers with trading companies with banks, large manufacturers developed vertical *keiretsu* with suppliers. By relying on suppliers to develop parts, cut costs, and improve quality, big companies could create new products faster and more cheaply. The interlocking networks of firms also provided so-called patient capital. Large firms typically owned pieces of suppliers and provided those suppliers with access to credit. The relationship between banks and customers went far beyond "relationship banking" in the United States, which, in any case, was giving way to transactional banking. The government also coordinated action in strategic industries, forcing companies to cooperate with one another. The system worked, particularly in manufacturing.

As the 1980s wore on, the Japanese machine hummed ever faster. By 1990, due largely to exchange-rate shifts, Japanese wage levels had passed American ones, and Japanese companies, facing a labor shortage, had introduced robots onto the shop floor. (The United States had led the robot industry in 1983 but largely abandoned it by 1990.) The use of robots grew rapidly. This industrial success gave way to financial success as Japanese manufacturers piled up money in Japanese banks and brokerage firms, which, with the help of the rise in the yen, soon became the largest, by far, in the world, despite operating in a manner and with technology that struck many American financial executives as old-fashioned.

Cheap Japanese Capital

Japan had a secret weapon whose importance is often overlooked: low-cost capital.

One explanation for Japan's success was the country's alleged long-term perspective. According to this view, so-called patient capital let Japanese firms take the long view. In contrast, quarterly reporting in the United States was said to encourage pursuit of the fast buck over long-term value. However, it so happens that interest rates dictate time horizons through the algebra of discounted cash flow analysis. While Japanese companies did think long-term and develop effective management techniques, particularly in manu- facturing, much of their success in the 1980s can be chalked up to cheap capital. Japanese managers reacted rationally to their low cost of capital by thinking long-term; American managers acted rationally by thinking short-term.

Why was Japanese capital so cheap? The Japanese people's high savings rate created a large pool of capital in Japan. In a totally free market, this money would have fled the country in search of higher returns abroad. But the market wasn't free due to constraints on flows of capital, so the money stayed in Japan. Minimal require- ments for military spending because of Japan's antimilitarist con- stitution further reduced competition for capital.

Thus, while there were other reasons why Japanese firms ac- cepted low returns relative to their American counterparts, a pri- mary one was their access to low-cost capital. If you can borrow at 1 percent, you can make money on a 3 percent return. In contrast, if you have to borrow at 10 percent, you need a 12 percent return to make a similar spread. Likewise, if the interest rate is a paltry 1 percent, investors have little choice but to invest in business. At 1 percent, capital is patient; at 0 percent, it is virtually dead. Lester Thurow points out that when Honda began to make automobiles, it accepted a 3 percent return on investment for years, a return that would have put it out of business in the United States.[19]

Japanese firms were also beneficiaries of a virtuous cycle of appreciating stock values during the 1980s. The prospect of ever- rising stock prices on Japan's market let firms cut their cost of acquiring capital to practically nothing and even let them borrow at negative interest rates. The trick was to sell bonds with stock warrants attached. The warrants generated the cash to pay interest.

In effect, the stock market boom let firms pay interest costs out of future equity. While this bubble popped in the early 1990s, for a while it created an incredible level of liquidity or, in laymen's terms, money from nothing.

OTHER LOW-COST COMPETITION

Japanese management methods drew much of the fanfare during the 1980s, but other countries did well, too. In the 1970s, South Korea ran trade deficits with the United States; by 1988, it was running a $10 billion surplus. South Korea even began selling cars in the United States. The country owed its good fortune not to any special management methods but to old-fashioned low-cost labor and overhead. The Reagan administration's high dollar gave it a foot in the American door. South Korea's story was similar to that of Taiwan, Hong Kong, and other Asian countries, whose exports to the United States soared after 1982.

The United States was getting beat two ways, the first way by Japan, new and terrifying, the second way by South Korea, Taiwan, and China, all too familiar.

The Asian countries had been making steady progress for some time. But in the 1980s they moved into high gear. One day, Indonesia was making sweaters; the next, it was making semiconductors.[20] The remarkable acceleration of technology diffusion resulted from a combination of improved communications technology, which let multinationals set up shop easily in far-flung areas, and the embodiment of more technology in machinery. In the past, technology had often had a strong craft element; engineers had often had to "tweak" a process to get it to work at all.

In the 1950s and 1960s, Americans pioneered the concept of franchising as a way to clone simple businesses such as retail stores and dry cleaners.

By the 1980s, companies had learned how to get complex factories up and running in a matter of months anywhere in the world, cloning plants the way McDonald's cloned restaurants.

In some countries, such as Malaysia, large-scale manufacturing had begun in the 1960s and had reached a critical mass—in terms of support services and skill base—by the 1980s. Improved information technology also made it possible to move capital far more rapidly than before. The accelerating speed of industrialization and globalization led people such as writer James Fallows to question the very theory of classical economics.

A FEAR OF CONVERGENCE

The possibility of convergence—the United States going down while Indonesia and Thailand went up—was particularly disturbing to anyone who worked for a salary. Reagan and Bush policy makers—who were more responsive to the needs of capital than to those of labor—lost little sleep over this problem. Supply-siders openly argued that the poor and middle class in the United States should have to work harder than the rich.[21] They viewed the increasing workload of those at the bottom as healthy.

There are many ways for a rich country such as the United States to trade with a low-wage country such as Thailand in order to lift the standard of living of both. The key is to let the low-wage country do the labor-intensive work and the rich country do the highly productive, knowledge- or capital-intensive work, so that each country can exploit its strengths. But by trying to keep wages down (the U.S. minimum hourly wage did not budge from \$3.35 between 1981 and 1990) and reduce safety and other regulations that were hampering old, seat-of-the-pants-style manufacturing, some Reagan policy makers appeared determined to compete with countries like Thailand in the low-end part of the job. In the early 1980s, economist Milton Friedman nostalgically recalled the days of the American sweatshop, when capitalists had easily been able to make money off immigrant labor, unhindered by regulations. Later, George Bush's first secretary of commerce, Robert Mosbacher, reportedly remarked, "What's the difference between wood chips and computer chips? They're both chips."

Many Americans began to get the sense that they were headed

downward. Their feelings found voice in books such as Juliet Schor's *The Overworked American*. Anger was directed at workplace competitors: white men focused on new workers—immigrants and women, as well as minorities—while the latter focused on white men or on one another. Meanwhile, those at the top were making fortunes. Junk-bond kings, corporate raiders, savings-and-loan operators, and others able to get their hands on the capital sloshing electronically around the world profited handsomely from the Reagan policies, though not always legally. More officials were indicted during the Reagan administration than during any other administration since that of Ulysses S. Grant.

"Greed is good" became the motto of the 1980s. Recalling the saying "In Adam's fall, we sinneth all," inscribed on Puritan school-children's hornbooks, the film *Wall Street* and the novel *Bonfire of the Vanities* railed at the new America. On Thursday, October 19, 1987, the stock market dropped 508 points, and while it subsequently recovered, the crash further rattled Americans' nerves. Also in 1987, an alarming number of savings-and-loan institutions began reporting problems. By 1989, hundreds were filing for bankruptcy, triggering the S&L crisis. Critics of lax regulation warned that commercial banks were at risk as well.

Magnifying all these threats to the American economy was the very speed of change, a function of improved information technology. It is one thing if a country's trade deficit edges up slowly. It is another if it goes from $38 billion to $155 billion in three years. The clear implication—an accurate one—was that the United States could no longer rest on its laurels for even a moment. Rapid change, change without respite, lay ahead. Americans were going to have to adjust to competition from developing countries and, some worried, work as hard and for as little as people there.

As though to confirm the predictions of doom, the economy went into full-blown recession in 1991. Companies that had loaded up on debt through leveraged buyouts, such as Federated Department Stores and Pan American Airlines, went bankrupt. As the recession veered toward a double dip, unemployment soared.

General Motors, besieged by foreign competition, announced layoffs of 130,000 workers, enough to fill two football stadiums. Economists warned that this new recession was different from all others and that America seemed pointed downward and headed for the certain disaster that doomsayers feared.

Chapter 2

America's Core Advantages

Had America continued on the path it was on at the beginning of the 1990s, it might well have experienced the disaster many feared. It didn't. By exercising resilience and self-corrective abilities, America changed course. As specific causes of its competitiveness problems, such as the high dollar of the mid-1980s, the Reagan deficits, and the S&L crisis, receded in time, America said no to decline, summoned up its resources, and reinvented its future. Year by year, industry by industry, and state by state America reclaimed leadership in the global economy and put itself back on track. The American Renaissance is only beginning and is full of opportunity and the chance of wealth. In later chapters, I will describe how it will unfold in different sectors and different states. But the companies and individuals that will make the most of the next few decades will leverage off of America's advantages. That means starting, investing in, or working for companies in industries that will thrive, studying subjects in which America will excel in the twenty-first century, and locating in regions that will fare the best. America's advantages, fortunately, are considerable.

From Sea to Shining Sea

Sheer size has long been a source of America's strength. The image of a continent rolling westward, up for grabs, full of opportunity, enthralled Europe's poor and fascinated aristocrats such as Alexis de Tocqueville. During the Civil War, an American visiting Paris proposed this toast: "I give you the United States, bounded on the north by the Aurora Borealis, on the south by the precession of the equinoxes, on the east by the primeval chaos, and on the west by the Day of Judgement!"[1] Since the country's founding, size has been not only a metaphor for the very audacity of the American enterprise but also a real source of advantage.

By any measure, the United States is a singular piece of real estate. It is bigger than Europe, not including the former Soviet Union, and three times the size of the European Union. It's about twenty-five times the size of Japan. Whereas smaller countries must purchase commodities, the United States exports everything from grain to lumber to cigarettes. The country is big enough that the presence of lucrative resources doesn't stunt the rest of the economy, as, for example, oil has done in smaller countries by bidding up prices.[2]

Geography and size have shaped the American economy through their role in driving expansion. During the second half of the nineteenth century, when the railroads boomed and the United States doubled its income, geography was no less than destiny.

The railroad boom—a real estate boom, more than anything else—drove frenzied activity on Wall Street and a wholesale revolution in commerce as companies arose to supply a national market.

America's huge size enabled it to benefit from the railroads more than other countries did. Large farms and ranches, bigger than those in Europe, produced both the need and the wherewithal for settlers to purchase tools, housewares, and firearms. As rail lines linked and towns grew, newly standardized products appeared to supply a national market. In the early part of the twentieth century,

America invented everything from canned foods to packaged cigarettes to national grocery chains such as A&P to mass production
and the very idea of brand-name products. To sell the products,
America invented modern advertising, which underwrote magazines and modern media.

**Besides goods, railroads moved people. Personal mobility kept
America from developing rigid social hierarchies.**

In the 1950s, geography became destiny once more, when Eisenhower's federal highway system further knit the country together.
Freeways replaced rails as the new arteries of national distribution.
The automobile industry thrived, and roads created a real estate
boom in the suburbs. McDonald's and other franchises began to
sprout up along the roadsides. National retail chains grew even more
popular and set up shop in a related invention, the shopping mall.
Franchising of everything from oil changes (Jiffy Lube) to tuxedo
rentals (Mr. Tux) soon branded services as well as burgers.

**In coming years, the United States will experience another eco-
nomic boom, thanks to electronic networks. And as with railroads a century ago and highways in the 1950s, the information
superhighway may be remembered more for the real estate
boom it drives than for anything else.**

In the 1980s, improved communications and air-conditioning
opened the South to development and industry. Today, new information networks have begun to carry economic activity to even the
furthest-flung reaches of the country. No other advanced, industrialized country has as much land for development as the United
States, which, in many ways, remains a developing country. One
third of the country is still owned by the federal government (one
half, west of the Mississippi), and much private land is "unim-
proved." America has the capacity to undergo undreamed-of levels
of development—at a cost to the country's beauty, to be sure, but to
an extent impossible in Japan or even Europe. The fastest-growing
states are now Nevada, Idaho, and Alaska.

Consider just one state, Utah. In 1847, the Mormons settled one of the least desirable places on earth, the area around the Great Salt Lake. They went there to escape persecution after their leader, Joseph Smith, and his son were shot dead in Illinois by a mob unhappy with their religious beliefs during the Second Great Awakening. They picked a place where they doubted anyone would bother them, and for more than a century they were right. An ethic of industry and a link to the railroad led to modest prosperity. But the Mormons' very isolation in the middle of a desert in the middle of the country limited their economic interaction with the rest of the world. In the days when proximity to a river or ocean guaranteed wealth, Salt Lake City, the capital of Deseret, as the Mormons called their state, was off the beaten track.

The construction of interstate highways, several of which cross in Salt Lake City, spurred growth in the 1960s and 1970s. Still the city remained comparatively obscure. But the growth of electronic networks and the knowledge economy has changed all that. Salt Lake City and the area around Provo and Brigham Young University have become a global software mecca and will grow in importance for years to come (see Chapter 7). As the economy has boomed, the area has gained population, housing, malls, commerce, and other multipliers of wealth. Whereas companies once looked for natural resources such as minerals, cheap energy, and proximity to transportation as foundations on which to build a business, increasingly they will look for inexpensive land in a temperate climate, universities, and an educated workforce. Utah sends the highest percentage of students to college of any of the fifty states.

Throughout the United States, plentiful land will facilitate the development of the exurbs.

The development of the information superhighway and retail innovations such as warehouse stores like Home Depot, Office Depot, and Wal-Mart will make it easier to live beyond the suburbs. New satellite cities such as those that have popped up in northern Virginia, outside Washington, D.C., enable people to work closer to where they live. But in many cases, it will be easier simply to work at home. Just as the railroads and highways let America take advantage of its physical size, so the information superhighway will make America's size an advantage once again. In contrast, Japan has no land available for economic growth and expansion, so exurbanization that takes advantage of the information highway is not a development option there.

The Japanese will have difficulty raising the quality of their housing due to the lack of buildable land and the sheer population density of the island.

According to some economists, successful trading economies such as Hong Kong and resource-poor countries such as Japan prove that physical endowments such as land and minerals no longer matter. But this viewpoint ignores the strange ways in which resource-poor countries must grow, if they grow at all. Hemmed in by their constraints, they grow in odd directions, like trees blocked in by walls. Japan's shortage of land, for example, is largely responsible for its poor housing stock relative to its wealth. To this day, housing advocates and developers must battle rice farmers, who control much of the developable land on the island. Japan's dependence on imports of raw materials accounts, in part, for its clinging to an outdated obsession with trade surpluses, which penalize consumers. And while a few countries such as Japan and Singapore have transcended their geographic limits, many in Africa, Asia, and Latin America have not.

Each generation of the Toyoda family, founders of Toyota, has started a new line of business. The current heirs have entered the business of prefabricated homes on the theory that the new generation needs homes the way the previous generation needed cars. Small Japanese homes do not comfortably support office activities and partly explain why "salarymen" stay out so late. Even those wealthier Japanese who build American-style houses must typically compromise on size; new Japanese houses are significantly smaller than those in the United States.

Not only are American homes larger than those in Japan, they are cheaper. In fact, housing is far more affordable in the United States than in any other industrialized country. According to PHH Home Equity, a Wilton, Connecticut–based relocation firm, "An upscale four-bedroom house costing close to $400,000 in the U.S. goes for a million in the outskirts of Paris and two million or more in the Tokyo area."[3]

Europe has more land available for development than Japan does, but again the continent's desire to remain self-sufficient in agriculture (and its limited land area) inhibit significant development. History and zoning have also imposed limits on change. In Italy, old houses are zoned as national treasures. While Europe remains a beautiful part of the world, development will play a smaller role than in the United States for the foreseeable future and drive considerably less growth and creation of jobs.

Possessing two coasts, the United States is uniquely poised to participate in both the older Atlantic and newer Pacific economies.[4]

How can the United States' advantage in physical size help the individual American? It will drive growth in both construction and retail commerce in coming years. (The specific directions this growth is likely to take are discussed in Chapter 7.) U.S. agriculture will continue to thrive as the General Agreement on Tariffs and Trade (GATT) and the North American Free Trade Agreement (NAFTA) open markets around the world. The growth of the information highway, combined with America's ample supply of land, will lead to the development of the new American homestead (see Chapter 7). More and more houses will be living/working space, containing provisions for a home office and souped-up terminals connecting to the information superhighway.

But some of the greatest benefits of America's size will be indirect. Services that cater to the new use of America's space will become huge international industries.

Just as McDonald's and Kentucky Fried Chicken first appeared in the United States following the creation of the national highway system but, a few years later, expanded overseas, so exurban innovations such as Home Depot and Wal-Mart are going international.

Wal-Mart is opening stores in Latin America. Electronic retail services developed to serve exurban dwellers will likewise find markets
overseas. Already, CompuServe dominates on-line commerce in
Europe. In an earlier era, America's size created products such as
canned foods (which could be shipped long distances), frozen
food, Sears, Roebuck catalog sales, the Western Union telegraph,
cheap cars, cheap mass-produced revolvers (far from civilization, guns were important), branded restaurants and hotels, aircraft, and airlines.

More recently, the size of the country has hastened the deregulation of long-distance telephone service, the development of on-line
and Internet services, cable television (to reach rural areas far away
from antennae), sport utility vehicles, and even credit cards (to
facilitate doing business in a country this large). In the future,
America's size will promote far more sophisticated on-line services,
even better networks, more warehouse stores, and a wireless revolution. Thus the long-term effects of America's size advantage may be
far greater than what immediately meets the eye.

Population and Market Size

The large size of its population is another advantage the United
States possesses over its principal competitors. America has about
twice the population of Japan, more than three times the population of Germany, and about as many people as Germany, Great
Britain, France, and Italy combined. It is not as big as Europe or
even the European Union, which now contains about 369 million
people. Were the European Union truly to unify, it would have the
same advantage in size over the United States that the United States
enjoys over Germany or France. But the United States is a unified
nation, whereas the European Union is only a trading bloc made of
disparate countries. The size and freedom of the American market
are, of course, what the European Union was designed to copy. But
while the E.U. will grow more functional in years ahead, the United
States' size and homogeneity will give it an advantage for decades
to come.

Furthermore, the American population is growing relative to that of other developed countries.

By 2025, the U.S. population will have risen by about 15 percent to 300.8 million, while the European Union's population will have dropped by about 1 percent.

The European Union may grow by acquiring new members, but then again so may the NAFTA trading bloc. Due to Japan's lack of land and an aging population, its population will fall as well. This means that the United States will enhance its size advantage over Japan by more than 15 percent and narrow the gap with the current European Union by a similar amount. As discussed at greater length in Chapter 3, the United States will also have more working-age people able to support the elderly and young in the early part of the twenty-first century than either Europe or Japan. It will see a rise not only in the working-age population but also in the quality of its workforce as a decline in the average age of workers due to the baby boom is reversed.

The size of the U.S. market helps nourish local producers, distributors, and sellers. It gives them a huge outlet for their wares and services, one they can reach without undue difficulty. To some extent, foreign firms have managed to take advantage of the transparency of the U.S. market as well. Sony, for example, was initially excluded from Japan by Matsushita's lock on distribution channels. To succeed in Japan, founder Akio Morita first built his business in the United States. To the very end of his life, he divided his time between New York and Tokyo. Honda, likewise, built its car business in the United States before taking it back to Japan. Nevertheless, U.S. entrepreneurs have an obvious advantage over foreign ones in exploiting the local market. Individual entrepreneurs also have more opportunities here than in other countries.

Of course, Japanese companies have privileged access to the large, homogeneous Japanese market, which is all but closed to outsiders in certain industries, though open in others. This large, protected home base gives Japanese firms a considerable advantage in their global dealings (at the expense of Japanese consumers). The Japanese system of distribution also favors large, established firms. While access to the Japanese market would be valuable, the U.S. market remains twice as big, and it's open to the "little guy."

The U.S. advantage in population size also translates to an advantage in GDP. After years of rapid growth, Japan's per capita GDP levels have reached or exceeded those in the West, including the United States. But Japan's explosive growth is over. It has dropped to (and recently below) the levels found in other industrialized countries. As a result, Japan's GDP will track, not gain on, that of the United States for the foreseeable future.

Since the United States has more than twice as many people as Japan (and the American population is growing rather than shrinking), the U.S. GDP would still be equal to Japan's even if the Japanese per capita GDP were twice that of the United States. Over the long term, the U.S. GDP is likely to gain on that of Japan by about 1 percent per year, the rate of U.S. population growth.[5]

Cultural Openness

In 1827, the German romantic writer Johann Wolfgang von Goethe wrote a poem that begins with the line *"Amerika, du hast es besser"* (America, you have it better). He praised Americans for *not* looking backward. He wrote, "No useless memories, no vain feuds of the past disturb thee from living in the present."

Abraham Lincoln made a similar point when he said, "I do not care who my grandfather was, but I care who my grandchildren will be." Walt Whitman wrote "Have the elder races halted? . . . wearied over there beyond the seas?" He answered, "We take up the task eternal . . . Pioneers! O pioneers!" America's focus on the future, not the past, is still a source of advantage. To this day, immigrants from Lebanon, Haiti, Russia, Yugoslavia, Ireland, Ethiopia, and other turbulent parts of the world put aside political battles in their quest, almost immediately upon arriving in America, to get rich. Economic class differences, while real in the United States, carry far less weight than in other countries, particularly Europe. Here they can disappear within one generation, whereas in much of Europe they can endure for centuries.

Freedom from the dead hand of tradition has spurred American innovation in everything from technology to music to the creation of new art forms such as movies, animated cartoons, and CD-ROMs. It encourages movement, cultural assimilation, and workforce flexibility. Americans have been willing and able to make changes in almost everything they do, from coming to America in the first place to going to college in different parts of the country, marrying outside their religion or their race, and moving around by plane, bus, or U-Haul to try new jobs, careers, and lives.

Freedom from class barriers, geographic limits, and age-old prejudices has created one of the most meritocratic societies on earth. In America, what you can do counts for more than who you are. Once upon a time, America was called "a melting pot," and while it turns out that many of the disparate elements in our society did not entirely meld (in particular, strong differences in race and religion persist), ethnic and cultural differences have faded. Today, rampant capitalism continues to level the country, blurring accents, building up a common experience with malls and chain stores, and creating more national products. The country's two largest newspapers, *USA Today* and *The Wall Street Journal,* are distributed nationally; the New York *Daily News,* for years the nation's largest paper, has declined in circulation in its local market. The Internet is encouraging national commerce. Futurists who predict that the country will split up along regional, local, or ethnic lines are wrong. More and more common experiences bind Americans together, which means that what works in one part of the country can increasingly work in another.

A Dynamic Labor Market

In most other industrialized countries, to get a job is to keep it for life. The good side of this is security for workers. The bad side is less flexibility and an inability to adapt to economic change. Lifetime jobs also perpetuate class differences.[6]

In Germany, France, or England, the loss of a job is a major tragedy. People who lose a job after age forty may never hold one again. It's a good thing European countries provide such generous welfare benefits. Otherwise, they might face revolutions. In Japan, larger companies offer "permanent employment" and no one expects to change jobs, although even there the system is under pressure to change. In the United States, changing jobs or even careers is extremely common. Americans change jobs on average about once every two years; Japanese, once every *thirty* years.[7] When technology or the economy changes, Americans have an unusual capacity to change with it. Workers pick up stakes and move. Fired executives start their own businesses. America's dynamic labor market is an advantage in adapting to change. In the late 1980s and early 1990s, this ability to change allowed U.S. firms to react to the global recession far faster than those in Europe or Japan.

There are a number of reasons why Europeans rarely change jobs. Unlike Americans, they never physically moved away from a feudal society, and while feudalism is long gone, its class distinctions as well as its vestigial rights and customs linger, even among the staunchest champions of equality. Today's wealthy societies still maintain rights and traditions developed when they were poor. One arcane tradition is that of "Madame Pipi," as she is known in France, a woman who looks after a public restroom. In the United States, it would be difficult to find someone willing to spend his or her life in a restroom. However, in France, this humble profession has a distinct place in the social system. "Madame Pipi" rules over her domain as a sovereign.

Both the poor and the rich have rights, and in Europe rights are serious matters. In European offices, it is common to say that a superior does "not have the right" to do something. By contrast, in the United States, most office workers would admit that the boss can do anything he or she pleases (except lose money or commit sexual harassment). The improvement in the condition of the working classes over the nineteenth and twentieth centuries led to increasing standards of living that reached their peak during the golden age from 1950 to 1973. But welcome as postwar equality was, it often took the form of specific new rights that only added to an already rigid, inflexible, class-based system.

Even Germany's famous apprenticeship system perpetuates class differences. At a young age, students who enter the program are tracked toward a blue-collar future. While the system may produce highly competent technicians, it is inherently inflexible. Graduates of the apprenticeship program, although guaranteed a job in industry, have scant hope of ever surpassing their preordained limits to achievement. Even the most socialistic countries in Europe—Sweden, and Denmark, for example—still have sharp divisions between blue- and white-collar workers. While they may enjoy similar union and social benefits, a blue-collar worker has little chance of ever escaping his or her station.

In Europe, downward mobility is blocked as surely as upward mobility by a rigid system. Blue-collar workers cannot hope to become white-collar ones. But workers are also loath to accept less well-paid or less glamorous jobs if they are laid off, even as a temporary measure. During the 1980s, thousands of laid-off autoworkers in the United States took lower-paying jobs rather than go on welfare. But in France, which lost 5.3 autoworkers per thousand of the working-age population in the 1980s, the highest level of automotive job loss in any country, laid-off autoworkers did just that.[8] One of the reasons for the difference is that social welfare benefits in Europe are simply better. If they were abolished tomorrow, worker flexibility might increase. But they won't be abolished—and if they were, Europeans would protest violently because much of their social station and identity is bound up in their job and its attendant rights. The average European autoworker would rather be an unemployed autoworker than an employed cab driver.

Tradition has also slowed the introduction of new technology and new working methods in Europe. At the outset of the computer age, pollsters assessed the views of workers in a number of countries toward using computers. About half the respondents in Germany and Great Britain said that they had no interest in using a computer. Only 29 percent of American respondents were similarly disinterested. These polls had a shock effect on European policy makers, who promptly launched programs to encourage acceptance of the computer.[9]

Hit the Road, Jack

Americans all come from somewhere else. As the country was settled, many moved further west in search of riches or on the lam from the law. A nineteenth-century frontier song entitled "What Was Your Name in the States?" asked, "Did you murder your wife and fly for your life?" The West was America's safety valve. Besides the steady migration west, Americans moved south, north, up to Alaska and even back east in the course of the country's first two centuries of existence.

The first Americans moved by foot, horse, and wagon train. Later, railroads carried them west. By the 1930s, when drought and the Depression sent dust-bowl midwesterners to California, they packed up their belongings and moved by truck and car. Hitting the road became a part of America's culture, celebrated in such epic books and movies as Steinbeck's *The Grapes of Wrath* and even Kerouac's *On the Road.*

Today, the tradition of moving continues little changed from pioneer days, although the wagon train has given way to the jet plane. Half the population of the United States moved from one home to another between 1985 and 1989. Since 1960, nine out of ten households have moved at least once. Reasons range from availability of jobs and housing to the short duration of unemployment benefits to the country's range of climates and conditions to the size of the economy, which can boom in one region while going bust in another.

America's size and immigrant history have produced a legacy of mobility that contributes to the willingness and ability to adapt to economic change. Not by coincidence are air and bus fares, rental car rates, and, most important, gas far cheaper in the United States than in any other developed country.[10]

A Tradition of Entrepreneurship

It is not surprising that the United States leads the world in entrepreneurship. In countries such as Great Britain, Germany, and Japan, rigid control systems guide and channel economic enterprise. Imposed by government, which until the Industrial Revolution was synonymous with the aristocracy—and therefore the rich—these controls remain sympathetic to the status quo. The tradition of strong European governments' being allied with economic power goes back centuries. Modern social movements have done little to chip away at this link.

As a result, European governments typically support and coddle large "national champions" and look askance at individual upstarts. New money remains suspect, and entrepreneurs who might upset the apple cart face large obstacles. To this day, when European entrepreneurs succeed, they receive limited social recognition. For example, British billionaire Richard Branson, founder of Virgin Atlantic Airways and Virgin Records, was the victim of a nasty smear campaign waged by British Airways under the stewardship of then chairman Lord King of Wartnaby. Lord King called the then-forty-four-year-old Branson "too old to rock and too young to fly." And British Airways spread rumors that Virgin was insolvent and attempted to infiltrate its computers, for which it eventually had to pay Branson $1 million in damages.[11] Likewise, in Japan, the close relationship between government and business does not extend to the individual businessman. (In classical, pre-Meiji Japan, the businessman was at the bottom of the upper classes, the soldier at the top.) The central ministries work to promote the success of Japan's largest firms but pay little attention to the unknown entrepreneur, who enjoys less social prestige.[12] Restrictions on imports preserve domination of the distribution system by larger firms.

In contrast, government in the United States was somewhat weak from the beginning and never achieved the legitimacy it enjoys in Europe. Nor was it ever run by an aristocracy. Business, which during the nineteenth century grew faster than government, has always considered government a nuisance. Government, for its part, has tended to view big business with suspicion. In 1887, it intervened on the side of small goods distributors against the railroads by creating the Interstate Commerce Commission (ICC).[13]

While government cooperation with large companies in Germany and Japan has helped large producers, it has harmed entrepreneurs. Today, there is little question that, of all the older, industrialized countries, the United States provides the most supportive environment for entrepreneurship. Competition for the honor of world's most supportive government for entrepreneurs comes only from new countries, notably Hong Kong, Singapore, and Taiwan, all predominantly Chinese countries in Asia. Taiwan's companies, for example, tend to be smaller and more family-oriented than those in Japan. (Recall that in ancient China, businessmen were not excluded from society as they were in Europe and Japan but ranked above servants and soldiers, though below the mandarins.[14])

The United States has fewer regulations on business than Europe, Japan, and most of Asia. In Europe, it can take six months to charter a company. In Germany, the minimum investment needed to start a *Gesellschaft mit beschränkter Haftung* (GmbH), or corporation, is $35,000; the minimum needed for an *Aktiengesellschaft* (AG), or public company, is about $70,000. In the United States, by contrast, creating a corporation can be done over the Internet or a toll-free telephone number in minutes, and there are no capital requirements. The difference between the U.S. and European systems is not just red tape. In Europe, there is the lingering notion that a feudal "right" has to be "accorded." Although it is accorded more readily than in feudal times, it must be granted nonetheless.

The invention of the self-chartered corporation was a milestone in capitalism's development. After the American Revolution, New York State required a separate act of the legislature to create a corporation, barring the party out of power from this form of business. In 1811, however, it began to allow the secretary of state to grant charters, depoliticizing the process.

In Europe, however, sovereigns recognized the value of controlling the licensing of businesses and held on to this authority as long as they could. Russia, for example, discussed reform in 1825, but the czar dismissed it. More than a century and a half later, says Professor Jeffrey D. Sachs of Harvard, the Russian Parliament held discussions similar to those held by the Duma in 1905 about whether to permit self-chartered corporations.

The difficulty of starting new companies unquestionably feeds Europe's unemployment. The McKinsey Global Institute recently studied the job creation problem in Europe. One single law, France's 1984 *"loi Royer,"* has blocked the creation of retail jobs for over a decade. France's Carrefour hypermarkets have stopped trying to expand in France in favor of building stores in "less regulated" markets such as China.[15] Europe's educated workforce and showpiece infrastructure should attract capital investment and high-paying jobs. Instead, its strict regulations have caused capital to leave or ignore it.

In Japan, it remains almost impossible for a foreign firm to buy a Japanese company. That's as true for an Italian who wants to buy a restaurant as for T. Boone Pickens, who could not get a seat on the board of directors of a Toyota affiliate even after he became the largest shareholder in the company. The number of foreign takeovers peaked at forty-three in 1992 and has since declined. Starting a *kabushiki kaisha* (KK), the Japanese equivalent of a corporation, requires about $30,000 in capital. In South Korea, it takes more than $60,000 to start a firm.[16]

As a result, the United States possesses more businesses per capita than its major competitors. The relentless downsizing of U.S. business in recent years, combined with the personal-computer revolution, has compelled many executives to start businesses of their own. American entrepreneurs have started the businesses that have provided many of the jobs created in the last ten years, and they will start many of the businesses that will put people to work in the future. According to Dun & Bradstreet, small businesses created half the new jobs in the country in 1995. They also constitute a huge market for supplies and services from Wal-Mart's "Sam's

Wholesale Clubs," Office Depot and Staples. The continuing phenomenon of entrepreneurship will be an important American asset in coming decades.

A House in Order

Contrary to current fear mongering, the United States has its fiscal house in order—compared with other countries and with itself historically. Some of the biggest political issues in recent years, the deficit and our rate of taxation, are chimerical. Consider the following facts.

THE U.S. DEFICIT IS RELATIVELY LOW

Is the size of the U.S. federal deficit a source of competitive advantage for the United States? Yes, since every other major competitor except Japan runs a larger one and Japan's about equals ours, as a percentage of GDP. In 1994, as a percentage of GDP, Italy's deficit was five times ours, Britain's was 3.5 times ours, and Germany's was about 35 percent higher than ours. If certain politicians are to be believed, the size of the current U.S. deficit will soon lead to bankruptcy. In fact, it is low by historical standards and dropping.

The current U.S. deficit is half the size of deficits during the Ford administration and *one eighteenth* the size of the deficit after World War II.

Historically, wars create deficits, peace, balanced budgets. The deficit hit 35 percent of GDP during World War II, but then tumbled into balance. Since its peak in 1983 at 6.3 percent of GDP, it has dropped to 1.8 percent of GDP, thanks to the end of the Cold War and the deficit reduction measures taken in 1993. A balanced budget deal would only shrink it further. The Organization for Economic Cooperation and Development (OECD) wrote in 1994, "The last two years have seen the biggest annual declines in real Federal purchases since the aftermath of the Vietnam War twenty years ago."[17]

Were it not for interest on debt contracted during the 1980s, America's budget would be in surplus.

Fear over the size of deficits is a hangover from the huge deficits of the Reagan years, which *were* threatening and which made interest payments a large item in the budget. But after a sharp rise, the military budget fell back to its 1980 level in 1990 and has kept on dropping. From 23 percent of the budget when Reagan took office, it soared to 28 percent but is now down to 20 percent. The decrease is saving us $113 billion a year in today's dollars in direct budgetary expenditure[18]—less than the $200 billion per year the United States pays in interest on the debt, but no small change.

Americans have not yet recognized the vast improvement in our fiscal picture that has occurred since 1991. Assuming supply-siders do not get control of the government, the deficit is likely to continue to decline, and its low level will give the United States another advantage over competitors in years to come.

The U.S. Federal Debt Is Relatively Low

Can the U.S. federal debt (what we owe overall), as opposed to the deficit (our annual budget shortfall), possibly be an advantage? Yes again, when compared to those of our competitors. While our deficits have tumbled since the end of the Cold War, the debt accumulated during the Reagan buildup lingers. Currently, U.S. debt is about 50 percent of GDP. Although it is twice what it was before Reagan took office, it is half what it was after World War II.[19]

A comparison of debt levels shows that, as high as this may seem, it is moderate when compared to other countries'. Our debt level of 50 percent of GDP is well below those of Japan (57 percent), the Netherlands (64 percent), Italy (84 percent), Singapore (89 percent), and Belgium/Luxembourg (106 percent). They are only slightly above those in the United Kingdom and Germany. After alarming growth in debt during the Reagan years, the situation has dramatically improved.

U.S. Taxes Are Relatively Low

Notwithstanding the hysteria about taxes, U.S. taxes are by far the lowest of the Group of Seven (G-7) countries, even below those of

Japan. At about 31 percent of GDP, U.S. taxes are below Japan's at 33 percent, Great Britain's at 37 percent, and Germany's at a whopping 47 percent. Taxes in countries such as Sweden and Denmark are much higher still.

Furthermore, U.S. taxes are low by historical standards. Top tax rates first peaked during World War I and were 94 percent from 1944 until reduced by Johnson in 1965; today the top rate is only 31 percent. What has increased are payroll taxes—which go to Social Security—but overall taxes and taxes on the wealthy remain low by international and U.S. historical standards.

U.S. SOCIAL EXPENDITURE IS RELATIVELY LOW

The low level of social expenditure might count as a negative in terms of the social commitment of the country, but it counts as a positive fiscally. The only large country whose social expenditures are lower than the United States' is Japan (whose large companies provide far more benefits than do U.S. companies). The lower level of social expenditure also means that while the government does not take care of people in the United States as well as some other governments do, people have more money of their own to look after their needs. At 15 percent of GDP, U.S. social expenditure is marginally higher than that in Japan (12 percent) but only about half that in Germany (27 percent), France (28 percent), Belgium (27 percent), and most other European countries.

U.S. INFLATION IS RELATIVELY LOW

America has the lowest inflation of any G-7 country with the exception of Japan, with which it is approximately tied. The 1995 core inflation rate (not counting volatile food or energy prices) of 2.6 percent was the lowest since 1965. General inflation, at 2.7 percent in 1994, has been less than 3 percent for the last four years.[20] A number of factors are fueling disinflation, including productivity gains resulting from the use of computers and networks and global trade. New and more efficient distribution channels such as Wal-

Mart, Home Depot, and the like allow consumers to pay as little as possible for goods.

Japan, of course, has a low inflation rate despite having fewer computers and grossly inefficient methods of distribution, proving that monetary policy remains the best check on inflation. High inflation was a disadvantage for the United States during parts of the 1980s; low inflation will prove a U.S. strength in years ahead.

A Retooled, Reengineered Industry

In 1968, in his famous book *The American Challenge (Le Défi américain)*, French author Jean-Jacques Servan-Schreiber wrote, "Fifteen years from now it is quite possible that the world's third greatest industrial power, just after the United States and Russia, will not be European industry but American industry in Europe." The reason: American management. Servan-Schreiber's fear of the specter of American domination struck a chord in Europe. His book sold more copies in its first three months than any other book published in postwar Europe.

In the mid-1980s, his prediction might have seemed wrong. American industry was reeling from the combined assault of unfavorable exchange rates, new management methods in Japan, and global competition from newly industrialized countries as manufacturing capability spread like wildfire. Nobody wanted to copy U.S. management. Japan was all the rage.

Ten years later, however, Servan-Schreiber's comments again seem prescient. Why? American industry has reinvented itself, so much so that Japanese managers are now studying American companies while European companies envy American flexibility. As Servan-Schreiber wrote over a quarter century ago, "American firms have made more mistakes than their competitors—but they have tried hard to correct them. And an American firm can change its methods in almost no time."[21] In the 1980s and 1990s, U.S. firms studied their Japanese competition and adjusted.

Bit by bit, sale by sale, U.S. firms have reclaimed competitive ground through the upgrading, reengineering, and reconfiguration of their businesses.

The main elements of this process are now familiar territory to business observers. Total quality management, which U.S. firms adapted with a vengeance in the 1980s, empowerment of workers, improved cycle time (the time between receipt and fulfillment of an order), better relationships with suppliers, design-in product development, the use of strategic alliances, a focus on core competencies, and reengineering have transformed U.S. industry. These management improvements have been the focus of countless books and articles and millions of hours of billable management consulting. In retrospect, they seem almost obvious. For example, when labor accounted for a large percentage of the cost of a product, it made sense for Henry Ford to break down jobs into the simplest possible tasks in order to use the cheapest labor available. Now that labor accounts for a small percentage of the cost of high-tech products, it makes sense to train workers to use sophisticated equipment. But there is another innovation that has received no attention. A key enabler of change was an improvement in accounting that was comparable, in its way, to the invention of double-entry bookkeeping. That invention: activity-based accounting.

A little-known, little-celebrated improvement in accounting, activity-based accounting made possible outsourcing and much of the last decade's downsizing wave.

What is activity-based cost accounting? It's a way to keep track of profits and losses in a company at a micro level, and to look outside the company as well at the value chain. It lets managers of large companies peer inside the workings of their gargantuan operations to see what tasks are making money and what tasks can be done for less by others. The computer made this feasible.

Before these improvements in accounting, companies often wavered on whether to deal with subsidiaries at arm's length or to cross-subsidize through preferential deals. Often, pricing was downright arbitrary. Many companies had no idea which operations were making money and where their costs really lay. Activity-based accounting has enabled units to deal with one another at arm's length and put an end to most unintentional corporate subsidies.[22] No longer do firms pay extra to in-house suppliers for supplies, confident they will gain with one hand what they give with the other, or force sweetheart deals on money-losing captive suppliers. With every unit a profit center (or strictly accountable for performance) and compensation linked to results, the manager of one business unit is no longer likely to stand idly by while he subsidizes another manager. More than anything else, activity-based accounting has given companies the ability to cut waste, outsource functions, and do all the other things that companies have begun to do.

Dynamic Venture Capital Markets

The United States has the most dynamic venture capital markets in the world. In 1994, American firms raised $633 billion in debt financing[23] and $45.5 billion in initial public offerings.[24] Over the last ten years, they have received billions more from venture capital funds and private investors. American firms have been leaders in developing new methods of venture capital financing involving warrants, debt, and other complex financing instruments. Recent innovations include venture leasing or financing of equipment, as opposed to a company itself, and even the sale-leaseback of patents, where a venture capital firm buys a patent from a start-up company and then leases it back to that company.

The U.S. venture capital system surpasses those in other countries for many reasons: American entrepreneurs are willing to work long hours. Their enthusiasm is part of the recipe for success. And the United States has a critical mass of people who understand venture capital arrangements. Superior universities also create new technologies that lend themselves to venture capital financing.

But, most important, the U.S. public markets are liquid, honest, and sophisticated enough to permit investors to cash out at the end. A lucrative exit strategy, the proverbial pot of gold at the end of the rainbow, is what encourages venture capitalists to lend out money. The U.S. public markets provide the ultimate liquidity, or "takeout," that lets venture capitalists cash out profitably and unload their risk onto others. Observes Robert J. Kunze, a well-known venture capitalist, "Germany and Japan have amazingly similar deterrents to venture capital. The governments and banks in these two countries control and regulate the markets. Only a token public stock market is available to emerging companies. . . . Existing venture capital funds are therefore invested in second-rate opportunities and have no clear path to liquidity. . . . Venture capital is just talk in these countries."[25] As for emerging markets such as Taiwan, Singapore, and Mexico, Kunze argues that the absence of exit strategies in these countries has forbidden a true venture capital market to develop in any of them.

The United States will continue to lead the world in venture capital for the foreseeable future for the simple reason that none of its competitors will liberalize their markets sufficiently to create enough liquidity and market efficiency to "take out" early investors.

Great Britain is the only country that has truly deregulated its capital markets and tried to get venture capital going. But, according to observers, the market has failed to develop because of cultural barriers to working the eighty-hour weeks often necessary to create successful start-ups.

Superior Universities

For the sheer number and quality of its universities, no other country can match the United States. However, universities do more than produce educated graduates. They draw the world's best and brightest to America. In particular, Asian students flock to the United States to study math, economics, and the sciences. Each year, 100,000 Indians take exams for 2,000 places in the Indian Institutes of Technology. The very best of these then go to America. In general, foreign students do not cut and run after graduation. Instead, they provide an important "brain gain." Seventy percent of those who get Ph.D.s stay in the United States after graduating.[26]

American universities also produce new businesses. Large high-tech enclaves surround universities in California, Boston, and North Carolina, while smaller enclaves surround universities elsewhere. The presence of Stanford helped create Hewlett-Packard and eventually Silicon Valley. MIT and Harvard helped create Digital Equipment, Wang Laboratories, and Route 128, where many electronics firms are located, near Boston. It is estimated that the United States possesses more than two thirds of the top hundred universities in the world. Knowledge will drive much of the growth of the next quarter century, and the United States is particularly well positioned in this area.

From 1960 to 1993, twenty-five of fifty-four Nobel Laureates in chemistry were American or had done their work at U.S. research institutions. In physics, Americans garnered thirty-seven of eighty Nobel Prizes.

Since 1950, the United States has produced 160 Nobel Laureates, the United Kingdom 44, Germany 24, and Japan only 4.[27]

According to the OECD, "The diverse system of higher education—featuring institutions that run the gamut from world-class research universities and colleges offering vocational certificates and remedial education programmes—is a major competitive strength for the United States."[28]

Sixty-six percent of U.S. students attend college, compared with 41 percent in other large OECD countries.

Accordingly, 2.4 percent of U.S. GDP goes to colleges compared to an OECD average of 1.5 percent. We spend twice as much per student in relation to GDP as Germany, France, and even Japan (compared with about the same amount at the primary and secondary levels). The federal government picks up 32 percent of college costs but only 7 percent of the tab for primary and second-ary education, a fact that explains part of the difference in quality between U.S. universities and lower education.

An American specialty is the two-year community and technical college. Between 1963 and 1990, enrollment in such institutions increased more than sixfold, from 740,000 to 4,900,000. There are about one thousand community and technical colleges spread fairly evenly across the country. Companies such as GM, Ford, Chrysler, Nissan, Toyota, and Honda have established some five hundred apprentice programs in these colleges.

Why is America's university system so good? The country got its head start with the Morrill Land-Grant College Act in 1862, which gave states federal lands on which to create land-grant colleges.[29] The Morrill Act was an amazingly farsighted gesture. Up to that time, universities around the world had been elitist institutions serving a handful of well-connected students. Today, seventy-two land-grant colleges exist. But while the Morrill Act increased ac-cess, college remained difficult to afford through World War II. The G.I. Bill opened it up to returning veterans. Since then a variety of federal grant and loan programs has made a university education available to the largest number of people in history.

While U.S. universities clearly lead the world, critics often point to primary and secondary education as areas of weakness. They point out that despite the fact that the United States was the first country to guarantee universal education—and thereby gain a considerable advantage—we have fallen behind other countries. Standardized tests place U.S. students, on average, below counter-parts in many other countries, particularly in math and science. However, the problems are not universal. Students in some parts of the country and some schools do well.

Students in midwestern agricultural states and parts of the Northeast do better, on average, on tests than the fabled South Koreans.

Twenty percent of American children and teenagers go to private schools which often are excellent. And in rich suburbs private schools provide competition for public ones, enhancing their quality.

A principal reason for the poor performance of American students compared with students of the same age elsewhere is that the average school year in the United States is shorter than in most other industrialized countries, a legacy of the day when most Americans worked in agriculture and children were needed, come summer, to work on the farm. However, in general American students stay in school more years than their counterparts in other countries, and learn just as much once they have been in school an equal number of hours (which may take an additional year). American secondary school students graduate at the age of seventeen or eighteen, compared to sixteen in many other countries. Moreover, a higher percentage of twenty-five- to sixty-four-year-old Americans has completed secondary school than in other OECD countries. The OECD believes that this more relaxed pace of education, in which schooling is spaced out over more years and mixed with sports and work over the summer, is more compatible with the flexible U.S. economy than the more regimented systems found elsewhere.

Given the higher levels of secondary school and higher education in the United States, Americans are, overall, as well or better educated than people living in its principal competitors. Certain groups and regions, however, remain far behind. The lowest levels of schooling and achievement are concentrated among minorities. However, the past is not the future. The least educated members of the labor force are now relatively old. Of the 33 million Americans over age twenty-five who had not finished high school in 1990, 71 percent were over the age of forty-five and 56 percent were over fifty-five.[30] Most of them will have retired by 2005.[31] Sounding an upbeat note, the OECD writes, "Clearly, the next generation of Black and Hispanic workers will be much better educated, on average, than the current generation, as the less-schooled older workers retire."[32]

In the conclusion to his otherwise alarmist book on education, *Inside American Education*, Thomas Sowell writes:

All the ingredients for a successful educational system already exist in the United States: some of the leading scholars in the world in numerous fields, masses of college-educated people capable of teaching in the public schools, and a public whose willingness to provide financial support for education has far outstripped educators' willingness to buckle down to the task of teaching academic skills to the next generation.[33]

A Dynamic System of Technology Creation

The United States is still the world's largest technology exporter. No other country can create technology as readily. Japanese and European firms shop for technology in Silicon Valley, Cambridge, Princeton, and elsewhere. But with capital no longer tied up in leveraged buyouts and heightened military spending, the United States is in a better position to take advantage of its own technology.

The United States leads the world in most of the new technologies, including biotechnology, software, artificial intelligence, virtual reality, central processing unit (CPU) design, and memory chip design. In the 1980s, the United States had problems with turning technology into products. It invented the VCR and liquid crystal display (LCD) but failed to commercialize their technology. In most such cases, American firms could not find the capital needed, or else they faced competition from Asian manufacturers willing to accept minimal returns in exchange for gaining market share. (Negative interest rates in Japan helped Japanese firms win in capital-intensive industries.) There is little doubt that the United States remains the world's largest technology producer, notwithstanding figures that pessimists like to quote showing that Japanese firms are obtaining more and more patents in the United States.

The main reason Japanese firms rack up so many U.S. patents is that they are adept at playing the game of "patent *go*."

In the ancient game of *go*, two players try to encircle each other's stones. When an opponent's stone is entirely encircled, it is captured. To guard against this, players protect their stones by arranging them to avoid encirclement. In the game of "patent *go*," the idea is to circle one's opponents' patents and to protect one's own. Players obtain patents around patents to anticipate and block one another's technological progress and to protect their own patents from competitors'. Aggressiveness in playing this game is not synonymous with true technological accomplishment although U.S. firms should take note of this strategy's benefits.

Recently, U.S. firms have retaken some ground in patents. In 1993, IBM reclaimed the number one spot and Eastman Kodak placed fourth after several years during which Japanese firms took all the top positions. Hewlett-Packard credits an aggressive patent strategy for part of its success with ink-jet printers.

Japan has made progress in product technology, building on its accomplishments in process technologies. Germany is strong in chemicals and automotive technology, Switzerland and England in pharmaceuticals, France in telecommunications. But the United States remains firmly in the lead overall. A 1993 German government report on world technology concluded, "The USA is still the uncontested leader. Japan has caught up considerably in the science area (basic research), but compared with the size of the country and the number of scientists, it still has a sub-average publication rate."[34]

Other GDP measures confirm the United States' strength in high technology. Gross research and development expenditure in America is more than twice that of Japan and more than four times that of Germany. R&D expenditure per capita is higher in the United States than in any other country.[35] Critics of America like to point out that the private share of R&D is lower in the United States than elsewhere. In 1990, 73.1 percent of Japan's R&D was private, compared with 50.6 percent in the United States. However, the *total* amount of U.S. private R&D expenditure is still 40 percent larger than that of Japan.

Furthermore, the overall flow of technology is out of the United States and into other countries. Japan is the world's largest importer of technology in the form of licenses and other payments, spending $3.6 billion more than it took in in 1990; Germany ran a $1.9 billion deficit.

The United States not only runs the world's *biggest* surplus in technology, $12.7 billion, it runs the world's *only* technology surplus.[36]

It's easy to see why America creates so much more technology. There is no equivalent to Silicon Valley in Japan or Germany. America's advanced university system and developed venture capital system spawn and nourish new technology companies in clusters throughout the country. In Silicon Valley, pioneers at one company have promptly moved on to start others. A genealogy of the disk drive industry—one still dominated by U.S. firms—shows the same names popping up in one trendsetting firm after another. Again, it is the dynamism and flexibility of the U.S. economy that set it apart.

American technology companies will fare well in years ahead as the U.S. technology sector continues to outstrip the rest of the world's. Engineers, microbiologists, and others who enter this sector will benefit. While it is impossible to predict which companies will do best two decades from now, technology firms as a whole will prosper in years ahead, and their success will benefit the regions that spawn them (as discussed in Chapter 7).

Leadership in Information Services

The United States also leads in information infrastructure and information services, the backbone of the global economy.

The United States has almost four times the number of personal computers per capita of Japan and two and a half times the number of personal computers per capita of Germany.[37]

Computers have indeed been slow to catch on in Japan, in part due to the difficulty of rendering the Japanese language via keyboard. Many large Japanese companies still use word processors, called *wapuros*, all of them made in Japan, instead of networked computers (in which the United States leads). The gulf between the United States and other countries in the installed base of computers is even greater than the per capita gulf: eight times as many computers as in Germany, seven times as many as in Japan.

AT&T reports that the United States possesses about 20 percent more telephone access lines per capita than either Japan or Germany. In Germany, Touch-Tone service is still rare, itemized phone bills cost extra, and more than half the system is analog. Toll-free numbers are undeveloped. Deutsche Telekom handled only 110 million such calls in 1993, less than AT&T handles in *two days*.[38] U.S. phone companies themselves have a strong presence in Europe: AT&T has 21 percent of the market for calling cards, a doorway to its network, and American firms as a whole have 35 percent of the European calling card market.

Office automation (OA) is the term used in Japan to describe computing in the office. The term itself says a great deal about how the Japanese see office technology. OA recalls computing in the United States about a decade ago, when firms such as American Data Processing first began to automate office payrolls and newspapers used the Harris and, later, Atex word processing systems. OA in Japan remains highly proprietary, largely because of reluctance on the part of Japanese firms to accept the Microsoft standard for personal computing. Rather than using the American system of stringing personal computers together on local-area networks (LANs) that run common programs such as WordPerfect, Lotus, and other DOS- or Windows-based applications, Japanese firms have persisted in trying to develop their own proprietary systems. The failure of such systems to win wide acceptance is why so many Japanese firms still use nonnetworked word processors.

U.S. industry, in contrast, has made massive investments in information technology. According to the OECD,

> *Most of this increased spending went into purchases of computers—partly because corporate "re-engineering" required increased computer intensity, and also because computer price declines of 10 to 18 percent annually (corrected for quality improvement) allowed firms to stretch their investment dollars further via computer purchases. Over the past two years, overall*

> *gross equipment investment has increased to record levels rela-*
> *tive to GDP.*[39]

This huge investment has just started to pay off in productivity gains, which have surged in the last two years[40] (see Chapter 3). In coming years, U.S. investment in information technology is likely to remain high. The huge installed base of computers means that American market needs will continue to shape the evolution of computer software, as well as the development of peripherals and such vital technologies as computer memory. American investment in information technology will not only help all industries perform better but will create opportunities in information-related businesses.

WIDE-AREA AND VALUE-ADDED NETWORKS

The United States is far ahead of its competitors in creating the information superhighway. Planners at Japan's Ministry of International Trade and Industry (MITI) neglected to work on networks, and Japan has no indigenous equivalent of the Internet. Hiroshi Inose, director general of Japan's Center for Science Information Networks, estimates that Japan is ten years behind the United States in networks.[41] Slowing the implementation of even local-area networks in offices is the incompatibility of Japan's computers. NEC, Fujitsu, and Toshiba each uses a different way of storing data; thus their disks and files cannot be swapped. Apple Computer is an important player in Japan, but its machines are incompatible with other formats. The market share of U.S. firms in personal computers has dramatically risen since the introduction of a Japanese version of Windows. But while the Intel/Microsoft standard is growing, the installed base of personal computers and software remains a patchwork, retarding network development.

Europe is still well behind the United States in the development of multimedia as well as the information superhighway. Says Carlo De Benedetti, head of Italy's Olivetti, "Europe is lagging enormously."[42] While European universities are linked to the

Internet and some institutions such as the European Center for
Nuclear Research (CERN) played critical roles in its development,[43] Europe as a whole has no strict equivalent. U.S. scientists
designed the Internet to safeguard communications in the event
of a nuclear attack. Messages get broken up into packets of data,
which are routed over excess capacity along the nation's phone
lines and reassembled at their destinations. The Internet uses
excess long-distance capacity purchased at cut rates from long-
distance carriers as well as trunk lines. Cross-subsidies in Europe
that keep long-distance rates high to fulfill policy objectives (similar to those in the United States before telephone-service deregulation) make long-distance service expensive. As a result, private
industry has yet to make significant investments in creating services for the information superhighway. Although European companies will soon compete with CompuServe and other U.S.
players, they are just getting started.

France's Minitel system is an interesting exception to the rule.
Launched in 1984, the state-sponsored system has been fantas-
tically popular in France. For a while after its inception, France led
the world in the development of on-line services. It was possible to
check railroad schedules, shop, chat, flirt, or even meet your mate
on the system. The French telephone company distributed actual
Minitels, small telephones with screens, to most of the households
in France. The system never required personal computers.

However, while on-line services have been developing elsewhere,
the French system has stayed the same, becoming a dinosaur of
sorts. The Minitel system remains entirely text-based. Its terminals
are dumb and slow. The large installed base means that any improvements must be backward-compatible. Accordingly, France will
have trouble upgrading the Minitel system. The lack of processing
power on the part of its terminals now bars access to much of the
Internet.

Bandwidth

In general, the United States has far greater bandwidth than other
countries—with one proviso. Much of the European effort to build

the information superhighway has been targeted toward the introduction of integrated services digital network (ISDN) technology, a way of squeezing more data through copper wires. However, the European strategy of trying to get businesses to adopt ISDN has ignored consumers, who are leading the development of networks in the United States through services such as America Online and the Microsoft Network.

One of the biggest advantages the United States has over its competitors is the sheer number of U.S. telephone companies, wireless firms, and cable providers, each offering different technologies. Intense competition among these players will spur more innovative solutions. MCI stands for Microwave Communications, Inc., and originally the company's main offering was microwave communications. It has since expanded into fiber optics and other technologies. Overlaid across the big networks owned by AT&T, MCI, Sprint, and others, companies with names such as Encore Communications, Mid-Com Communications, Frontier Communications, Cleartel Communications, LODS-Metromedia Corp., and Econophone package and resell service. NYNEX offers local customers a choice of about seventy long-distance carriers. Dozens of other firms offer wireless and/or cellular service.

Everyone's building networks. IBM sells time on its network. Westinghouse's network services blue-chip customers. General Electric's GEnie service is yet another network. The only countries that come close to matching U.S. network capability (on a much smaller scale) are Singapore and, in cellular services, oddly Finland, where conventional lines are expensive due to the climate.

Favorable Exchange Rates

The United States is emerging as the low-cost producer in many industries. American manufacturers are benefiting from the sharp decline in the cost of labor and the low prices of their goods abroad. The cheap dollar is also luring foreign companies to invest in the United States. While the dollar may rise and fall from time to time and began rising in 1996, it is unlikely to soar as it did in the

1980s—barring any abrupt shift in ideology in Washington. The low dollar will also help U.S. exporters continue to regain ground they lost following the Reagan-era run-up.

The unusual flip-flop in exchange rates in the 1980s was a one-time event.

For eight years straight, U.S. exports have hit record levels. As a percentage of world exports, they have sharply increased, passing Germany's, which pulled ahead in the 1980s.

An analysis of the ingredients of America's balance of trade reveals that while consumer electronics and auto parts have gotten the most attention, about half of the deficit is due to oil. The United States runs a surplus in CPUs, aircraft, and scientific instruments (and agriculture, which in America is a high-tech industry). This cloaks a hidden opportunity. Since oil imports have been steady, providing prices don't surge (which they should not, due to measures such as the strategic petroleum reserve that were put into place after the 1979 shock), an expansion in trade should reduce the deficit.

Moreover, the United States runs a large surplus in services, which have traditionally traded less than goods. And as services have grown more important to the U.S. economy, it is not surprising that we have experienced pressure on the balance of trade in goods. As the information superhighway develops, trade barriers fall, and services trade more freely, the United States should export more services. Only trade barriers (and poor protection against the pirating of intellectual property) are keeping the United States from exporting huge quantities of television programming, telecommunications, and content for the information superhighway. Looked at by country, trade with Japan accounts for about half of the trade deficit, while trade with China accounts for another quarter. The United States actually runs a trade surplus with Europe.

The main trade problem remains Japan and its closed markets, but as GATT and NAFTA boost trade with the rest of the world, trade with Japan will decrease as a percentage.

Commentators often marvel at how easily Japan has adjusted to the rising yen. Ignoring rises in the value of the yen, Japan's trade surpluses have steadily increased. As Lester Thurow puts it, Japan is the only country where water runs uphill.[44] If Japan can adjust to a rising yen, the question arises, why couldn't the U.S. export sector cope with the rising dollar in the 1980s? The answer is that Japan's producer economy and attendant trade barriers made adjustment easier for Japanese exporters.

In the United States, when the dollar rose, manufacturers got hit two ways: by a reduction in exports and by erosion of sales at home. In Japan, when the yen rose, trade barriers kept out imports of finished goods, while imports of raw materials like oil and glass grew cheaper. This combination actually increased profit margins on some domestic sales. These earnings could then be used to subsidize sales overseas in order to maintain market share. The Japanese companies' system of buying components from affiliated suppliers also let them shift the pain. Vertically integrated U.S. firms had to take more of the hit themselves. (Recently, of course, the United States has begun to explode its value chain through the use of outsourcing and alliances.)

During the high-dollar phase of the 1980s, the U.S. trade deficit soared. But when the dollar came back down, the trade deficit with Europe (including Germany, a highly competitive exporter) disappeared. It did not disappear vis-à-vis Japan because of the country's determination to rack up trade surpluses and huge institutional biases toward that end. Japan's membrane is permeable in only one direction: for goods going out. But the Japanese system has a cost: while guaranteeing a favorable balance of trade, it penalizes consumers and reduces overall efficiency. Our system benefits consumers and small businesses, including retailers and distributors— in short, the "little guy."

Finally, much of the current trade deficit reflects the strengthened U.S. economy compared with sluggish economies in Europe and Japan. As those economies move forward in the business cycle and the American economy peaks, the trade deficit will fall.

Chapter 3

The Brave New

Workplace

I n 1980, IBM, a paragon of industrial America, struck a deal with a West Coast entrepreneur to provide the operating system for its personal computer. Only a few years earlier, an upstart company named Apple had beaten IBM to market with the first popular home computer, the Apple II. Annoyed, if not shocked, by Apple's impertinence, Big Blue decided to outsource its new machine's components to get its product to market faster. It licensed its operating system from two Harvard dropouts based in Seattle who had good connections and a flair for computing. Their names: Paul Allen and Bill Gates. Fifteen years later, the stock market value of Gates and Allen's firm, Microsoft, passed Big Blue's, and Gates had become the richest man in America. Somehow IBM goofed.[1]

On July 17, 1995, the day Microsoft passed IBM as the most highly valued U.S. technology firm, it is interesting to compare the two companies, one a symbol of America's postwar might and vertical integration, the other a symbol of America's future. For their differences speak volumes about how changes in American enterprise will revolutionize the labor market.

In 1995, IBM had 240,000 employees; Microsoft had 15,000. Manufacturing was critical to IBM but of little account to Microsoft. IBM sold mainframes, minicomputer and personal-computer hardware, printers, software, and computer support and offered financing to clients, and did all those things in house; like GM, Ford, AT&T, and other giants, it employed all sorts of people from executives to cooks to truck drivers. Microsoft just did Windows (and other software) and hired mainly software engineers. IBM had more levels of management than Microsoft. IBM's sales were twelve times Microsoft's, and its software revenues alone exceeded Microsoft's entire sales. Indeed, by every measure but two, IBM dwarfed Microsoft in size. Only in consistency of earnings and earnings growth did Microsoft outperform IBM—but these are the measures that matter to markets. Capital, in the form of market value, flocked to Microsoft while IBM's stock price and capitalization languished.

IBM has slashed jobs and layers of management in recent years, consolidated products, and regrouped so that it is by any measure a global aggressor. Nevertheless, the trajectories of the two firms, from nothing to preeminence in the case of Microsoft, from fat to thinner in the case of IBM, illustrate the massive changes affecting U.S. enterprises and, with them, the labor market. To keep hold of today's ever-restless capital, American industry is moving from vertical to horizontal, from big to small, and from the world of hard, material objects like big iron mainframe computers to the disembodied realm of software and the information highway. These trends are revolutionizing the American workplace.

The Flattening of American Enterprise

No change is more pervasive than the flattening of American enterprise. It is said that inside every fat man there lurks a thin man waiting to pop out.

Over the last decade, from out of America's fat men has popped an entire army of thin ones.

During the golden age after World War II, large institutions, often categorized as Big Business, Big Government, and Big Labor, ran America. Vertical integration with a top-down command and control system was the dominant mode of organization. The model was so strong that it even took hold in crime. Not by coincidence, in the late 1950s, Robert Kennedy and the McClellan Committee discovered organized crime and the Mafia. Before then, crime was considered an individualistic endeavor, symbolized by the FBI's ten most wanted men. Americans in the fifties were fascinated to learn that instead of "Pretty Boy" Floyd and Al Capone, the real problem was the Syndicate or Murder, Inc.

The huge vertical organization came into being because it generated economies of scale. But to keep everything working smoothly, the command organization needed layers of managers to pass information up and down. Computer networks have now squashed the pyramid. A few examples:

- The number of employees of *Fortune* 500 companies has dropped from 16.2 million in 1974 to 11.8 million today.

- GM shed 100,000 jobs between 1990 and 1993 alone.

- Union Carbide slimmed down from 110,000 workers in 1984 to 10,000 in 1994, a 90 percent reduction.[2]

- Today, even in the midst of a recovery, the *Fortune* 500 are continuing to reduce their head counts.

Does downsizing mean that American jobs are disappearing? Hardly. Doomsayers focus on layoffs at the big firms but ignore hiring at smaller ones. Between 1980 and 1990, America created 21 million jobs. During the first three years of the Clinton administration, it gave birth to eight million more. This phenomenon, unique in the world (Europe lost private-sector jobs during this period) has been called the "Great American Job Machine." The new jobs are not at the older firms like IBM or GM, but at the Microsofts or the potential Microsofts, small firms that have outsourced work from big ones or have discovered niches that the big ones missed. They are not all low-paying. Many are far better than the jobs they replaced.

America is witnessing the simultaneous downsizing of big business and upsizing of small and medium-sized business. American industry is also broadening. Overall, in 1980, the average number of workers per business establishment was 16.5. In 1992, it was 14.7. The statistics show that American industry and employment are spreading out across more and more firms. American enterprise, and with it the distribution of jobs, is growing less centralized and more diffuse. In Marxist terms, industry is growing less concentrated—the opposite of what Marx predicted.

This is not to say that vertical integration is dead in America. To dispel that notion, just look at Wayne Huizenga's creation, Blockbuster Video. In the mid-1980s, the VCR launched a rush to open video rental stores across the country. Most such stores were mom-and-pop ventures, but Huizenga, who had cobbled together Waste Management from small garbage carting companies, saw that the video rental market was ripe for branding. His chain of Blockbuster Video stores, backed by national systems, scale, and advertising, soon outstripped the mom-and-pop vendors. Huizenga followed in the path of Rexall Drug and A&P, which in an earlier era had created drug and grocery chains. Blockbuster then moved upstream vertically and began to buy into movie production, acquiring two studios. Only Blockbuster's purchase by Paramount Communications stopped Huizenga from following in the footsteps of Louis B. Mayer, who went from exhibiting films to being a Hollywood mogul. Sumner Redstone, now head of Viacom, America's largest media conglomerate, also started out exhibiting movies and moved upstream.

But Blockbuster and Viacom differ from the vertical giants of the past in their lean management style. And while new empires will continue to spring up, the overall trend in the United States points away from large vertical organizations such as the old GM toward flatter, nimbler firms. Growth companies such as Microsoft and Blockbuster are taking pains to stay lean. Big firms are slimming down to focus on core competencies by outsourcing noncore functions to specialists. Everywhere firms are substituting alliances and supplier relationships for direct ownership of corporate functions.

If diversification means not putting all your eggs in one basket, the core competencies/alliances model, to quote Mark Twain, says "Put all your eggs in one basket and then *watch* that basket."

Following business's example, government has begun to downsize, in part due to the same technological changes that squashed the private pyramid, in part due to the end of the Cold War. Long before Social Security and Medicare, government taxed the public to pay for war and repaid soldiers with booty and pensions. The end of the Franco-Prussian War led to Bismarck's socialist experiments with workmen's compensation, sickness insurance, and old-age insurance—the beginning of the welfare state. Throughout history war has been a driver of government, peace a curb on it. In the United States, an absence of hostile neighbors permitted rapid demobilization after early wars. The first U.S. income tax, passed in 1861 to pay for the Civil War, was repealed in 1871. After World War I, an income tax of up to 77 percent was quickly scaled back as the United States turned isolationist and rapidly demobilized. World War II was a different story. The advent of total war posed a new challenge: how to repay unprecedented numbers of veterans and, indeed, the entire country.

The size and breadth of World War II and the Cold War that followed it, forced governments to pay unusual attention to the masses who had fought it.

The G.I. Bill, Social Security, Medicare, and other initiatives were America's reward to its people for fighting World War II, while the Cold War perpetuated government control in the United States as well as the USSR. Now that the Cold War has ended, the U.S. government is at last able to shrink. (It grew during the Reagan years but has shed 200,000 workers since 1993.) Due to the presence of well-armed neighbors, European governments are shrinking more slowly. Only one thing can reverse the shrinkage of government in the United States: another major war.

Yesterday's typical employee worked at a large organization, whether business or governmental. Tomorrow's will work at a small organization supplying a specific service or product to others.

Large organizations are still the locomotive pulling the train of the economy. But tomorrow's jobs will not be in the locomotive but in cars down the line.

The Migration of Business Toward Services

Related to the flattening of U.S. industry is its continuing migration toward services. In 1973, Daniel Bell identified this trend in his book, *The Coming of Post-Industrial Society: A Venture in Social Forecasting*, noting that fewer people were working in manufacturing and more in services. But Bell saw only the beginning of this phenomenon. Public and private services now account for three quarters of U.S. jobs and will account for more in years to come. Services promote decentralization and the flattening of industry because they do not require the economies of scale of manufacturing, agriculture, or resource operations. It's possible to start up a service business with a staff of one. In contrast, manufacturing firms usually need a large complement of workers to be at all efficient. Thus the shift to services is responsible, in part, for the deconcentration of the American economy.

Of the thirty companies that make up the Dow Jones Industrial Average, seven are now service firms and three are oil companies that make much of their money from services. In recent years, Walt Disney has replaced USX, the successor to U.S. Steel, on the Dow; American Express has replaced Manville; and McDonald's has replaced American Brands. The other two Dow Jones indices, transportation and utilities, consist entirely of service businesses. And services themselves are changing from ones based on delivery or movement of things to ones based on information. Out of heavy industry and traditional services into knowledge: this is the direction in which America is rapidly moving.

The New Restless Capital: Mobility, Reorganization, and Relocation

Accelerating the transformation of America's employers is the new restless mobility of capital. No longer faithful to a given company, capital has become restless, promiscuous, and fast.

Once content to keep the home fires burning for the large companies of the world, capital now roams the world over the electronic net in search of action.

I call this phenomenon "capital's new mobility," and it too will dramatically transform America's labor market over the next quarter century.

Capital's restlessness and promiscuity are a direct result of new technology that permits the rapid transfer of funds, goods, enterprises, and employees. It's a new phenomenon in the world, driven partly by the ability to move money over wires but also by the ability to communicate and travel easily overseas. Once upon a time, going "in country" was left to a disappearing breed, the old-fashioned expatriate. The expat's trip by boat out to the region might take weeks. Visas, vaccinations, banking, and other matters were a complex affair. Once overseas, the expat had minimal contact with people back home, and some "went native." Only a decade ago, telex was the predominant means of communicating with many countries and business cards bore telex addresses. Today, anyone with a credit card, a passport, and a laptop computer can hop on an airplane and get to work. This expedites the flow of capital across borders.

During the postwar years in the United States, détente among government, unions, and business as well as growing regulations put the brakes on capital. But that world is slipping away. Over the last decade, information technology and relaxed regulations have freed capital of many of its bounds. It has become easier than ever for a capitalist to move or shutter a plant. The embodiment of more and more technology in machinery makes it feasible to locate even the most sophisticated semiconductor plants in low-wage countries. Today, a high-tech manufacturer like Texas Instruments, Hitachi, or Intel can open a new facility in virtually any country in the world that offers the right mix of incentives.

Cloning a high-tech factory has become almost as easy as franchising a doughnut shop, a far cry from the day when technological competence had to be built up slowly and required long periods of apprenticeship.

But the change goes deeper than that. No longer are wealth and enterprise primarily a matter of plants and machinery. As the world advances further into the information age, capital need not be invested in land or factories at all. More and more money can be made through information itself, without investing in bricks and mortar. The financial markets now generate huge value added from moving paper alone. And that is only the beginning. Telephone companies recognize that new revenues will come not from calls alone but from information *about* calls and callers, whether through Yellow Pages revenues, caller ID services, or more sophisticated billing. Indeed, billing skills are the phone companies' biggest weapon in their coming battle with cable firms and others to provide access to the information highway. Federal Express believes its tracking services provide more value to customers than the actual movement of packages.

In a very real sense, more and more capital has entered cyberspace where it can move around free of impediments.

Eventually, most of it must touch back down on earth—in the form of a thing or service, since capital, by definition, is convertible into goods of some kind. But some goods—for example, information that people buy over America Online or data they buy from Bloomberg—need never come back to earth. Less and less capital is locked up in plant and equipment; more and more in organization, information, and other floating intangibles.

What this means is that capital's mobility has exploded, permitting fantastic new efficiencies in capital allocation as it roams the world by day and night in search of higher returns (often by-passing old intermediaries such as banks). The world and, in particular, America are moving toward real-time capital allocation.

Capital's New Advantage over Labor

Capital has always fled older industries, leaving makers of buggy whips high and dry, while flocking to makers of the horseless carriage. But the new speed of this activity is unprecedented, and it gives capital a new advantage over labor, particularly the traditional worker. Capital increasingly resides not in fields, bricks, or iron but in cyberspace, where, free of conventional restraints, it can roam the world at the speed of light.

Labor, in contrast to capital, remains stuck in marriages, mortgages, and the real world.

While the airplane has speeded up travel and people can now work on line, they remain less flexible than capital. On balance, this has tipped the scales, at least initially, in capital's favor. Bear in mind that capital's mobility should, in theory, help labor—indeed, everyone—by creating more efficient markets. And it does help labor as a whole throughout the world. If a plant closes in one country and opens in another, one group loses but another benefits. The problem is that movements of capital are disruptive to people; when a plant closes and people have to find new work, there are high transaction costs to pay: forced sales of homes, broken families, and unemployment.

Capital Versus Labor through History

Before the Industrial Revolution, when most capital was tied up in land, aristocrats had few alternatives to operating their estates. During hard times, it was easier for peasants to leave the land in search of better prospects in America or London than for a lord to move his capital to get a higher return.

Industrialization increased capital's mobility, giving capitalists more leverage over workers. European capital went to America to fund railroads, to Malaysia to plant rubber trees, and to India to build textile factories. Still, steel plants had to be located near iron and coal reserves, rubber plantations in suitable climes, and textile mills near running water. As industrialization progressed, large plants proved easy targets for unionization. A union could some-times literally block off the only road to a factory, making it easy to shut it down.

Cities, crammed full of workers, for their part, radicalized politi-cally. The fixed location of plants and their resulting vulnerability encouraged capitalists to seek labor peace. By the third quarter of the twentieth century, a new breed of professional managers for hire could enjoy lucrative, lifelong careers at a single company, while unionized workers could attain a middle-class lifestyle.

Over the last decade, thanks to technology, the decline of unions (which have failed to internationalize to compete with interna-tional capital and never will since people are less fungible than money[3]), better capital markets, and the growth of the service economy, it has become easier than ever for a capitalist to move his or her capital. In Eastern Europe, the collapse of communism has removed the last major bulwark against the movement of capital. Everywhere, capital has opened up a lead over labor.

Capital moves fastest of all in the United States, where officers of pension funds are legally required to move it as fast as they can.

Indeed, more and more money is controlled by funds that by law must seek out the highest return available from public markets around the world. Many such institutions face no tax consequences when buying or selling. Their transaction costs for moving money are virtually zero.

True, workers can move to seek jobs in other locations. The single largest group of illegal aliens in New York is not from the Caribbean or Asia but from Italy. Most travel to New York by airplane on tourist visas, look around, and, if they like it, get a job. There were 30,000 such illegal Italians in New York recently.[4] Labor's mobility has increased from the days of booking steerage passage months in advance and packing all one's possessions into trunks. But its mobility can hardly compete with that of capital moving over satellites and phone lines at the speed of light.

The results of this new balance of power can be read in how labor and capital are dividing up the spoils in America. Capital is helping itself to more and more profits, labor to less and less. In 1994, corporate-sector operating profits hit 15 percent, their highest level in two decades. The rate of return on capital after inflation went up to 6.5 percent, the highest rate in a quarter century.[5] Meanwhile, wages and benefits have dropped to 81 percent of profits, the lowest level since 1969, and wages and salaries to 67 percent of profits, the lowest level of the postwar era.

In other countries, labor gets even less of the spoils. In Japan, for example, capital helps itself to a much higher percentage of return, and most capital is reinvested. Indeed, the fact that capital is gaining leverage over labor does not automatically mean that capitalists will begin spending more money on yachts and gold-plated faucets. It's up to the capitalists themselves to determine whether they build their capital or consume it. In the 1980s, in the United States, they consumed it. However, when tycoons waste money, it is usually other people's, notably the government's. For example, the government paid for the S&L bubble and, through tax credits, financed the consumer binge of the 1980s. Free-spending moguls become as tight-fisted as anyone else when their own after-tax money is at stake. In the 1990s, evidence suggests, they have begun to conserve and invest it.

This is not to imply that labor mobility is bad for capitalists. It's good overall. In the nineteenth century, imported Chinese and Irish labor enabled capitalists to build the transcontinental railroad. Today, mobile Mexican labor benefits California growers. The ability of Mexicans to cross the U.S. border helps Mexican workers and American capitalists but hurts Mexican capitalists and American workers.

While mobility of both capital and labor contributes to overall efficiency and benefits everyone in the long run, in the short

run, it helps those who have it and hurts those who don't. At the moment, capital has more of it than labor.

The collapse of communism has eliminated the largest political barrier to global capitalism. And with communism gone except in a handful of countries, it's clear that capitalism will be the protagonist of the next quarter century. But who or what will be the antagonist? Who, if anyone, can apply the brakes to capital? It won't be organized labor. Labor will play a role in the future, perhaps most violently in such countries as China, but in the more advanced countries its power has peaked. Barring a major war, it won't be government either. The main potential brakes on capital are religion, tribalism, and environmentalism. None will significantly challenge capitalism in the near future, although they may mount a serious challenge later in the twenty-first century, as discussed in Chapter 8.

The New Balance of Power

The change in the balance of power from labor to capital affects managers as well as workers. It is largely responsible for the shareholder rights movement. It has emboldened owners to demand more and more from managers. Those who control capital—rich individuals, pension funds, and speculators—are increasingly using their power to force changes in corporate management. And downsizing, a consequence of capital's new efficiency, has reduced the status of those who found security in the old order, upper-level managers and workers alike. (Large CEO salaries reflect participation in capital flows through stock options designed to unite CEO interests with those of shareholders.)

The change in the balance of power between capital and labor has huge implications for anyone trying to chart his or her economic future. First, those with capital have a clear advantage over those without it. People with capital are in luck. But the very power of capital means that capitalists must increasingly think about building it rather than blowing it. Those without capital face a less predictable world and less security.

All those anxious to control their future should no longer put their faith in a lifetime of work for someone else's concern.

Instead, they might think about taking advantage of capital's powers themselves. Alternatively, those who want to work for others must figure out ways to even the score. For the situation is not static. Labor is adapting to capital's new mobility, nowhere more than in the United States.

The truth is, both capital and labor are still struggling for power in the new world that information technology is building. Both entrepreneur and employee can benefit from a better understanding of the labor market. Despite capital's new mobility, there are ways for labor to level the playing field. And capitalists, to compete against other capitalists, must understand how to make the most of capital's advantages over labor and the coming changes in labor itself.

How Labor Is Coping with Mobile Capital

At first glance, capital now appears to hold all the cards vis-à-vis labor. Companies can restructure, move overseas, or simply liquidate and shut down. The unemployed can find other jobs or go on welfare. Unions have dramatically declined, not only in size but in popular esteem. Job security, in the old sense, is a thing of the past. The threat of foreign competition and job loss are powerful inducements to employees—all the way up to the CEOs—to do whatever capital wants.

According to Bureau of Labor Statistics data, of workers who lost permanent jobs between 1991 and 1993 and found new jobs, 53 percent made more than before, 47 percent less. Twenty-seven percent were making at least 20 percent more, 26 percent between 0 and 19 percent more.[6] In other words, more than half of the people who found new jobs ended up better off than before. Not bad! However, the broad statistics hide what happened to certain groups. While women saw a rise in salary, males between ages twenty-five and fifty-four who lost jobs in the 1990s took a 20 percent hit on average.[7] The U.S. job system, though more flexible than any other, is still imperfectly equipped to handle lateral movement. Even under the best of circumstances, changing jobs is difficult. The difficulty of getting another job with equal pay, even with unemployment at only 5 percent, has made many Americans grateful for any job they can get.

Compounding the problem, holding one job has been no bargain. Real wages began to stagnate after 1973. While women's wages have risen as men's have dropped, married women realize that they must now work for their families to enjoy a level of security that a husband could once provide alone. Thus, American workers, on the whole, are dissatisfied. They have lost the security and stability of the golden years after World War II, a consequence of the new mobility of capital and economic change. Keeping one job is no longer the ticket to prosperity it once was. By contrast, salaries for those at the top have increased exorbitantly. CEOs, Wall Street executives, baseball players, and, most of all, owners of companies make more than ever before. But this provides little consolation to the majority of Americans, whose reaction to the high incomes of those at the top is a mixture of resignation and anger.

Some people look longingly to other countries' systems, but a reality check is in order. Unemployment in Europe is 11 percent, compared with 5 percent in America. The much-vaunted training system in Germany has done precious little to boost employment, while perpetuating differences between classes. Japan has a low unemployment level but also a low standard of living. Its producer economy has protected workers from the winds of capitalism, but only at the cost of sky-high prices for goods, almost no lateral movement for labor, restrictive immigration policies, and what in the U.S. would be unacceptable constraints on women. The head of Japan's New Frontier Party recently complained that Japanese firms treat their workers like pets. Discontent and dissatisfaction are higher abroad, on average, than in the United States.

Yet an objective assessment of the new economy reveals that while mobile capital has reduced security, it has created immense new opportunities in the United States that the old system could never have provided.

At the same time that capital has grown more mobile, it has grown far easier to obtain.

The deverticalization of industry and the growth of small business have created vast new opportunities for entrepreneurs. It has driven a sea change in the workforce: an explosion of entrepreneurship as employees turn into capitalists. This is a phenomenon that has not occurred in either Europe or Japan and is another area in which Americans have a distinct advantage.

Entrepreneurship: If You Can't Beat 'Em, Join 'Em

Not long ago, when large organizations dominated the economy, Americans who wanted to get ahead dreamed of going to work for IBM. Today, more and more people dream of starting their own businesses—and many do. The new models of success are not organization men but entrepreneurs like Bill Gates of Microsoft and Michael Dell of Dell Computer. Neither of these men had a traditional job history of working for someone else. Both of them built huge fortunes. For every successful billionaire entrepreneur, countless others are trying to emulate their success. Again, technology has facilitated the change.

In the old days, the everyday chores of running a business, including answering phones, sending out letters, and keeping the books, were jobs unto themselves. Before 1979, there were few answering machines. The IBM-PC did not arrive until 1981. Well into the 1980s, in order to hang out a shingle, a would-be entrepreneur needed, at a minimum, to rent office space and hire a secretary. Small businesses were forever fighting battles to appear legitimate.

But today, to go into business, all people have to do is change the message on their answering machines. An up-to-date personal computer can handle correspondence, phone mail, E-mail, accounting, faxing, and the other basics of business. New word processing programs create customized stationery with a few clicks of the mouse. Many businesses—both blue-collar ones like plumbing, electrical work, and contracting and white-collar ones like law—benefit from pagers and cellular phones. But that's only the beginning.

Personal digital assistants (PDAs) can now do telephoning, faxing, paging, word processing, scheduling, and almost every other office task, and can be carried around in one's pocket. Future versions of the Apple Newton MessagePad, HP palmtop, and other PDAs and personal communicators or digital phones will further refine the concept of the portable digital secretary. A software program called Wildfire can page you, screen calls, type memos, and do almost everything secretaries do.

The growth of small businesses has fueled an explosion in services that cater to them. Over the last ten years, a raft of magazines for business owners has appeared, including *Entrepreneur, Inc., Home-Office Computing, Kiplinger's Money Report,* and others. More and more computer programs are directed at the smaller business. Rather than invest in phone lines, today's entrepreneurs can get a telephone number with voice mail for a few dollars a month, in major cities, with no up-front charges. Some such services provide multiple mailboxes, options to callers, and even operator backup that let tiny companies appear as professional as big ones. Shared offices have become big business. In many large cities, visitors in town for only a few days can rent an office.

Legal and technical barriers to opening a company have been lowered. The Company Corporation in Delaware now lets people form a company over CompuServe or by phone in minutes. In numerous ways, barriers to entry have tumbled. Accordingly, the number of new businesses is growing dramatically. In 1984, America had 4.9 million incorporated businesses; in 1993, it had 3 million. Fifty-four percent more firms filed tax returns in 1990 than in 1980.

The number of people per business in the United States dropped from 18 in 1980 to 12 in 1990.

This is a sea change in the American economy, and the growth of small business has, to a significant extent, come at the expense of big business. In 1994, small business played a pivotal role in blocking health care reform in Congress, while much of big business supported reform. That same year, small business started its first caucus in the House of Representatives. As small business grows, its purchasing power grows too, and it commands even more support in the way of services, products, and help from lawmakers. In terms of influence, small business has achieved a critical mass.

Today, even low-skilled workers have the option of starting their own business. Janitors start janitorial service firms. Hospital orderlies tired of emptying bedpans start health care service firms and employ others to empty the pans. Of course, starting a business requires some capital. But it takes less and less capital, and more people are taking the risk.

People who have studied small-business behavior point out that small-business owners often act irrationally by working harder than the return would justify. On average, they argue, small-business owners would do better to take jobs. What these studies ignore is that starting a business provides an outlet for hard work and the opportunity to make additional returns that salaried jobs do not. Further, small businesses can take advantage of numerous legal ways to reduce taxes. And finally, there is a big payoff to starting a business that does not exist when working for a salary. If a salaried worker makes $50,000 a year and a business generates $40,000 a year in profits for the owner, you might argue that the salaried worker is earning more. However, if a small business takes off, its income stream becomes an asset that can be sold. A business generating $40,000 in profits is worth $400,000 at a 10 percent capitalization rate. Small businessmen dream about this payoff when they work long hours. More and more people, meanwhile, are starting businesses in the hope of franchising them.

The economic incentives for starting a small business have grown stronger and will grow stronger still in years ahead. Today, retail businesses account for about one quarter of the business establishments in the United States. Most require considerable overhead in the form of rent, salaries, and inventory. But just as national chains have begun to sell goods over networks, paying rent to network providers such as Prodigy and Microsoft, so smaller businesses will begin to sell on line, paying a reduced rent for their "storefronts" on local networks or Internet service providers. By creating a virtual storefront instead of a real one, companies will slash overhead.

The network revolution makes it easier to locate a business in a low-cost area but sell into a higher-cost one.

Electronic retailers can sell into Manhattan, for instance, through electronic storefronts from operations based in New Jersey, the Bronx, or Texas. Dial-A-Mattress, the New York area company that sells mattresses by phone and guarantees delivery by truck the same day, pioneered the use of a virtual storefront using an old technology: the telephone. The company keeps prices in check by eliminating retail locations and doing all its selling via a toll-free number.

Virtual storefronts using computer technology are just beginning to appear. Credit cards have made it easier than ever to raise the money to start a small business. In coming years, barriers to starting a new business will continue to drop, increasing opportunities for people who want to control their own capital to try to do so. Starting a business is one of the main ways Americans are evening the score with restless capital: They are becoming capitalists themselves.

Going Mobile

Another trick that Americans (as well as people everywhere) will use to keep up with capital is an old one: they will move. America was founded by people who moved. To this day, people from all over the world continue to flock to America in search of the American Dream. And from pioneer days, Americans have migrated within the country in hopes of a better life. They are still moving in a way unheard of in most of the rest of the world. America is still a restless, rootless country.

Americans don't hesitate to go where the jobs are. Over the last decade, 40 percent of Americans have moved.[8] Between 1980 and 1990, the population of the fastest-growing state, Nevada, increased 50 percent while that of the fastest-shrinking state, Iowa, decreased almost 5 percent. By county, the percentages are even more dramatic. They're fleeing taxes, unions, cities, and the aging buildings of the North for new construction down south. In even greater numbers they're moving west. As Americans move in search of jobs, economic activity, or retirement, they generate other activity: the construction of malls, roads, and housing.

What makes America such a popular destination for foreigners and what encourages Americans to move within the country is the wide-open nature, both geographic and cultural, of the country, nowhere more than out west. While residents of the state of Washington may complain about new arrivals from California, Seattle's mayor during the late 1980s, Charles Royer, a former TV newscaster, moved to the city only a decade before he ran. Royer, originally from Oregon, points out that in Boston a newcomer without roots could never be elected mayor. On the West Coast, it's different. The capitalist ideology and America's cultural openness to newcomers permit more mobility. In Europe, in contrast, mobility is drastically curtailed by tradition and a closed-mindedness toward recent arrivals that reflects not only the settled nature of the continent but a static economy. In Japan, few foreigners are even allowed to work on a temporary basis, and movement by nationals is complicated by a shortage of land and housing.

Thus, in the United States, the country where capital is most mobile, labor is also mobile, partially evening the score. Still, the increasing mobility of capital in recent years has outstripped the ability of people to move by car and plane. However, Americans have another trick, less available in other countries: the ability to work over wires.

Telecommuting

Not long ago, IBM's Cranford, New Jersey, sales office decided to change the way it serviced customers. It had been servicing customers from the office. Its sales staff would make calls on clients, but they also spent a lot of time sitting at desks. Besides spending less time with customers, IBM's deskbound salespeople ate up company overhead. The firm decided to kick its staff out of the office into the field. IBM being IBM, it didn't just ask them to work at home. Instead, it redesigned a facility to accommodate mobile workers.

The resulting reorganization of space has saved the company a bundle and pushed salespeople into the field. IBM has replaced 400,000 square feet of offices with 100,000 square feet. Cubicles are assigned as people check in. At first, the unit's 600 salespeople were assigned to areas corresponding to departments, but now they are assigned cubicles randomly, which encourages them to meet more people, a concept called hot-desking or hoteling. About 150 support people send out paperwork, which mobile employees can order up by computer from the field.

Telecommuting—living in one place while working in another—has become an important trend in the labor market, one that will accelerate dramatically in years ahead. The phenomenon is only in its infancy and is far more advanced in the United States than in any other country for a number of reasons:

• U.S. firms are more lenient about work and anxious to cut overhead through innovative means than most firms abroad.

• Use of personal computers (as well as other new technologies) is far higher in the United States than elsewhere.

• U.S. homes are bigger than those in Japan and most of Europe.

- Traffic and air problems have driven some states such as California to offer incentives to work from home and the EPA to order urban firms to cut solo car trips.

- U.S. telephone charges are cheaper than in other industrialized countries.

- On-line services are far more advanced.

For these reasons, increasing numbers of Americans are no longer working in an office. Freed of geographical limits, they have improved their bargaining position with capital.

Working by wire enables an individual to keep up with capital.

Indeed, labor in the United States can sometimes be more mobile than capital. How? While capital moves at a breakneck pace in some sectors, in others, it remains tied to locations, networks of distributors, and other physical realities. In such situations, people who can work over a wire may actually have an advantage.

Many Americans are beginning to move out of high-cost areas into low-cost ones but still perform work for companies based in the high-cost areas. With the adroit use of information technology, they are improving their standard of living by a process I call "arbitraging places" (see Chapter 7). A top executive who reports to corporate headquarters each day and spends a third of the year on airplanes may still earn more than an advertising executive who does his Los Angeles client's work from Montana. But the Montana-based advertising consultant will probably have a lower cost of living and an easier life than one who fights Los Angeles traffic every day. Telecommuting, combined with starting an independent business, provides the most protection from the new mobility of capital, at the cost of traditional security. Whether it's better or worse than a traditional job (and really less secure) will depend on the job in question.

Electronic bulletin boards will further add to mobility by making it easier than ever for employees to meet up with employers.

In coming years, America will move toward a virtual labor market, consisting of stateless transactions on a net.

This is not high-tech mumbo jumbo but a real development. Just as the World Wide Web on the Internet is effectively stateless, permitting people to communicate on a constantly changing web of connections that take advantage of excess telephone capacity, or just as NASDAQ now pairs buyers and sellers of stock all over the country, so capital and labor will increasingly meet in cyberspace on a network that exists independently of the geographic world.

Workers will bid for work in competition with workers around the country. Companies will bid for labor in competition with other companies in different locations. Obviously, manufacturing workers who must report to an assembly line every day will not be able to participate in this cyberauction. Similarly, executives responsible for supervising plants and other physical assets will continue to work at a traditional office building or factory (although many are already serving huge territories by means of the airplane and the phone). But people who can work over a wire—sales staff, accountants, technologists, lawyers, writers, and so forth—will increasingly interact with a national (and eventually even global) base of employers. When executive search firms are able to hunt heads all over the world, the resulting labor contracts or transactions will be more efficient, and both labor and capital should benefit.[9]

In short, capital is more mobile in the United States than in other countries; labor is more mobile as well. On balance, this helps the United States relative to its competitors: capitalism benefits from fewer constraints, while labor's options mitigate the unsettling effects of restless capital.

Avoiding Global Competition

One last trick is open to American workers, one many will use without realizing it. Imports still account for only 12 percent of the economy. Whereas the manufacturing sector is open to imports and requires cooperation from buyers overseas, some sectors remain insulated from trade and foreign competition. These include construction and retail and wholesale merchandising, as well as many technical jobs servicing installed equipment. Such sectors will tend to look kindly on American workers, particularly as labor shortages crop up from time to time. In 1995, for example, long-haul truck drivers were in such short supply that trucking firms were increasing their benefits and raising their pay.[10]

Not that any sector can escape capital's new mobility: Shrinking demand or a higher return in any industry anywhere in the world will cause both capital and jobs to disappear or move. Even housing starts depend on complex factors with global origins while jobs in the export sector pay more, on average, than other jobs. But, that said, sectors such as construction, when they boom, will reward local American workers. Even prefabricated houses have to be assembled by someone. Insulation from global competition may dampen productivity growth in these sectors but will tend to preserve jobs and, if the service is a necessity, wages.

The Greater Size of the U.S. Workforce

On balance, the U.S. labor market will be a source of strength in coming years. Over the next quarter century, the American workforce will grow far larger than it is today, a development that will help employers as well as the economy as a whole. The working-age population, a key determinant of a country's prosperity, will rise in the United States over the next quarter century both in absolute terms and as a percentage of the country's total. In 2010, the working-age population of the United States will be about 3 percentage points higher than Germany's and 5 points higher than Japan's, the opposite of what it is today.

The working-age population in America is rising at precisely the same time it is falling in Japan, Germany, and most of America's competitors.

Employers will benefit from this larger pool of labor. But it will help the nation as a whole. As the working-age population rises over the next quarter century, the United States will have more people to support the young and the old. This means that working people, on balance, will pay fewer taxes and have fewer expenses at home.

This trend bodes extremely well for the United States. But what most people have heard and focus on is that the U.S. population is aging. And the aging of the country is often held up as a dangerous development. In fact, the United States is currently too *young* and is aging into a superior age configuration. However, that trend has been twisted by some to suggest that the numbers of retired elderly will soon swell to levels at which working people can no longer support them. That is not the case. The false idea that America is somehow aging itself into poverty has contributed to pessimism about the future.

America's working-age population is rising as a percentage of the total, not declining. The rise in the working-age population between 1990 and 2010 will increase the size of the workforce by more than 25 million people.[11] What economists call the "economic dependency ratio" (the ratio of those too young or old to work to those of working age) will plummet. This ratio has been declining steadily since 1975. Between today and the year 2005, it will further decline, from 96.4 percent to 89.7 percent. While the retirement rolls will start to grow faster than the working-age population when the baby boomers hit retirement age in 2015, the total number of dependents per worker will shrink.

Working-age people will have more elderly people but fewer children to support over the next quarter century.

Children, not the elderly, consume most of a society's resources. They don't have houses, investments, retirement plans, pensions, or other assets that retirees tend to have. In the year 2020, retirees will own more than $10 trillion in assets. Unlike children, they can also work. Moreover, the average annual income from Social Security is currently about $12,000; the average cost of raising a child is far more.

Germany currently has more people of retirement age than the United States will have in 2020 as a percentage of its total and is not experiencing any crisis. The only way Social Security payments will pose a problem is if wages fail to grow. If wages grow at 2 percent annually, as they did up to 1973 and have during the first years of the Clinton administration, the Social Security Trust Fund will be flush with money when the boomers retire.

Finally, America will find it easier to care for children in coming years as the number of women of childbearing age declines as a percentage of the workforce. Economists track this indicator because it measures the need for daycare and other services for working mothers. In 1948, women of childbearing age made up only 20 percent of the workforce. In the 1970s and 1980s, their numbers soared until, in 1987, they represented 33 percent of the workforce. Since then, their number has begun to decline. By the year 2005, they will make up only 29.8 percent of the workforce, reducing demand for services.[12]

Compared to other developed countries such as Germany and Japan, the United States is aging more gracefully for two main reasons: the size of its baby boom, which dwarfed those elsewhere, and its diverse population, which contains more immigrants. In the United States, the baby boom ran from 1946 to 1964; in war-ravaged Europe and Japan, baby booms never got off the ground. The large bulge of boomers in the United States is serving as a counterweight to the generation ahead of it, the group that in Germany and Japan is pulling the average age off the scale. Meanwhile, American baby boomers' children, a boomlet themselves, will also moderate the aging trend.

Improved Quality of the Workforce

Not only is the U.S. workforce growing, its levels of quality and experience are improving. This is a positive trend for everyone: workers, employers, and the economy as a whole.

In the 1970s and 1980s, the United States experienced an unusual demographic triple whammy when three groups of predomi-

nantly unskilled workers suddenly entered the workforce. The first
new group was immigrants, who began to come to the United
States in significant numbers after immigration policy was changed
in 1965. The new arrivals tended to be young, unskilled, and non-
English-speaking.

**Since 1970, a total of 17 million immigrants has entered the
United States.**

The largest group, almost 8 million, has come from Mexico. About
2 million have come from the Caribbean, notably from Jamaica, the
Dominican Republic, and Cuba. Six million have come from Asia,
notably from the Philippines, China, South Korea, and Vietnam.
Europe has contributed about 2 million, about 300,000 each from
the United Kingdom and the former Soviet Union. The legal immigrant population has been supplemented by illegal aliens.

The second group to enter the workforce consisted of baby
boomers. Technically, the baby boom began in 1946, immediately
after the war, but it did not really take off until 1950. Significant
numbers of boomers did not come of working age (sixteen years)
until 1966. College-educated boomers began to enter the workforce in 1971, but as a result of the Vietnam War, which drafted
some male workers and kept others in college longer than usual,
the baby boom first began to hit America hard in about 1973. As the
1970s and 1980s progressed, the wave continued; the last of the
baby boomers hit the age of sixteen in 1980 and if they completed
college got their first jobs in 1985. Statistics bear out the onslaught.
The overall number of workers in the United States increased by
about 700,000 per year in the 1950s and 1.3 million a year during
the 1960s. Then, in the 1970s, the rate doubled to 2.4 million,
reaching 3 million for a few years at the end of the decade. The
overall labor supply surged 29 percent in the 1970s before tapering
off in the 1980s. Today, growth is in line with the growth during the
1950s. From 3 percent annual growth in the 1970s and 1.7 percent
growth in the 1980s, it has fallen to close to a one percent annual
growth rate, the rate of growth in the population.

The third new group to hit the workforce was women, a sea

change that began in 1970, when labor-force participation by women began to accelerate. One contributing factor was a technological change in the workplace. In 1960, 34 percent of workers were in services, including finance and retail; by 1970, this figure had reached 42 percent. While women had always worked in services and certain types of manufacturing, men possessed obvious physical advantages for jobs as laborers or in heavy industry. The expansion of the service economy offered new opportunities for women.

From an employer's point of view, women willing to work full-time were a dream come true: comparatively well educated, underemployed, and available to hire for less than men.

Second, the end of the baby boom freed women from child-rearing duties. By 1975, the first boomers were twenty-nine and the last boomers were eleven. The influx of women into the workforce was accordingly two-pronged. Having already raised their children, the mothers of boomers returned to the workforce. Labor participation by women aged thirty-five to forty-four (whose children had typically reached their teenage years) jumped from 43 percent to 66 percent between 1960 and 1980. Meanwhile, their daughters, the baby boom women, began to marry later and have fewer children. The labor-force participation rate of women aged twenty to twenty-four jumped from 58 percent to 69 percent between 1970 and 1980.

Third, improved methods of birth control gave women more control over when they had children. And fourth, on a cultural level, the very institution of marriage came under assault in the 1960s. Out-of-wedlock births began to accelerate sharply in the mid-1960s, not only in the United States but in England and almost everywhere else. From a historical level of 4 percent, out-of-wedlock births have steadily risen in the United States to 30 percent today. Indeed, the rates of out-of-wedlock birth in several countries are far higher than in the United States. Out-of-wedlock births may simply reflect an increase in the number of working women, or they may have been a reason why more women went to work. What is irrefutable is that the number of out-of-wedlock births correlates with the number of women working.

Fifth, labor-saving devices and an explosion in the 1960s and 1970s of restaurants and other businesses offering services that women had performed in the home made it easier for women to work.

American households outsourced housework in the 1970s and 1980s to restaurants, frozen food firms and others.

Finally, the women's liberation movement of the 1970s encouraged women to return to the workforce. Bottom line: the labor force participation rate of women soared from 1975 to 1991. About 1.3 million new women entered the workforce each year during the 1970s and early 1980s. In 1977, 2.3 million entered the workforce. The female labor participation rate rose from 43% in 1970 to 58% in 1990.

Twenty-five million more women were working in 1990 than in 1970.

The largest influx of immigrants, baby boomers, and women occurred at the bottom rungs of the workforce, the lowest-paying band.

As with any commodity—wheat, tobacco, coffee, or people—a huge surplus of workers lowered their price.

This surge in the supply of labor, not any fundamental problem of American industry, stymied wage growth. In contrast, America's major competitors experienced no such phenomenon.

- No other country experienced U.S.-style immigration.

- Japan never had a baby boom. Fertility rates of Japanese women dropped steadily after the war and by 1955 had already declined to 2.0. Germany had a moderate baby boom, but its fertility rate never topped 2.5. In contrast, the U.S. rate was 3.5 in 1950 and by 1955 had soared to 3.8; not until 1970 did it drop back down to 2.0.

• In Germany and Japan, whether for cultural reasons or because their economies remained largely industrial, female labor-force participation rates did not increase to the degree they did in the United States.

Not surprisingly, real German and Japanese wages increased sharply during the 1980s though in Germany at the cost of some unemployment.

But today the U.S. economy has absorbed this flood of workers and fitted them out with jobs. The baby boom is over. The labor-force participation rate of women has almost reached parity with that of men. Women's wages have also risen so that they are no longer undercutting those of men (who have shouldered wage stagnation). No new influx of native unskilled workers can dampen wage growth in coming years. Indeed, a shrinking labor supply at lower age levels and in lower-level jobs will buoy wages in years to come. Generation X-ers will see their wages rise sharply as labor shortages set in.

The situation with foreign-born workers is less clear. If immigrants continue to arrive in the United States in large numbers, employers of low-wage workers will benefit but productivity and wages may suffer. Already, McDonald's and other fast-food restaurants that hired high school students in the 1970s now hire immigrants in their stead. However, there is a growing political movement that would ban or severely reduce immigration. If that occurs, the third pig in the python will disappear, too. But even if it doesn't, the absorption of baby boomers and new female workers has taken a lid off wage growth. This bodes well for people who work for a salary and will reduce capital's advantage over labor in years ahead.

Finally, mention should be made of the fourth group of people who entered the workforce in the 1960s, the 2.7 million workers who left the farm in a previous wave of agricultural "downsizing." Disproportionately African American, this group arrived in the cities only to face harrowing competition from immigrants as well as baby boomers and women, many blessed with the full complement of middle-class advantages, from stable families to college educations. The difficulties this group faced in adjusting, difficulties exacerbated by competition for jobs, fed the growth of the economic underclass in the 1960s and 1970s. In coming years, less competition from boomers and new female workers will help descendants of agricultural workers find jobs in the service economy. They would get another boost from limits on immigration. However, the social problems created by one or two generations of life in the underclass mean that a solution will not occur overnight.

The Aging and Seasoning of the American Worker

The end of the baby boom has led to another trend that is good for the economy, for labor, and even for employers: the aging of the American worker.

In 1960, before boomers began to enter the workforce, the average age of the American worker was forty. After dropping precipitously, it will attain that level again in 2005.

Forty is a good age for workers. They are knowledgeable, seasoned, responsible, and still young enough to be comparatively healthy. An average age of forty implies a rough balance between those just entering the workforce at sixteen and those leaving it at sixty-five.

From a benchmark of 40 when John F. Kennedy took office, the average age of workers began dropping in the early 1960s because of the boomers, slowly at first, and then sharply in the 1970s, reaching its nadir of 34.7 years in 1979. Not surprisingly, low-skilled, low-wage jobs in service businesses such as McDonald's and Domino's Pizza proliferated during this period. But today, the average age is 38, and over the next ten years it will continue to rise, reaching 40.5 again in the year 2005.

This will have positive consequences for the country. Seasoned workers have more skills, experience, and knowledge than younger ones. They drink and use drugs less and miss work less often. They commit fewer crimes and save more money. They also earn larger salaries.[13] These things should benefit both the economy and people's standard of living.

Even employers should benefit from a higher-quality workforce. Fast-food chains may find it harder to attract staff and may have to invest in productivity improvements. But other employers will have access to more experienced workers. Higher savings rates among older workers should feed the nation's pool of capital. And the aging of the American workforce will, paradoxically, help younger workers the most since they are increasingly in short supply.

The number of men aged 24 to 34 will decline absolutely by nearly 2.9 million between 1992 and 2005, a drop of 14.7 percent.

A Note on Inflation

A particular group of pessimists, typified by Martin Feldstein, who was chief economic adviser to President Reagan, worry that with too few people out of work, employers will bid up wages, causing inflation. But in a free economy wage increases, unlike commodity increases, are not by definition inflationary. All economists, including Feldstein, agree that wages can experience *real* growth—that is, increase more than inflation. The question comes down to whether employers deal with wage increases by launching productivity measures or pass them on to consumers; inflation alarmists always assume the latter.

In the current environment, however, Feldstein is wrong to worry about wage inflation. Low unemployment has not caused inflation yet. Nor have labor shortages at the lower end of the workforce. In today's global economy, higher wages, except in special cases, do not pose a serious inflation risk. While employers may want to pass wage increases on to consumers, they can't. American consumers will not oblige them; they have the option to buy from someone else. As a result, higher wages force employers to invest in new plant and equipment or redesign work processes to improve labor productivity. High wages have historically driven productivity increases, which have permitted higher wages still.

To do more with less, a company may have to lay off workers. But the remaining workers get paid more. And higher productivity increases growth, which allows those laid off to find work elsewhere—even at the same enterprise if productivity gains boost sales. For example, Denny's, like other fast-food chains, has run up against the problem of disappearing cheap labor. Denny's competition was not other fast-food chains, which face similar costs, but other sources of food such as frozen meals and conventional restaurants. Competition kept it from passing higher wages on to consumers. This meant that Denny's had two choices: close stores or increase productivity. It chose the latter and has radically redesigned work processes.

Similarly, Taco Bell has engineered major improvements in productivity by shifting an entire level of food preparation, the manufacturing part of cooking—crushing beans, shredding cheese, and the like—out of individual restaurants to outside contractors that specialize in high-volume food processing. This maneuver has not only cut the cost of preparing food but, more to the point, cut required kitchen size by 40 percent, reducing real estate costs, freeing up space for seats and permitting stores to open where space is limited—for example, in airports.[14] Likewise, Pizza Hut is testing the use of large cheese disks on its pizzas in place of shredded cheese to speed preparation and make pizzas uniform. Appetizing, maybe not; more productive, definitely.

This virtuous cycle is the opposite of the vicious cycle that can occur when wages drop, diminishing investment in productive plant and equipment and leading to lower wages still, what happened during the Reagan years. Of course, this vicious cycle can continue only as long as there is an ample supply of cheap labor—which there was in the United States for most of the last two decades. But as the labor supply has tightened, this cycle has come up short.

Inflation numbers in recent years bear this out: in 1994, core inflation (inflation not counting volatile food and energy prices) reached its lowest level since 1965. And while inflation in manufac-

turing was modest, inflation in services tumbled from 3.8 percent
to 2.9 percent, proving that upward pressure on costs has led to
improved productivity, not inflation.

**The virtuous cycle of higher wages spurring productivity and
making possible still higher wages will be good for the economy
and good for those who sell their labor for a living.**

It will even be good for employers, once they adjust, since it will
force them to become more productive.

Better Training

One last thing can benefit labor (and U.S. employers): training.
Workers with training have an advantage over those without it. For
the individual, whether laborer or executive, education has become increasingly valuable. M.B.A.'s make more than B.A.'s. (The
so-called oversupply of M.B.A.'s has done nothing to narrow this
gap.) B.A.'s make more than high school graduates. Anyone who
fails to graduate from high school is in tough shape indeed. It pays
to get a good education.

At the same time, many U.S. companies are beefing up their
training. "Training and high quality go hand in hand," says Kodak
CEO George Fisher. "As you empower workers, you must train
them."

**Computer companies estimate the half-life of an education to
be only eighteen months.**

They know they must keep sending their engineers back to
school—not necessarily college but through programs run by the
company—to keep them up to date. Empowered workers on up-to-
date assembly lines require training too. As a result, *Fortune* 500
companies today do more training than ever before.

But the *Fortune* 500 companies are shrinking as a percentage of
the economy, and smaller businesses have fewer resources for training. Government efforts to promote lifelong learning, meanwhile,

have long been hampered by the congressional committee system, which encourages powerful chairmen to protect pet programs at the expense of a national training system. While training remains a hot-button issue, supported by some and fiercely opposed by others, there are some prospects for reform.

The Productivity Payoff

All these changes in the labor market mean that U.S. productivity, after a long lull, has begun to climb. Economists waited for years for the big productivity payoff from information technology. For years it didn't happen. Now it's finally happening. A generation of people have emerged who understand how to use computers. Stand-alone computers only marginally increased productivity. But as computers have become networked, at least in the United States, permitting the sharing of information and documents, they are boosting productivity. Stanford economist Nathan Rosenberg points out that it took forty years for the electric motor to translate to improved productivity.[15] Rosenberg and Paul David, also of Stanford, found that electricity had little impact after its discovery in 1879 well into the 1920s, when managers finally reconfigured factories to use the new technology and productivity jumped ten-fold, from 0.5 percent to 5 percent.[16] That's finally happening with productivity in telecommunications, which jumped 6.4 percent per year during the early 1990s.

Now that the three pigs in the python have been absorbed, upward pressure on wages will also lead to higher productivity.

The end of cheap labor (and the beginning of upward pressure on wages) will force firms to invest more in machinery.

The flip side of downsizing is an increase in labor productivity. Why is productivity growth so important? At 1 percent growth per year, it takes about seventy years for a nation to double its output; at 3 percent growth, it takes only twenty-three years. Productivity growth leads directly to wealth.

A nation that experiences 3 percent growth in productivity will be four times as rich in seventy years as one that experiences only 1 percent growth.

The following numbers bode well for America's future wealth. Growth in non-farm business productivity, which limped along at 1 percent per year during the 1980s, topped 5 percent in the last half of 1993 and has averaged close to 2 percent over the last few years. Manufacturing productivity has been rising at a 3.8 percent annual clip since 1991,[17] a threefold increase over rates in the 1970s and 1980s.

Will other countries get the same boost in productivity the United States has recently? Probably not. Critical to improved productivity from information technology have been networks, in which the United States leads the world. In time, Europe and Japan will realize productivity gains from their information technology investments (which still lag behind those in the United States). But the United States will lead in information technology implementation for the foreseeable future. Furthermore, neither the Japanese nor the European economies had the same surplus of cheap labor that until recently blocked U.S. productivity growth.

For the first time since World War II, the United States is leading Japan in productivity growth.

In fact Japan's manufacturing productivity has actually been falling! While Japan made huge productivity gains over the last few decades, the United States was the world's most productive economy even before its recent productivity surge. In 1990, the average American worker produced $46,900 in goods and services; his or her German counterpart produced $5,000 less, his or her Japanese counterpart $10,000 less.[18] Studies by the McKinsey Global Institute conducted with the help of Nobel Laureate Robert Solow and Harvard economist Francis M. Bator, using data from 1989 and 1990, reveal that U.S. productivity was about 12 percent higher than Japan's and 27 percent higher than Germany's in manufacturing, and 4 to 92 percent higher than Germany's and 30 to 127 percent higher than Japan's in various services.[19] The key factor identified by the McKinsey team as contributing to productivity was exposure to international competition. In explaining the overall results, William Lewis, head of the institute, noted, "Of the three countries, the US was the most exposed to trade, transplants (foreign direct investment) and foreign mergers and acquisitions."[20] In the end, once more, it is America's openness and flexibility that lie at the heart of its strengths—and that will drive further progress in the future.

We do not live in a zero-sum world. What benefits the United States will also benefit others. Higher productivity in the United States will make possible higher profits and higher wages, which Americans will use, in part, to buy foreign goods, benefiting the standard of living everywhere. That said, Americans will be the biggest winners from improved U.S. productivity. People who live in a country with high productivity get to spend their time doing higher-paying, more glamorous work than those in low-productivity countries.

While the macroeconomic indicators are good, rosy figures alone don't provide employment. It's up to specific businesses operating in specific places to do that. And American companies in every business all over the country have recovered from the problems of the 1980s and changed the course of America's future.

Chapter 4

A Renaissance in the Production of Goods

In the spring of 1985, things looked bleak for Intel, then a $1.6 billion American maker of computer microchips. From bright beginnings as one of the leading lights of the industry (including a noble lineage that reached back to the beginnings of America's silicon industry at Fairchild Semiconductor in the 1960s), Intel had fallen mightily. The firm was facing its first loss in years and the prospect of red ink for the foreseeable future. The Santa Clara–based company was not alone. In the mid-1980s, the entire U.S. silicon sector seemed on the brink of collapse. After having invented the microchip industry little more than a decade before, U.S. players were facing blistering competition from cost-cutting Japanese companies that had come from nowhere to lay siege to the market.

The Japanese firms had gained their advantage a year and a half earlier, when several factors converged to give them an edge over American manufacturers. A foreign exchange windfall, a mandate from Japan's Ministry of International Trade and Industry (MITI) which had targeted the industry, cheap capital, sheltered markets at home, and, perhaps most tellingly, the 1982 U.S. recession, which slowed American investment, gave NEC, Hitachi, Fujitsu, and Matsushita, the Big Four of Japan's semiconductor industry, a window. The four decided to move in for the kill. They made massive investments in expensive state-of-the-art facilities for making the next generation of dynamic random-access memory (DRAM) chips, the memory building blocks of computers, video games, and other electronic devices. Companies must invest in the next genera-tion of chips two years in advance of their introduction. Now the Japanese companies' investments were paying off. Already, they had driven National Semiconductor, Motorola,[1] and AMD out of memory chips.[2] They were also slashing the prices of EP-ROMs.

The problem, as Intel saw it, was the nature of DRAMs, a product that had grown frighteningly competitive. Even apart from the exchange-rate problem, variable margins made factors like yield (the percentage of chips that come out right) critical. Due to the complexities of chip production, only a certain percentage actually work.[3] By relentlessly "tweaking" the process, Hitachi, Fujitsu, and others were pushing up their yields. In a business as competitive as this one (with high fixed costs), a few points in additional yield, like extra passengers on an airplane, went straight to the bottom line. The cost of R&D for DRAMs was also mounting.

Faced with losses, Intel executives made a do-or-die decision to abandon the business Intel had pioneered, DRAM chips, and turn to the small but growing business of making central processing units (CPUs), the "brains" of personal computers. It was a risky decision.

The latest generation of CPUs, such as the Intel 80386 and the Motorola 68030, contained far more transistors than DRAMs, cre-ating huge manufacturing challenges. While Intel had a supplier arrangement with IBM, its chip was not yet the confirmed standard. Intel's top executives, including Gordon Moore and Andrew Grove, decided to bet the company on advanced technology.

They shut down plants, licensed out their CPU designs to others (such as NEC and AMD[4]), and laid off 30 percent of the workforce in a desperate effort to survive. Amazingly, the strategy worked.

After six loss-producing quarters, Intel's 1987 profits hit $248 million, and have largely continued to rise ever since. As Intel recovered, it became the most profitable electronics firm in the world, earning up to 63 percent profit on its CPUs, a far cry from the 1 or 2 percent margin on DRAM chips. Intel's success proved to be emblematic of that of the industry as a whole. Helped by a government-sponsored consortium, Sematech, which supported U.S. chip-making infrastructure, such as the production of lithography equipment, as well as a bilateral trade agreement that forced Japanese companies to buy 20 percent of their semiconductors from U.S. firms, the American silicon industry bounced back.[5]

Meanwhile, Japanese firms, stuck making lower-technology, interchangeable DRAM chips, began to encounter intense competition from South Korean firms such as Samsung, Hyundai, and LG Semiconductor. The South Korean firms, for their part, had to pay 5 percent of their revenues in royalties for technology.[6] By 1994, the U.S. had totally recovered from a state of near collapse and was again dominant in the world.

Today the United States leads the semiconductor business in almost every way: overall dollar volume, market share, profit margins, and the technology mix of its offerings.

America's strengths are in the fastest-growing, higher-margin parts of the business, namely, CPUs, Reduced Instruction Set Computing (RISC) processors, flash memory chips, and other advanced components, while its main competitors, Korea and Japan, are fighting for market share in the lower-margin segments.[7] In recent years, U.S. firms outinvested their Japanese rivals. There is no room for complacency. U.S. firms could easily lose their advantage if they slough off for several quarters. But it is up to them to lose or keep it.

The U.S. renaissance in semiconductors is only one example of a broad revival in the manufacturing sector. Helped by improved quality control, better supplier relations, and a host of manufacturing improvements, U.S. firms are again major players in the most desirable, demanding manufacturing industries.

During the 1980s, Asia's success in manufacturing caught U.S.

industry off guard. American firms had grown unaccustomed to even competing on manufacturing skill. After World War II, the unionization of most large industries, with its practice of "pattern bargaining," which made wages across firms virtually identical, had virtually removed manufacturing from the stakes. Firms competed on things like technology, marketing, and service.

In the third quarter of the century manufacturing became an invisible part of the American corporation, like personnel or accounting.

Japan's success made manufacturing a battleground once more and provoked a wholesale revolution in U.S. practices. Since then, firms such as Intel have studied the Japanese methods, mastered them, and even improved on them. Helped by favorable exchange rates, U.S. firms are now the world's most efficient manufacturers. And they have the added advantage, in many cases, of superior technology. Intel, for example, didn't beat its competitors with manufacturing alone; it merely negated their advantage in manufacturing and beat them with new technology.

Today the United States has a bright future in the manufacture of high-value-added products, which can be seen in the strategies of farsighted firms:

- Motorola, in trouble during the mid-1980s, has struck back with a vengeance, besting giants like NEC and Matsushita in telephones and trumping them hands down in the low-priced, high-volume pager market—a market many thought would prove a Japanese walkaway.

- Hewlett-Packard has taken over the high-volume market in low-cost printers with its DeskJet series.

- Xerox now makes cheaper and better, low-end as well as high-end, copiers than Canon.

- Once-sleepy Kodak, now revitalized, is moving back into consumer goods with digital and disposable cameras that are challenging Japanese domination of that market.

- Compaq, GE, and others are also proving that U.S. manufacturers can win.

These success stories are important because manufacturing remains the single most competitive skill of the Asian region. Japan
has made a massive investment in robots to help it win the manufacturing wars of the future. China thrives on cheap labor but is also
encouraging more capital-intensive investments. Countries such as
Malaysia, Indonesia, Hong Kong, and Singapore have moved from
low-wage manufacturing to high-tech manufacturing. Since Asia's
strongest suit is manufacturing, the American comeback is doubly
significant.

**Data networks are proving to be a key ingredient in the superior
performance of many U.S. manufacturers.**

Networks, a particularly well developed asset in the United States,
can bring order and sales information directly into the manufacturing process. For example, Motorola makes the Bandit pager at a
facility in Florida that is almost entirely automated. Each pager is
unique and made in response to specific order information pro-
cessed in Chicago. Likewise, Rockwell's Allen-Bradley has pioneered a lights-out, paperless factory. By using data properly,
companies can streamline the entire product fulfillment process,
from sales to ordering to manufacturing to distribution.

But it is not just the *Fortune* 500 that have returned or will excel in
years ahead. Within industries, large firms are driving smaller
ones—their suppliers—to speed up technology implementation
and improve manufacturing. They are going on line with suppliers
and customers. Entrepreneurs are devising new products, while
niche companies are thriving on information technology that lets
them identify and service smaller markets.

**The growing importance of networked as opposed to conven-
tional manufacturing is shifting the global playing field to one
where the United States has an advantage.**

Instant Manufacturing

The future of manufacturing lies in making smaller lots to higher and higher specifications and quality standards in quick response to customer orders. As a New York manufacturer of sports uniforms recently put it, "Things have changed so much. Ten years ago, there were no Herman's or sports chains. The only store was Paragon. Say you made a basketball shirt. You call the guy up, a guy you know. The choice is red or blue. He tells you so many blue, so many red. You make 'em and sell 'em for, say, $2.50. The next year, the only thing different is, the price goes up a quarter to $2.75. That was inflation." Today's manufacturing is a far different world. "Today," he adds, "you need a five-page brochure to sell shirts—in all different styles—and you get $25 for one."

Tomorrow's manufacturing will be far different still as new technology lets manufacturers give their customers exactly what they want when they want it, in as little as several minutes.

Blockbuster Video and IBM, for instance, plan to make CDs that can be ordered in stores in less than a minute.[8] Customers will be able to choose any title they want from a catalog or even order a mix of songs. This is bringing manufacturing to the customer.

During the height of the industrial age, mass-produced, nationally distributed cookies replaced those made at bakeries. But today, cookies, muffins, croissants, and everything else are made locally before your eyes. Likewise, once upon a time, people took film to be developed to a store, which sent it out to a lab. Today, developing can be done on premises at a one-hour photo store. Kodak recently introduced CopyPrint stations, which enlarge photos from prints, not negatives, in seconds and let customers correct red eye and other flaws. Indeed, digitized photos as well as software are now available for sale and delivery over the Internet. In this case, manufacturing occurs in your home or office and is truly instantaneous. Moving manufacturing closer to the customer "is the biggest trend in manufacturing today," says Kodak CEO George M. C. Fisher. The decline of wages as a percentage of cost is a further incentive to manufacture locally for your customer.

Agile and flexible manufacturing will give way to what I call instant manufacturing.

Even in capital-intensive industries such as steel, production is moving closer to the customer and away from central locations. Whereas once production could take place only near deposits of coal and iron ore, new minimills can be located anywhere. Bringing manufacturing to the customer and doing it to order makes as much sense when building heavy machinery, assembly lines, or power plants as when turning out photographs, music, or software.

Mass, or volume, production has not disappeared; it's still as important as ever. The difference is that mass production must now include ways to differentiate products for different customers or cram in so many features that the product satisfies everyone. For example, Hewlett-Packard's ink-jet printers come in numerous variations and can print in color or black and white. The myriad variations on a single theme help Hewlett-Packard manufacture in volume and give it economies of scale that let it undercut competitors in the marketplace.

Localized Trade and Continental Economies

Implicit in the trend toward instant, localized manufacturing is localization of trade. In the 1980s, Americans imported millions of television sets from Asia. Ten years later, over half the TVs bought in America are made here. Why? Shorter cycle times and larger picture tubes have made the long-distance shipment of sets uneconomical. Localized manufacturing collapses the two functions of manufacturing and distribution into one. The shorter the life cycle of a product and the greater its weight to value, the more advantageous local manufacturing becomes and the more trade becomes local.

The much-ballyhooed trend toward globalization of trade in the

1980s stemmed from a unique set of circumstances: cheap labor abroad and the new ease of technology and industry transfer. Today, shifting plants and technology is still easy but cheap wages have become harder to find, even in Asia, and shorter product cycles mean that customers won't wait around for goods to travel by boat. In some industries, wages' share of product cost has declined so much that savings on wages no longer justify the cost of tying up inventory, not to mention transport. Yet a funny thing happened as wages rose in overseas manufacturing sectors: newly industrialized economies became important markets themselves. The result is that global companies are investing in overseas markets less to take advantage of cheap labor than to manufacture for local customers. Over the next quarter century, capital investment and wealth will spread to the furthest parts of the earth, creating a large middle class in such places as Chile, Malaysia, and India.

Mercedes-Benz and BMW have opted to make cars in the United States to serve the U.S. market. Japanese firms are investing heavily in Europe, using London as a beachhead (due to their familiarity with English), and are investing in the United States and Mexico to serve the North American market. U.S. firms are investing in Mexico and Asia. Local investment, of course, protects firms from tariffs and currency vagaries. The upshot of the trend toward localized manufacturing and trade is that regional economies are growing up.

Asian countries will increasingly trade goods within Asia, American countries within the Americas, and European countries within Europe, creating new continental economies.

Consider the following:

- In 1987, Japan sent only 27 percent of its exports to developing countries in Asia; in 1993, it sent 38 percent. Japan's exports to the United States, meanwhile, dropped from 37 percent to 28 percent of its total. Asia has replaced the United States as Japan's principal trading partner.

- Canada, with 26 million people, is the United States' largest trading partner. Over the last six years, U.S. exports to Mexico have tripled from $14 billion in 1987 to $42 billion today. The United States' trade with Mexico is now about the same as its trade with all of Europe.

- In 1987, South Korea did three quarters of its trade with the industrialized countries; today that figure has fallen to half. Meanwhile, South Korea's trade with the developing countries of Asia has leapt from a tenth to a third of its total.

Free trade areas such as the European Union and the NAFTA region are only strengthening the trend toward continental economies.

- In the Americas, NAFTA will expand to include Central and South American nations. The first country expected to join: Chile.

- In Europe, the EU will admit new members or form reciprocity agreements with organizations such as the European Free Trade Association (EFTA) until it encompasses much of the continent. Already, it has expanded to fifteen members.

- Israeli Prime Minister Shimon Peres has called for the formation of a Middle East regional economy and announced that he will work to create one.

These new continental economies, strengthened by free trade agreements, will offer insiders preferential access. In the future, you won't win it if you're not in it. Certain countries will naturally dominate activity by virtue of their size—the United States in the Americas, the European Union in Europe, and Japan (already girding for a struggle with China) in Asia.

A system of modern mercantilism is emerging, with lead countries dominating their respective continental economies.

While goods are trading more and more locally, services, hitherto largely domestic, will trade longer distances as they migrate from conventional person-to-person services to electronic ones that move over wires. These trends bode well for the United States due to its dominance of the Western Hemisphere and proximity to both of the other major continental economies and to the Pacific Rim economy to the west and the Atlantic economy to the east. By contrast, the silk road that once linked Europe and Asia has been bypassed by air and water transportation.

The American Auto Renaissance

The car industry is a critical one because it drives so many others. Car companies purchase steel, fabrics, tires, and parts and, increasingly, electronic components. The car industry employs almost 1.2 million manufacturing workers directly, and new-car sales alone represent 3.6 percent of GDP. Yet only a few years ago, the poor quality of U.S.-made cars was legendary. Battered by unfavorable exchange rates and less-than-stellar products, U.S. firms lost point after point of market share to Japanese competitors. In 1985, U.S. firms made 500,000 more cars annually than Japanese firms. By 1991, they had traded places and Japanese firms produced 4.3 million more cars annually than America's Big Three. In 1991, the Japanese share of the U.S. market passed 30 percent. The U.S. auto industry had its back to the wall.

Led by Ford, however, U.S. firms have staged a remarkable comeback. In 1993, U.S. domestic sales rose by 17.4 percent while imports declined by 8.5 percent. In 1994, the Big Three sold 78 percent of the cars bought in America; Toyota and Honda sold only 6 percent each. In 1994, the United States reclaimed the honor of world's largest automobile producer,[9] making 13 million cars to Japan's 11 million, the first time it had led since 1986. The picture is even more striking in the fastest-growing segment of the industry, sport utility vehicles. Here U.S. firms enjoy an 82 percent market share. The Ford Explorer, Jeep Cherokee, and Chevy Blazer have most of the market to themselves. In minivans, U.S. firms control

93 percent of the market. Exports of U.S.-made cars and trucks have also been growing and may reach 1 million vehicles by 1998,[10] a far cry from the 48,000 exported in 1986.

America once again builds the most cars in the world—and many of the best ones.

In a face-off in *Motor Trend* magazine in 1995 that pitted American against foreign cars, the Cadillac Seville beat out Japan's best car, the Lexus LS400, and the top-of-the-line Mercedes-Benz E420, although the Cadillac costs $11,000 less. *Motor Trend,* which had openly chastised U.S. cars a few years earlier, rated the Oldsmobile Aurora the clear winner over the Lexus GS300 and the Mercedes-Benz C280, although it lost out to the Mazda Millenia.[11] And *Motor Trend* gave the nod to the Chevy Lumina over the Toyota Camry and the Chevy Blazer over both the Isuzu Trooper and Land Rover Discovery.[12] How did the United States do it? The answer lies in new methods of quality manufacturing, a changed relationship with suppliers, and new team methods of product design. Leading the way was Ford.

FORD

In 1986, Ford engineered what, in retrospect, marked the turnaround of the U.S. car industry with its successful launch of the Taurus. That launch followed the introduction of a total quality effort that permeated every part of the company as well as suppliers (and drove total quality change throughout the *Fortune* 500). Since then, Ford and Detroit, in general, have been turning out hit after hit.

The Taurus

In most respects, 1986 was not a good year for the U.S. car industry. It marked the beginning of a slump that got worse before it got better. But the launch of the Taurus would prove to be the seed of eventual recovery. The Taurus represented a major departure for U.S. manufacturers. The first aerodynamic car, it proved an immediate styling hit. It contained features such as a net in the trunk to keep suitcases from wobbling around, a coffee holder on the dashboard, and superior ergonomics that took customers by surprise.

The secret behind the Taurus's successful design was a team approach that brought designers, marketing people, manufacturing people, and assorted engineers together from the very beginning under the lead of a single honcho, Lew Veraldi, Ford's then head of engineering. Previously, Ford had used a system—which now seems impossibly archaic—of passing design chores from designers to engineers to manufacturing to marketing; that is, across departments in linear succession. In developing the Taurus, Ford imposed a rigorous time schedule that served to focus and organize development and created a group whose sole responsibility was to optimize product development from concept to customer, or "C to C." Japanese firms had been using a version of this method for years; finally, Detroit caught on. The other side of the Taurus's success was its leap forward in freedom from defects. Good quality kept customers in later years coming back for more.

In 1989, Ford announced the SHO version of the Taurus. According to a *Motor Trend* poll of performance-car owners, "The Taurus SHO is a wonderful example of how domestic manufacturers have regained their status in the performance marketplace. Many respondents previously owned Porsches, Jaguars, and BMWs and agree that, 'dollar for dollar, the SHO is the best-engineered, reasonably priced performance vehicle on the road.' "[13] For the last few years, Taurus has been the country's best-selling car. The retooled, redesigned 1996 model has only continued the trend.

The Explorer

The next Ford hit, the Explorer, paved the way for the explosion of sport utility vehicles, a segment of the market the United States now dominates. It owed its success to a number of factors:

• First, Ford went the extra mile to surprise the customer. The Explorer was simply a better car than most sedans, let alone

Jeeps or trucks. It handled better, rode better, and had more
power, more features, and more built-in quality than any
other car on Ford's lot at the time.

• Second, the car successfully targeted the emerging baby-
boomers-with-children market. When the Explorer was introduced, the boomers were anywhere from twenty-seven to
forty-years old and in prime need of transportation for children. Explorers addressed part of the same market as minivans but added an adventurous touch.

• Third, the Explorer appealed to Americans intent on exploring their sprawling country. Rural Americans, as well as
affluent suburbanites or urbanites on weekend outings, liked
the ability to go off road, handle mountain roads in winter,
and even drive on beaches.

• Fourth, the Explorer targeted a market in which foreign
competitors were weak. Japan, which had never experienced
a baby boom and has far less terrain to explore, offers only a
small market for sport utility vehicles. In fact, Japanese four-
wheel-drive enthusiasts are so deprived of wilderness that
Toyota has constructed a wilderness theme park in Toyota
City called Savage Adventure Field. There, for a price, enthusiasts tackle meticulously detailed replicas of off-road trails
with names like "Devil's Incline," "Boulder Gully," and other
imitations of the wild.[14] Without a large home market to drive
production volume or permit cross-subsidization, Japanese
firms (as well as European ones) are at a disadvantage. Their
strategy has been to go after the upper end of the market with
cars such as the Range Rover and entries from Lexus and
Infiniti. In addition, the Big Three managed to get sport
utility vehicles classified as trucks, imports of which are subject to duties.

Finally, the success of the Explorer reflected its timing. It was the
second car Ford introduced after its discovery of total quality and
team design. Hence, it was a good car instead of a mediocre one.

*   *   *

Every Ford entry since the Explorer has drawn good reviews. The Mustang represented another success story. Ford CEO Alexander Trotman gave designers a mission: to reinvent the Mustang, which from its glory days had deteriorated into an ill-styled, under-engineered also-ran. The designers rose to the challenge, and the Mustang has again become a distinctive car.

The Ford Contour, also known as the Mercury Mystique, represented the fruition of a separate experiment, Ford's "world car" program. Both got positive reviews, but, as a measure of how far Ford has come, their high quality was taken for granted. These midsized cars went after the strongest Japanese market segment, that of the Honda Accord, Toyota Corolla, and Nissan Altima.

Ford has also unveiled a new model for the company itself: Ford 2000, the name of a new organization to carry it into the twenty-first century.

CHRYSLER

Chrysler took longer to reinvent itself than Ford but it had further to go. It needed a government bailout in 1980 to avoid bankruptcy. CEO Lee Iacocca resurrected it, thanks largely to the minivans, but by the late 1980s it had once more begun to slouch toward bankruptcy or the federal larder. Then, in the early 1990s, a radical new-product development strategy led to a series of new models, all of them rapidly and expertly engineered. These new models have since lifted Chrysler out of its ditch and to unprecedented heights.

In 1994 and 1995, Chrysler was the most profitable auto firm in the world and the fastest-growing automaker among the top five.

Chrysler pursues a leveraged strategy of product innovation and production that relies heavily on suppliers. It asks suppliers to provide entire systems, so-called gray boxes, for whose quality the suppliers take responsibility. In this respect, it leads Ford and, in particular, GM, which historically has done more of its research and built more components in house. Its experience in managing supplier and technology alliances has paid off for Chrysler. Faced with competition from a new Ford minivan, Chrysler was able to get air bags into its vans before Ford.

Suppliers like working with Chrysler because it rewards them for doing research. For example, it will build an R&D cost component into supplier contracts. GM, in contrast, is famous for asking a supplier to design something and then bidding out its production to others.

LH-Class Sedans

Chrysler's so-called LH-class sedans, which include the Chrysler Concorde, the Dodge Intrepid, and the Eagle Vision, were conceived, designed, and built in less time than planned using simultaneous engineering. The process used to develop these cars was an outgrowth of in-depth studies of Honda and Chrysler's partner, Mitsubishi, in the 1980s, as well as Chrysler's own experience in designing the no-frills Jeep. Chrysler decided to reorganize itself in a platform strategy. The LH team was charged with developing large cars, a traditional Chrysler strength, using a new "cab-forward" design. Chrysler "colocated" the team away from headquarters to free it from traditional barriers, politics, and other impediments to success, and cut the number of suppliers for the cars to only 230. The results were extraordinary. Today, Chrysler sells more than 100,000 Concorde and LHS cars alone each.

The Neon

Between the LH cars and the Neon, Chrysler had other successes, such as the Jeep Grand Cherokee, which now runs neck and neck with the Ford Explorer as the world's best-selling sport utility vehicle. The Neon is remarkable, however, for a number of reasons. Designed to compete against what was traditionally a Japanese stronghold, the Neon outperformed the Nissan Sentra and Honda Civic, according to many reviewers. Chrysler also designed and launched the car in less than three years for $1.3 billion, beating anything the Japanese automakers had accomplished. And the Neon was designed to be profitable—a first for a small American car. Thirty years after small cars first appeared in the United States, they remain problematic for American carmakers. Until recently, the Big Three kept small cars in their lineup more to cover that market segment and raise average gas mileage figures to conform with Environmental Protection Agency (EPA) requirements than to make money. Saturn broke that mold for compacts; Neon obliterated it for subcompacts. Since its introduction, it has been extremely successful. Chrysler now sells over 300,000 of them per year.[15]

How did Chrysler do it? Again, it colocated a product team away from headquarters. Design for manufacturability was a high priority, as was cost. One way the Neon design saved money was by not including a grill in front. The company relentlessly benchmarked itself against the Honda Civic and Nissan Sentra. At one point, a senior executive drove a prototype and sent engineers back to the drawing board to make sure the Neon was *better* than the competition. It worked.

Chrysler followed up these successes with its successful launch of the Cirrus/Stratus models. These two cars, like Ford's Contour/ Mystique entries, take on the heart of the Japanese lineup, midsized sedans such as the Honda Accord and the Toyota Camry. Although not developed as quickly or as cheaply as the Neon, the Cirrus and Stratus were turned out rapidly using Chrysler's new platform/team approach. Chrysler has even applied these techniques to its bread-and-butter minivans. While Chrysler invented this segment, its minivans suffered from quality problems throughout the 1980s. The new generation is winning better marks for quality and has been first to incorporate new features and technologies such as built-in child seats and air bags. Chrysler's goal is to include new features so quickly that customers come to *assume* that its cars will always lead the competition.

The firm struck gold again with its sports car, the Viper, a specialty roadster for which demand vastly exceeds supply. *Motor Trend* recently called the Viper the winner over imports in the "socially irresponsible retro roadster" category.[16] The company makes only a thousand or so a year, hence the Viper is not a factor in its financial comeback. But it demonstrates the rebirth of U.S. engineering and styling prowess.

GENERAL MOTORS

General Motors has had the most problems of the Big Three, largely as a result of its size, which has made change difficult to effect. In fact, by some measures GM is still floundering. Investors have called for its liquidation, its breakup into smaller firms, and other drastic solutions to its apparent long-term decline in value. Nevertheless, the world's largest carmaker has shown signs of recovery. It created an entire new division, Saturn, that is based on Japanese manufacturing principles and that is winning extremely high marks from customers (second only to Lexus and Infiniti in J. D. Power and Associates surveys) and making money. The Oldsmobile Aurora and the Buick Riviera have stolen away partisans of BMW, Lexus, and other imports. The Cadillac Seville is considered a major accomplishment by people in the industry. The Chevy Blazer has won high marks. In 1995, the restyled Chevy Cavalier and Lumina were well received by the market, and GM beat out Ford and Chrysler in the J. D. Power quality survey. The last quarter of 1995 proved to be GM's most profitable in history.

JAPANESE AND GERMAN DIRECT INVESTMENT

While American automakers are enjoying a renaissance, the United States has also proven fertile ground for foreign car manufacturers. Honda now makes all of its Accords here, and in 1994 it announced it would make all of its top-of-the-line Acura cars in Ohio. Toyota is expanding its U.S. production of Corollas and makes all of its Avalons, the firm's American-style, full-sized car, in Kentucky. It now makes 100 percent of the compact pickup trucks it sells in the United States at its New United Motor Manufacturing (NUMMI) joint venture with GM in Fremont, California. Imports by American and Japanese firms combined now account for only 7 percent of U.S. auto sales. During the Japanese recession in the early 1990s, imports from the United States (from Japanese affiliates, not U.S. carmakers) supplied Japanese auto firms with their only profits.

Mercedes-Benz will open a plant in Tuscaloosa, Alabama, and BMW already has one in Spartanburg, South Carolina. These new plants, together with Nissan's facilities in Smyrna, Tennessee, and the Saturn plant in Georgetown, Kentucky, are creating a new auto belt across the South. They are also proving to be important new customers for U.S.-made parts.

ELECTRIC CARS

The electric car has arrived, thanks to California's zero-emissions standard, which will force carmakers who want to sell in California to offer an electric model. GM began selling its first electric models in California and Arizona in 1996. By 2003, ten percent of new cars in California will have to have zero emissions. The new cars require electrical stations for recharges, a role gas stations will fulfill initially. The new electric cars, however, will create an entirely new market for auto parts and services, one the United States will pioneer. (Electric cars are not expected to debut on a large scale anywhere else for many years.)

The runaway leader among electric-car prototypes at the moment is GM's Impact. *Popular Mechanics* said of the Impact, "Performance is unlike any other electric vehicle we've driven. Previous electrics have been downright slugs, but the Impact scoots and handles like a sports car."[17] In 1994, GM loaned fifty cars to one thousand drivers for two- to four-week stints. The cars were so popular that GM had trouble getting them back. Currently, they can travel about ninety miles between charges. While GM has had its problems, most auto observers agree that its labs are the best in the world.

Ford's concept electric car is the Event. Volkswagen may intro-
duce an electric Beetle, and Nissan believes it can make a gas-
driven car that meets the zero-emissions standard. An even more
exotic technology involves fuel cells. For the moment, however,
GM's electric car is way ahead of the competition's. The Big Three,
meanwhile, are cooperating with electric power companies and
battery makers to make cleaner cars under the government-
sponsored Partnership for a New Generation of Vehicle, or so-
called clean car initiative.

TRUCKS

The resurgence of U.S. vehicle manufacturing is most dramatic in
the area of trucks. The new competitiveness of Ford and GM
trucks, sport utility vehicles, and minivans has vanquished Japanese
competition, which once was strong.

In part, the American victory in trucks reflects the 25 percent
tariff on imported trucks. But at the same time, what happened to
imports of trucks into the United States shows just how hard the
American comeback has been on foreign firms. The truth is that
Japanese firms have survived and hung on to market share in autos
in the United States only through dogged determination.

Between 1986 and 1992, Japanese exports of trucks to the
United States dropped like a stone, shrinking almost 90 percent
from 1,085,706 to 188,779, the lowest level since 1971. Japanese
firms pulled out the stops to hold on to market share in the
higher-profile car market by instituting below-market leases and
rebates and scrambling to shift production to North America.
Market share, after all, is the holy grail of Japanese industry. But
what they did for cars, they could not do for trucks. They could
have shifted truck production to the United States to escape the
tariff, but, with some exceptions, they didn't. In trucks, at least for
the time being, they gave up, which shows what tough competitors
the American firms, aided by the rise of the yen, have become.

Many Americans still don't realize how much better and more competitive American cars have become.

For example, consumers surveyed by J. D. Power and Associates still rank Toyota Corollas, made by the GM-Toyota NUMMI joint venture, above Geo Prizms made at the same factory, even though the cars are essentially identical. (J. D. Power, in a separate rating it does itself, called the Prizm assembly line number one in the United States.) The Mitsubishi Eclipse also outranks the Plymouth Laser, although these identical cars are made at the same factory in Illinois. These trends reflect a lag in perceptions. In coming years, the reputation of American cars will catch up with the reality.

THE FUTURE OF U.S. AUTO MANUFACTURING

Already, carmakers form a large market for advanced speakers, cellular phones, on-board computers, systems to cancel out noise, radar detectors, and other advanced technologies, in addition to traditional "auto" technologies such as spark plugs and rotors. They are adding navigational systems, global positioning technology, Internet links to facilitate access to maps, hotel and restaurant reviews, and other travel information, smart technology to manage traffic flow, and even movies for children sitting in the back. A liquid crystal display (LCD) screen on new navigational systems can show a map with restaurants or gas stations lit up. New versions will talk and understand speech. GM has introduced onboard diagnostic computers that let dealers upgrade the car's software when the customer brings it in for any reason. It won't be automakers themselves that supply this technology; most will come from vendors or be developed through joint ventures. GM's Delco Electronics, for example, offers an integrated stereo/navigation system that fits into existing stereo bays. Pioneer and Sony are providing systems in Japan using technology from U.S. firms Trimble and Motorola. And the technology is still in its infancy.

AUTO PARTS

How will enterprising individuals take advantage of the U.S. resurgence in automaking? Apart from buying stock in auto firms, which goes up and down with the business cycle, they will invest in or work for an auto supplier or other business that services the auto sector. The Big Three are exploding their value chain, buying more and more outside, and U.S. auto-parts firms are benefiting. Parts sellers are setting up shop in Spartanville, South Carolina; Tuscaloosa, Alabama; Georgetown, Kentucky; Fremont, California; and elsewhere to service foreign-owned factories. German firms will be large buyers of U.S. parts. Japanese firms, which at first imported most of their parts from *keiretsu* associates based in Japan, are now stepping up American purchases.

The United States is the best place in the world to make sport utility vehicles, thanks to its superior supplier base and because it's the sector's largest market.

Mercedes-Benz, for example, will build a sport utility vehicle in Tuscaloosa. Mercedes located in the United States partly to escape exchange-rate penalties on European manufacturing and tariffs but also to enter this fast-growing segment. More and more people will be learning German in Alabama and South Carolina or Japanese in Tennessee and Kentucky.

When Toyota decided to make all of its pickups at its NUMMI joint venture with GM in Fremont, California, Dana, the country's sixth largest auto-parts supplier, built a truck-frame plant in nearby Stockton to service the added capacity. Dana engineers then went to Japan to study what Toyota wanted and to learn about just-in-time delivery. The German and Japanese automakers' billion-dollar investments will create all sorts of secondary activity, from metal-fabricating shops and paint distributorships to restaurants and housing.

Entrepreneurs located in older industrial areas, such as Long Island, will not get much of this business. It will go to those willing to move to these booming areas to service them directly (see Chapter 7). Indeed, parts supply has evolved from a small-time operation to a global one. U.S. parts makers are finding it advantageous and even necessary to go global themselves; there's a demand for world-class parts abroad, and global economies of scale make them more competitive.

In the latest boom, parts makers such as GenCorp, 60 percent of whose output goes into sport utility vehicles, and Tenneco's Monroe Auto Equipment (which makes shocks and struts) have thrived. As companies cut back on their own parts production, they create opportunities for suppliers—but only for those that are truly competitive. Today, auto parts sales account for 3.4 percent of GDP but 4.5 percent of manufacturing employment, and these numbers are slated to rise.

Not all suppliers to the automakers are huge companies such as ITT, Du Pont, and TRW. Bose Technologies, the boutique manufacturer of speakers, has carved out a niche at the upper end of speaker supply to the industry. It recently debuted an entirely new speaker technology in a sound system for the GMC Jimmy, a four-wheel-drive vehicle. Called "Manta," the speaker system uses a transducer technology that is more efficient than previous systems. Smaller, specialized firms can enter the game through partnerships with others. Harman Kardon, the Long Island–based maker of stereos, realizes that navigation, noise cancellation, voice recognition, telephony, and stereo will all meld into one in future cars. Harman Kardon is very strong in noise cancellation and conventional sound but recognizes that it lacks competence in voice recognition and navigation. Accordingly, it is forming partnerships to fill in those gaps.

Of course, at the same time that American automakers have exploded the value chain, they have also narrowed their supplier base. To survive winnowing, suppliers must develop global economies of scale and meet more stringent quality specifications. Once a supplier is chosen, however, it receives better treatment than before—and suppliers need suppliers! Every dollar of expenditure on auto parts generates another $2.50 in expenditures throughout the economy.[18] Entrepreneurs just starting out may find their greatest opportunity in supplying the suppliers. Another option is the $90 billion auto aftermarket. The renaissance of American automaking will create opportunity on many levels in years ahead.[19]

Personal Computers (PCs)

Not long ago, it looked as if Asian firms would make major inroads into the world personal-computer market. Some observers thought they would walk away with it. But it never happened. U.S. companies still dominate the worldwide PC market. Here's why.

First, PCs are a technology-driven business. Since Japanese firms lagged American ones in key technologies, this placed them at an initial disadvantage. The first PCs used American CPUs and software. The American market also took off ahead of that in Japan. Nevertheless, Japanese firms might still have taken control of the market through manufacturing efficiency alone, as they did with VCRs, televisions, and other products, but they proved unable to do so. The reason has to do with standards.

In the early days of the PC business, there was no reason to expect it would grow up around a dominant open CPU and software standard. In fact, there was every reason to think it wouldn't. Mainframe and minicomputers made by different manufacturers were largely incompatible. (The Justice Department had been suing IBM for years to get it to open its standards, to no avail.) At the other end of the spectrum, the chips controlling VCRs, video-game players, and video cameras used a hodgepodge of incompatible standards that were invisible to the consumer. Early PC makers such as Apple, Commodore, and Atari used proprietary systems. It was only IBM's decision to let Microsoft keep control of its disk operating system (DOS)—perhaps because IBM feared antitrust action—that let the industry develop as it did.[20] How lucky for U.S. companies!

While IBM chose DOS for its first machine, giving it a huge endorsement, no one could be sure that it would become a standard as opposed to CP/M. Moreover, different versions of DOS proliferated at first. Computer makers thought that by changing the DOS standard subtly, they could put a proprietary stamp on their machines. Japanese firms moved away from IBM's PC-DOS, thinking that by aggressive pricing alone (the yen was still low in the early 1980s) they could rack up market share; and as they accumulated more market share, their variant standard would then become a barrier to others. But in the end, they all came back to a single standard.[21]

PC makers were forced to adopt a common standard by an unexpected source: third-party software developers.

IBM had always written the bulk of its software itself, as had Digital Equipment, Unisys, and other minicomputer and mainframe companies. The other chief developers of software were corporate customers, which employed teams of programmers to tackle problems. In the PC business, however, the huge number of customers and low sales prices changed the software equation. Multiple customers meant multiple needs and limited means, and it became clear that third-party vendors were better positioned to provide software to consumers than were hardware firms.

As the PC market evolved, it did not take long for consumers to realize that the ability to run third-party software, notably Lotus 1-2-3, was critically important. Consumers passed over machines from Epson, Sanyo, and others, no matter how inexpensive, that lacked 100 percent compatibility with mainstream DOS. In due course, U.S. software makers stopped adapting their programs to anything other than standard DOS. Soon, Japanese firms had no choice but to go back to this standard on all their American offerings.

No single PC company has been able to attain total control of the market because of the open third-party standard—or will be able to—as long as it prevails.

The open Intel/Microsoft standard has guaranteed a market for any company that can make computers cheaply.[22] This has created a unique set of market conditions. Each of an unusually large number of firms owns a small share of the market. Small companies pop up and vanish overnight. The open system has kept anyone from walking away with the game thanks to a short-term advantage obtained through manufacturing skills, a closed market at home, money-losing or subsidized pricing—all classic Japanese gambits— or some unique accessory technology. American consumers are also the world's most demanding. Their preferences and demands for applications set the pace for the rest of the world, putting the United States at the top of the food chain.

While PCs in the United States quickly converged on the Intel/ Microsoft standard, in Japan multiple proprietary standards developed that, until recently, kept American firms out of the market but also hampered Japanese companies overseas. To this day, the machines NEC and Toshiba make for the U.S. market are different from many they sell in Japan.

But not all Asian countries missed the boat. Taiwan signed on to U.S. standards early. As a result, Taiwan exports more PCs to the United States than do Japanese firms, particularly laptops, and is very active in Asia. U.S. firms, however, play a major role in Taiwan and in Asia as a whole. AST Research, a U.S. firm with South Korean participation, is particularly strong in Asia. Europe makes many of the PCs it uses itself but has been content to follow rather than lead. Much of the production of PCs in Europe is concentrated in Ireland and Scotland, which provide generous tax breaks to multinational corporations. U.S. firms operating there include IBM, Digital Equipment, Apple, and Intel. The Italian firm, Olivetti, and the French firm, Bull, use the IBM standard, but the German firm, Siemens, also supports a standard of its own.

Today five U.S. firms—Compaq, Apple, Packard Bell, IBM, and AST Research—control about half of the American PC market. Hewlett-Packard is also coming on strong. Worldwide, U.S. firms control five of the top six slots. In Japan, U.S. firms have almost a third of the market—twice what they had in 1994—and their share is growing. Since the introduction of a Japanese version of Windows in 1993, numerous American software vendors have set up shop in Tokyo to write applications. While NEC's 9800 series, a proprietary system based on DOS, has more Japanese-language applications and still dominates the market, the pendulum is swinging toward Windows, particularly since the introduction of Windows 95. A Japanese businessman with Korean roots, Masa-yoshi Son, educated at the University of California at Berkeley, has become a billionaire in Japan by selling U.S. software.

WHAT'S AHEAD?

PC technology is headed in two directions simultaneously: toward both bigger and smaller systems. Regular PCs will grow faster and more powerful still in years ahead. They are adding capabilities such as CD-ROM drives, multimedia, video cameras for video telephones, television reception, Kodak's new still camera, virtual reality, and artificial intelligence. Their graphics capability is increasing. More and more memory will let PCs run video, handle voice recognition, and embed voice and video in documents. The mouse interface will be joined by voice and virtual reality interfaces that will perceive motions of the hands and head. PCs may even get credit card slots to facilitate charges.

Credit cards themselves are changing from magnetic stripe to "smart card" technology with built-in microchips that can perform computer functions. It may soon be possible, for example, to re-charge a subway or metro card at your PC. The charge you add to your metro card would be deducted from your bank account by computer. As discussed further in Chapter 6, banks, financial institutions, and even the government are looking forward to cutting the cost of branches made of "bricks and mortar."

But at the same time, PCs are moving in another direction, toward the consumer electronics market. Newer and better portable PCs will use more wireless technology and be able to access the web. Laptops, computer appliances and variations on today's personal digital assistants (PDAs), will have phone, E-mail, fax, and networking capabilities. Because of thinner profit margins in the consumer sector, profits will come from the sale of peripherals or through recapture on services—just as cellular-phone companies today give you a free phone if you subscribe to their service. This is an old gambit: recall how John D. Rockefeller's Standard Oil gave away lamps in prewar China "to sell oil for the lamps of China." The computer wars are just beginning. But the successes of far-sighted firms suggest how they will be won. Consider the following examples.

BIG BOXES

One model for success in the United States is that of Packard Bell. Founded in 1986 by Benny Alagem, an Israeli-born graduate of California Polytechnic Institute, together with several classmates, this private company, which publishes no financial results, rocketed from nowhere into the top tier of U.S. computer makers. It sells more computers through retail channels such as Wal-Mart and CompUSA than any other PC maker.

How did Alagem and company do it? They started out selling low-end computers at Wal-Mart—a niche the big companies had ignored because of the high rates of merchandise return. To get a leg up on competitors, Alagem bought the name Packard Bell (a defunct maker of radios and televisions) from Teledyne. His strategy was to use retail channels to sell simple computers to ordinary people unlikely to enter a computer store. But Packard Bell soon began selling through computer retailers as well, such as Comp-USA. Its retail experience taught it to anticipate and bundle what people want—making its systems easy to use—rather than force them to worry about options. Packard Bell explicitly targets the home rather than the office market and calls its machines home appliances.

The company bundles a proprietary interface that's more pleasing to the eye than Windows is, lets consumers change color panels on its machines and color-codes the plugs and ports for easy setup. Packard Bell's other secret is speed to market. It has consistently come out first with new computers using new chips, larger hard drives, and other innovations (sometimes at the expense of quality, an area in which the firm has had problems). In 1994, when Compaq was complaining to Intel that Intel's ads for the Pentium chip were cutting into sales of its 80486 computers, Packard Bell was already shipping Pentium-based machines. The formula has been so successful that Packard Bell is going global. It makes computers in the Netherlands and in Angers, France. Its low profit margins have, however, driven it to seek cash infusions from deep-pocketed partners such as the French firm Bull and NEC, each of which owns 20 percent of the firm.

Michael Dell's Dell Computer is a success story with a different secret. While both companies specialize in quick cycle times and speed to market, Dell excels at what I call "instant manufacturing"—making computers to order and shipping them out within hours. Dell had the idea for his mail-order firm while still in college and started it before he was twenty. His $3.5 billion company owes its success, as much as anything else, to the existence of toll-free numbers. Dell reasoned that customers might like to configure their computer as they pleased and that, by selling directly, he could satisfy them for less. Dell got his start importing PCs from abroad, but today he builds and ships every one of his computers in the United States within twenty-four hours of taking an order. The company tried entering retail stores such as Wal-Mart and Comp-USA but found that paying a commission to retailers strained its made-to-order cost structure. Now it has gone back to selling customers exactly what they want, using catalogs and a toll-free number.

In coming years, the high end of the PC market will keep evolving, offering more to customers for less, with U.S. firms holding most of the cards. Standards will set the rules of battle, and standards, of course, are technology-driven. When IBM, Apple, and Motorola introduced the PowerPC microprocessor, threatening Intel's standard, Intel accelerated its product development beyond even its earlier accomplishments. It started development on its Pentium Pro chip while development of the Pentium was still under way and has done the same for its next-generation P7 chip, due in 1997 or 1998. The Pentium Pro rollout was the fastest in the company's history; the chip appeared only two years after the Pentium, which came out almost four years after the 80486 chip. The Pentium Pro is also continuing the trend of loading more and more functions onto CPUs, thus virtually turning them into computers.

The next few years will also see the debut of the Net computer (NC) or Net appliance, a stripped-down personal computer using a simpler chip designed to provide access to the Internet at an affordable price. The future of the NC will depend, in part, on the success of the Java programming language (see Chapter 6), which will let comparatively dumb terminals run programs embedded in Web pages or on network servers. NCs won't replace high-end PCs but may carve out an important niche at the lower end of the market. They're designed to open up the Net to the 60 percent of American households that don't have home computers.

The growth of networks has caused the sale of servers to explode. "Our sales of servers double every quarter," notes Edward R. Mc-Cracken, CEO of Silicon Graphics. "We have no Japanese competitors." The top makers of servers and workstations are all American and include Silicon Graphics, which is also a pioneer in virtual reality; Sun Microsystems, the inventor of the Java programming language; Digital Equipment; IBM; and Hewlett-Packard.

MOBILE COMPUTING

At the mobile end of the spectrum, the battles are shaping up differently. Here miniaturization and manufacturing skill will play a greater role. But standards will also prove critical, which poses an interesting dilemma. Japanese firms remain world leaders in miniaturized manufacturing, while U.S. firms lead in wireless technologies and the software needed to use them. Not surprisingly, this business has seen many trans-Pacific joint ventures.

While the Apple Newton MessagePad was widely judged a market disappointment, its installed base has reached 300,000 worldwide, 200,000 in the United States alone.[23] The PDA market will really take off when prices break the $300 barrier, the level at which products find broad consumer acceptance.

Motorola has no need to partner with others to compete in low-margin manufacturing and has considerable expertise in wireless technologies.

In coming years, more and more firms will enter this high-stakes, low-margin business. Given the problems of U.S. firms in low-margin businesses a decade ago, that might sound like cause for alarm. But the American ace in the hole with PDAs and NCs, as opposed to VCRs, is the importance of software. Shared or open standards such as those General Magic and Sun Microsystems are promoting (see Chapter 6) should keep any one company or group of firms from stealing the market. Whereas VCRs peaked technologically quite quickly, PDAs will evolve like computers, tracking advances in CPUs and software.

The main danger to U.S. firms would come if Japanese firms were able to shift the market to a proprietary standard and build units using their own chips, as they have done with video games.

What makes this unlikely is that unlike VCRs or game players, PDAs will be highly interactive, giving customers a major role in leading development. They will be highly technology-intensive. Thus PDAs will probably strain Japanese firms' ability to innovate. Like cellular telephones, PDAs are a product area in which U.S. firms will do surprisingly well, thanks to the importance of technology.

DISK DRIVES: DOMINATING A COMMODITY BUSINESS

If there was one industry that many observers thought would be taken over by Asian producers in the 1980s, it was disk drives. Disk drives struck some as a natural commodity part of the computer business, and the high-volume, low-margin sector seemed tailor-made for takeover by Japanese and Asian firms. Although U.S. firms had founded the business, it was thought that once most of them got a taste of Asian competition, they would make a quick exit. And in the mid-1980s, during the high-dollar period, Japanese firms did accumulate market share. But U.S. firms came back strong in the late 1980s as exchange rates moved their way. The U.S. firms' faster speed of innovation and greater adaptability out-weighed any cost advantages the Japanese firms enjoyed, and soon U.S. firms were back in the lead.

Today, U.S. firms enjoy about 90 percent of the $20 billion world market in disk drives.

Essentially, through faster innovation and world-class quality and manufacturing standards, they have blown the competition out of the water. Japan has retained a position in the industry primarily as a manufacturing subcontractor to one U.S. firm, Quantum, which outsources drives from Matsushita-Kotobuki Electronics.

The top five disk makers in the world are all American: Seagate Technology (which bought Conner Peripherals), Western Digital, and IBM. Of these, Quantum and Conner (within Seagate) make PC drives. Seagate, the industry's most profitable player, makes top-end drives for mainframes and workstations. Western Digital, the industry's fastest-growing firm, makes drives for large PC makers such as AST Research. IBM makes a variety of drives for itself. In effect, U.S. firms have sewn up every facet of the business.

The key to U.S. success in this fast-paced business is the rapid rollout of new technologies. The ability to innovate and forge close relationships with PC makers such as Compaq, Sun Microsystems, Dell, and Apple has enabled U.S. firms to reclaim dominance of the industry. In 1994, disk drives market share by worldwide unit volume[24] were as follows: Seagate Technology, 35 percent; Quantum, 23 percent; Western Digital, 13 percent; IBM, 12 percent; others, 17 percent.

OTHER COMPUTER-RELATED TECHNOLOGIES

U.S. firms have also staged comebacks in most other computer-related technologies. In semiconductor manufacturing equipment (SME), the machines used to make microprocessors, the United States has risen from the dead. SME is the equipment that the government-sponsored consortium Sematech was designed to save. Sematech worked. The U.S. government brought U.S. companies together and has since bowed out. U.S. firms now have more than 50 percent of the SME market, while Japanese firms have about 40 percent of the market. American firms' strengths are in the equipment used to make more advanced chips, mirroring their strength in advanced semiconductors. As the industry evolves, the outlook for American firms should brighten even further.

In supercomputers, U.S. firms continue to have a large lead in important technologies such as massively parallel processing. In mainframe computers, Japanese firms have made significant advances, but U.S. firms still have two thirds of the world's market. As usual, the Japanese firms have an advantage because their home market is virtually off limits to foreign firms. Everywhere else in the world, however, U.S. companies dominate.

The mainframe market is likely to decline as workstations and PCs grow more powerful, but experts agree it won't disappear entirely. Mainframes are still ideal for activities such as real-time transaction processing—for example, making airline reservations, managing cash machines, and performing other complex computing challenges.

In parts, U.S. firms will dominate the higher end—in particular CPUs, for which Intel and Motorola currently control almost the entire market—while Japanese firms will control the market for LCD screens (although Corning makes much of the high-quality glass used in LCDs). U.S. firms may have a shot at future flat-screen technologies.

With logic chips the domain of big players such as Intel and

Motorola and DRAM chips the province of cash-rich, government-supported conglomerates such as Samsung and NEC, is the silicon game closed to start-ups? Hardly. In recent years, a host of small firms with names such as LSI Logic, VLSI Technology, and Cirrus have been making chips that work with others' standards. While these smaller firms might like to create a standard to which others such as Intel and Motorola would have to bow, for the time being they are creating chips used in fax machines, VCRs, and PC boards that complement CPUs. Sony's Play Station, for example, uses an LSI logic chip.[25]

In coming years, chips will go everywhere, in light switches, toasters, door locks, and other industrial and home locations. Ten years ago cars had one microprocessor (in the engine); today they have five (in the engine, anti-lock brakes, radio, air bag, and climate control system); tomorrow they will have even more. The semiconductor business is still in its infancy.

THE DIGITAL NETWORKED REVOLUTION

The wireless revolution as well as the growth of digital networks will create still more opportunities for manufactured products. Motorola is a leader in this area, building on its expertise in wireless phones, as is AT&T in both the consumer and producer ends of the business. In coming years, investment in network infrastructure will create a demand for switches, computers, satellites, and other goods. Building the infrastructure for the U.S. information superhighway, as well as that in Arab and developing countries, is an enterprise that U.S. firms are poised to dominate. Only in countries that themselves make telephone equipment, such as Japan, Sweden, and France, are local firms better positioned.

But parallelling old-fashioned network development is a whole field of new network switching, which bears the same relation to the bigger, older networks that workstations bear to mainframes. Whereas the old national networks are still run by regulated or state-owned phone companies and administered by a priesthood of technicians, the new networks are flexible and can be set up by anyone with MIS experience. Servicing the new networks are small firms such as General DataComm Industries, ComStream, Cisco Systems, Cabletron Systems, and Newbridge Networks, which sneaked into the market while AT&T, Siemens, and other companies were napping.[26] The explosion of the telephone systems market, which parallels that of computers in general, will create vast opportunity for heads-up firms.

Networks are revolutionizing the consumer electronics business.

But networks will also create a whole new category of consumer products. Some will be entirely new and have an entirely new high-tech feel; others will be digitized versions of old stand-alone products. Products will run the gamut from digital assistants to Dick Tracy–style wireless watchphones. U.S. firms will enjoy an advantage in these products because of their dominance of the software that will link them up.

One digitized, networked variant of an old stand-alone product, the camera, is Kodak's new digital camera series. Kodak's Quick-Take camera, now sold by Apple, takes digital photos for personal computers. (From the other end of the spectrum, Kodak is chipping away at conventional cameras with its improved "throwaway" models, which are so sturdy they are not actually thrown away but recycled; its Advanced Photo System technology has also been well received.) Kodak has also released a $1,000 PC-connectable thermal photo printer.

New software has given Timex an edge in stealing market share back from foreign competitors such as Swatch, Casio, and Citizen.

Timex has introduced a Microsoft link for its Indiglo series of watches that enables them to communicate wirelessly with personal computers running Windows-based software programs. The technology let Timex leapfrog Casio and others, which have been putting phone number and scheduling functions in their watches for years without a PC hookup. In the same spirit, fax software is replacing fax machines as software stands in for hardware.

Networking will give U.S. firms a way to catch up to or even leapfrog today's makers of stand-alone electronic products.

OTHER OFFICE PRODUCTS

Copiers

Xerox has used total quality management and strategic vision to reassert itself as the dominant company worldwide in copying. In the early 1980s, Xerox almost went out of business because of competition from Canon, Ricoh, and others. Today, it can design and bring out new products twice as fast as Canon due to an investment in software technology that lets it rapidly upgrade machines. Rather than having to redesign all the hardware guts of the machine, Xerox can bring out an updated machine featuring new software capability. Its copier business has been growing at about 10 percent per year, and Xerox now has 31 percent of the North American copier market, compared to 16 percent for Canon, the runner-up, according to Dataquest data.[27] What's more, Xerox dominates the copier spectrum, from large copiers to small ones. Only in personal copiers does Canon still have a clear lead, though that lead is slipping.

Fax Machines

Only a few years ago, Japanese firms enjoyed a virtual monopoly on fax machines, a technology invented by the British. But fax machines were slow to take off. For faxing to be popular, many people have to have machines, which is called the "fax effect"; the more people who have fax machines, the more valuable the technology becomes. Fax machines reached that critical mass in the mid-1980s, when prices dipped below $1,000. The top manufacturers were Japanese.

Then, in 1991, Hewlett-Packard introduced a plain-paper fax based on its ink-jet technology, which rapidly picked up market share. In 1993, HP introduced its OfficeJet combination printer, copier, and fax machine, and today the company has 18 percent of the plain paper facsimile market, according to Dataquest, just three points fewer than Canon, the market leader. In 1994, Hewlett-Packard came in first in the J. D. Power and Associates survey of customer satisfaction in the computer industry following its triumphs in printers, workstations, and virtually every business it has entered. Xerox has 5 percent of the market in fax machines. And while Japanese firms still lead at the inexpensive, consumer end of the market, American firms have reclaimed a healthy part of the business.

Printers

Hewlett-Packard has been the dominant player in laser printers since it entered the business in 1984. However, the story of its ink-jet printer is even more dramatic. The key to the company's strategy is the combination of good technology with superior manufacturing. According to Richard Hackborn, the architect of Hewlett-Packard's success with ink-jet printers, in the old days the company would have steered clear of a market such as faxes or ink-jet printers in the face of Japanese competition.[28] But in the mid-1980s, the firm decided to take a flyer on ink-jet technology and target the mass market rather than niche markets, the traditional American response to Asian competition. It settled for slightly-lower-than-average profit margins and set about building up volume until it had developed economies of scale. Borrowing from the Japanese, Hewlett-Packard smothered its ink-jet technology with patents, playing the game of "patent *go*," and directly targeted Epson, then the market leader, for destruction. Company employees even wore "Beat Epson" T-shirts.

The strategy was successful. By 1991, Hewlett-Packard was the

only company offering a color ink-jet printer. It is now so strong
that it actually forced Canon to withdraw a printer in 1993 by
slashing its prices immediately before a Canon launch. Hewlett-
Packard now runs an $8 billion printer business and controls 40
percent of the total U.S. printer market, according to Dataquest,
and 55 percent of the world ink-jet printer market.

Consumer Electronics

In consumer electronics, U.S. firms collapsed during the 1980s in
the face of Japanese competition and remain a shadow of their
former selves. Consumer electronics manufacturing remains a
labor-intensive business, and these days much of the business has
moved out of Japan to South Korea, Malaysia, China, and other low-
wage countries. Nevertheless, in certain segments, U.S. companies
have made a surprising comeback, one that may accelerate in years
ahead. The domestic industry, which is made up of foreign-owned
firms as well as U.S.-owned ones, is larger than often realized.

Where U.S. industry has recovered and will excel in the future is
in areas where technology is advancing and networks are important. For example, the United States leads the world in cellular
telephones and digital cameras and will have a shot at the huge
high-definition television (HDTV) market. Indeed, the nature of
consumer electronics itself is changing.

**In 1994, a little-known revolution occurred when U.S. con-
sumers spent more money on home computers than on television sets.**[29]

Multimedia computing, a sector the United States dominates, will
soon cross lines with the conventional stand-alone TV and stereo
market.

**The multimedia computer will soon challenge the conventional
stereo and home entertainment center as the primary center of
home audio and video.**

No wonder Pioneer and Sony are actively seeking multimedia partners!

U.S. firms will get a boost from NAFTA, which has created a low-
wage manufacturing platform close to the United States. American
firms faced a disadvantage manufacturing in Asia during the 1980s
for purely logistical reasons. Because the Asian export platforms
were far away from domestic R&D operations, the strategy of moving production offshore failed. In contrast, Japanese firms, faced
with sky-high wages, had success in shifting production to nearby
low-wage countries. (More than half the color televisions sold in
Japan are now imported.) U.S. firms will derive an advantage from
more manufacturing in Mexico.

HIGH-DEFINITION TELEVISION (HDTV)

Only a few years ago, the United States seemed to have lost the
HDTV battle before it even began. American firms began leaving
the conventional TV manufacturing business in the 1960s. Hence,
it is not surprising that Japanese firms grabbed an early lead in
HDTV. Japanese firms brought the technology into production in
1990, and in 1991 Japan Broadcasting Corp. (NHK) began broadcasting eight hours of HDTV a day. At that time, U.S. firms were
not even in the running. They had one faint hope. A 1987 demon-
stration of Japanese technology in Washington alarmed a number
of congressmen, who asked the Federal Communications Commission (FCC) to take some sort of action. In a last-ditch effort to
save the industry, the FCC called industry executives together,
Japanese style, to see what might be done. The executives pointed
out that the Japanese standard was an analog standard, not a
digital one. They suggested that U.S. engineers could devise a digital standard and asked the FCC to hold off on endorsing a standard until American firms had a chance to propose their own.

Thus was born the contest to design a U.S. standard. A total of
twenty-three groups entered the fray, but three emerged as front-
runners. In one corner, the Japanese firms proposed the Japanese

standard known as MUSE, an analog standard under development
since the 1960s. In the opposite corner stood the proponents of a
European standard, including Philips and David Sarnoff Laboratories (the former RCA laboratories, spun off as a separate company
after RCA's takeover by General Electric).

Then, in 1991, General Instrument Corporation stepped into
the third corner with a proposal for a fully digital TV standard, a
technological coup that left the others in awe. The General Instrument coup forced all but the Japanese to propose a digital standard
of their own. The unlikelihood that an analog standard would win
drove the Japanese to withdraw from the competition. In short
order, the European and American groups formed a grand alliance
around the General Instrument standard made up of AT&T, General Instruments, MIT, the David Sarnoff Research Center, Zenith,
Thomson, and Philips, clinching its victory. In February 1994 the
Japanese group agreed to support the grand alliance's standard
as well.

The new digital standard will play a critical role in the living-
room terminal to the information highway (see Chapter 6). It will
also give U.S. firms a second chance to manufacture TVs. But one
should not underestimate the strength of the Japanese TV industry. Whereas in computers American firms are way ahead, in
picture-tube technology Japanese firms clearly lead. Nevertheless,
the new standard puts everyone back at a starting line of sorts. And
the domestic U.S. television industry is not as moribund as many
people think. Currently, five of the top six American brands are
U.S.-based (although foreign-owned). Only one of the top six
sellers of TVs in the United States—Sony—is Japanese, and Sony
makes its TVs in America.

The lineup is far different from what it was only a decade ago,
when Japanese firms dominated the list. Zenith, now 42 percent
U.S.-owned and 58 percent owned by the South Korean firm Lucky
GoldStar, no longer manufactures sets in the United States, but
does make tubes for large-screen TVs and performs R&D on HDTV
here. RCA, GE, and Tektronix do some fairly advanced television

work in the United States. U.S.-based TV manufacturing has in fact undergone a renaissance, thanks to the demand for larger sets, whose greater weight and size make long-distance transportation problematic.

From the late 1970s through the 1980s, few TVs were made in the United States. Yet today, almost half of the color TVs sold in the United States are made here (a percentage similar to that in Japan), and almost every global manufacturer has at least one plant in the United States, a prime example of the trend toward localized instant manufacturing.[30] Who will win the battle to sell HDTV sets to the world remains to be seen. However, it is now clear that it won't be the Japanese cakewalk some expected. The market share of the U.S. television set industry is as follows: RCA and GE (Thomson, France), 22.3 percent; Magnavox and Sylvania (Philips, Netherlands), 13.5 percent; Zenith, 10.0 percent; Sony, 7.0 percent.[31]

SPEAKERS

One niche market where the United States never lost out to foreign competitors is the speaker market. Speakers do not involve a great deal of assembly. They are technology-intensive; manufacturing efficiency does not make or break a product, and production is not dependent on ready access to electronics components. Bose Technologies, based in Framingham, Massachusetts, Harman International, the maker of JBL, Harman Kardon, and Infinity products, and Illinois-based International Jensen, the maker of Jensen, Advent, and Phase Linear speakers, control the bulk of the U.S. market. In North America, Bose is number one, followed by JBL; in Europe, Bose is tops; while in Japan, Bose alternates with JBL for the number one spot, outpacing Japanese firms. In Japan, U.S. firms benefit from a consumer perception that American speakers are best.

Traditional Manufacturing

The American comeback has not been confined to high-tech sectors. Some surprisingly old-fashioned sectors have lent themselves to the application of new high-tech manufacturing methods. As the twenty-first century unfolds, U.S. manufacturers will excel in all sorts of industries. In the steel industry, for example, U.S. firms are excelling despite government subsidies to competitors in other countries.

STEEL

Not long ago, the steel industry was yet another metaphor for America's decline. Devastated by foreign competition during the 1980s, it received tax breaks from Congress that failed to resuscitate it. USX (the former U.S. Steel) used one such break to buy Marathon Oil (in order to diversify out of steel) in one of the first big takeover battles of the 1980s. But a decade later, an amazing thing has happened: the U.S. steel industry is back.

In 1994, the domestic steel industry operated at an unprecedented 93 percent capacity. It made money and sold 75 percent of the steel consumed in the United States. In other words, foreign penetration of the U.S. steel market is lower than in many other industries. U.S. steel is now considerably cheaper after figuring in transportation than that produced in either Japan or South Korea. Productivity has risen a roaring 6.7 percent annually over the last decade, making U.S. steel plants the most productive, on average, in the world. The main reason a trade deficit in steel lingers is that American firms are producing at the peak of their capacity and can't meet the domestic demand.

If one company typifies the American comeback, it is Nucor. Based in Charlotte, North Carolina, and eschewing the old-fashioned blast furnaces that melt iron ore, Nucor in 1988 pioneered the use of minimills that melt scrap metal in high-tech ovens. Since it doesn't need ore, the company has been able to build its empire in the South, away from traditional steelmaking regions (and unions) and the high costs of northern states. Indeed, Nucor has placed a number of factories in areas that were previously rural, as opposed to industrial. In common with many other investors in greenfield ventures, it believes that people in rural areas have a stronger work ethic than those in cities. (Virtually all of the foreign auto plants have been sited in the rural South.)

Obviously, costs are less in rural than in traditionally industrial or urban areas. Taxes are lower, labor is cheaper, and, in the South, energy costs are less. In Arkansas, where Nucor has opened a plant in the heart of the cotton belt along the Mississippi, the company is able to pay workers $25,000 a year in base salary, three times the state's average, and offer productivity bonuses that can bring annual earnings to $50,000.[32] Even at that rate, Nucor still pays no more than in traditional steel areas but gets top productivity from its workers. In exchange for jobs, Nucor has often been able to negotiate low electricity prices with local utilities. A low cost structure, combined with the low dollar, has enabled it to undercut foreign competition. Nucor has also recently introduced a new way to make sheet steel, called thin-slab caster, that may cut costs by $80 per ton.[33] Other U.S. leaders in the industry include Chaparral Steel.

Railcars

Another surprise industry to boom over the last few years is the manufacture of railcars. The U.S. railcar industry virtually died in the 1980s. In 1983, deliveries of railcars limped along at a twentieth of levels in the 1970s. All at once, it has recovered, and in 1994 deliveries of railcars reached their highest level since 1981. Hear the story of Johnstown America Industries. In 1991, this small firm bought a dilapidated plant from Bethlehem Steel in Johnstown, Pennsylvania, in the center of smokestack America. Today, the newly spruced-up plant turns out a stream of gleaming coal cars, flatcars, and boxcars for delivery to railroads throughout the country.

Driving the railcar renaissance is a resurgent railroad industry that is the strongest it has been in decades. In the 1980s, thousands of U.S. railcars stood unused on sidings throughout the country. Today, most of the rolling stock is rolling. Companies such as Union Pacific are actually experiencing capacity shortages; hence the demand for new cars from firms like Johnstown. Other train producers seeing orders soar include Thrall Car Manufacturing of Chicago Heights, Illinois, which recently reopened a shuttered plant in Georgia, and Greenbrier, which is running at full capacity.[34]

What's behind rail's resurgence? New computerized systems known as automatic train control systems (ATCSs) are making rail transport more efficient than before and frequently more competitive than trucks.

Rail is newly competitive thanks to computer controls.

In addition, many trains now move double-stacked containers. Railroad productivity grew faster than productivity in any other segment of the economy, doubling between 1983 and 1992 for an 8 percent annual rate of increase.[35]

MACHINE TOOLS

Yet another "old-fashioned" industry in which U.S. firms have fought back with a vengeance and will do well in years ahead is the manufacture of machine tools. During the 1980s, machine tools were the case study of choice when chronicling America's decline. The failure of U.S. firms to invest in numerically controlled tools is perhaps the most oft-cited example of the nation's industrial woes. But the picture has changed. In 1994, U.S. manufacturers received the highest number of machine-tool orders since 1979; 1994 orders from U.S. firms were the second highest since 1960. Orders jumped 27 percent in 1994 alone. Despite the image many people have that a domestic machine-tool industry no longer exists and that U.S. customers import all their tools, this is hardly the case. The high dollar did decimate the industry in the mid-1980s, but, like so many others, this industry has come back from the dead.

After rising to two thirds of sales, imports now make up about half of U.S. machine-tool orders.[36] American makers supply the other half, up from a third a decade ago. However, U.S. manufacturers also export almost a third of their output. While a trade deficit lingers, it has shrunk dramatically. U.S. firms have made major technological progress. Says Eli Lustgarten, an analyst at PaineWebber, "There is a tremendous amount of new product coming out of U.S. machine tool builders." Illinois-based Ingersoll International recently secured a huge order from the German industrial giant Daimler-Benz. The new equipment lets automakers put different engines into cars without slowing down an assembly line. Ingersoll won the order thanks to superior technology. Says Ingersoll chairman Edson Gaylord, "Americans buy German-made machines, but the Germans don't buy American machines so easily. But Mercedes had a great need for flexibility and we had the new technology."[37]

For Sale: Surplus Cold War Technology

Boding well for manufacturing not only at the moment but for many years to come is the post–Cold War American military build-down, which will redirect resources into the civilian sector.

The United States disproportionately bore the weight of the Cold War and has disproportionately benefited from its end.

Consolidation of the defense industries will free up resources for civilian investments. General Dynamics sold its remote-technology division, its electronics division, its Fort Worth aircraft division, and its missile divisions, leaving submarines and tanks as its only remaining defense businesses.[38] GE went further and sold off its entire military and aerospace portfolio. Raytheon's nonmilitary revenues have grown to 65 percent of its total revenues, higher than before the Reagan-era buildup. Lockheed Martin has almost completed shifting its defense-to-commercial ratio from 7 to 3 to its goal of 1 to 1.

Motorola is using spinoff strategies to add punch to its consumer businesses. Successful in competing with Japanese firms in telephones, pagers, and other businesses during the 1980s, the company is now developing secure phones for consumers and other products using military technology. Raytheon is employing dual-use technologies such as superminicomputers and militarized workstations to reduce its dependency on the military.

The downsizing of the U.S. defense industry has put top, tough American players back into the consumer game.

Meanwhile, the U.S. military is selling, licensing, or outright giving away technology that until recently was hidden in classified labs. Just as the USSR is selling rides on MiG fighter jets, the American national labs are selling the equivalent of war-surplus technology. They are under pressure to find sponsors for their technology through cooperative research and development agreements (CRADAs). Entrepreneurs are finding valuable technology tucked away in the multibillion-dollar government labs.

The Coming Benefits of NAFTA

NAFTA will also prove a boon to U.S. manufacturing competitiveness over the next quarter century. Some low-wage jobs will leave the United States for Mexico (and Canada). However, the presence of a low-wage labor pool just across the border will actually help manufacturing as a whole. Just as the Big Three carmakers, which pay high wages, could not function without parts suppliers that pay considerably less, U.S. firms will benefit from the proximity of low-cost parts and components manufacturers. In addition, sales, design, and other managerial people—who far outnumber blue-collar workers at modern companies—will benefit from their firms' improved competitiveness. AT&T, for example, has made major inroads into the market for telephone answering machines, formerly dominated by Sony and Panasonic. Sony and Panasonic make their machines in Malaysia, Taiwan, and other low-wage Asian countries. AT&T has struck back with machines it makes in Mexico.

NAFTA will also help U.S. manufacturers by broadening the market for exports. Regardless of Mexico's short-term problems, over the long run Mexico and Canada will both prove to be huge markets for American exports. The United States has nothing to fear from Mexico.

Mexico has only about six thousand scientists and engineers. The United States overwhelms Mexico in technical capacity.

The same goes for agriculture: U.S. agribusiness has huge advantages over small farmers tending plots of maize. On balance, NAFTA will no more destroy American jobs than the single market in Europe will send German jobs to Greece.

Chemicals, Health Products, and Microbiology

While the U.S. steel, textile, and semiconductor industries suffered from global competition and foreign government support throughout the 1980s, chemicals and drugs did well. The pharmaceutical business is one in which intellectual property protections are strong and an advantage in manufacturing is rarely decisive. U.S. pharmaceutical firms own valuable drug portfolios. Not surprisingly, American companies have fared well and will continue to do so in the future. In biotechnology, U.S. start-up firms dominate the business so much that foreign companies must look to them even to enter the market. Roche, for example, purchased 60 percent of Genentech in 1990. Ciba-Geigy invested in Alza, inventor of the transdermal patch. Kirin, the Japanese beer company, formed an alliance with Amgen to help it develop Epogen, a drug to combat anemia. Foreign firms have helped fund this capital-hungry business. In the second quarter of the 21st century, as the baby boomers age and technology matures, this business may well explode.

Besides drugs, there's money to be made in other health-related products as the world ages. Technol, a tiny Fort Worth, Texas–based company, started out making conventional hospital supplies but, like any company, soon realized that success requires imagination. The company identified a niche: face masks for doctors and nurses. Fear about AIDS drove sales. Since 1989, the company's profits have risen 34 percent per year, and today it has 60 percent of the market. Its success has won it the sincerest form of flattery—imitation by huge firms such as 3M and Johnson & Johnson.[39]

Manufacturing Jobs

U.S. manufacturing jobs have gradually declined as a percentage of total employment, from 33.7 percent after World War II to 16.6 percent today, as workers' productivity has improved. Vigorous productivity increases in coming years will enable fewer workers to do more, further reducing manufacturing's share of the total. The good news is that the mix of jobs will improve from low-skilled to high-skilled and that pay will rise. As former AFL-CIO head Lane Kirkland put it, "These high-paying manufacturing jobs that everyone says are so great used to be low-paying and lousy."

Paradoxically, the main reason that manufacturing jobs pay better today than in the 1940s is that there are fewer of them.

The jobs that survive will require better skills and education. The very best jobs in the manufacturing sector are in management. In view of America's renewed competitiveness in manufacturing, executives at manufacturing firms will do exceptionally well.

As manufacturing has reemerged as a competitive weapon, managers and engineers who know how to do it right are in demand. Most of the growth in future manufacturing will occur in the service part of the business—designing products, engineering them, and managing the complex task of manufacturing customized goods using real-time networks to carry out "instant manufacturing." And because of the importance of alliances in manufacturing, people who know how to negotiate and form alliances will be well positioned in coming years.

The American Export Renaissance

In only one subsector, exports, will the number of manufacturing jobs genuinely grow. The number of jobs will increase because the volume of exports is growing so rapidly. Moreover, these jobs will pay well because the sector will be highly productive.

Export-related jobs pay better than other jobs, on average.

Why? Exported goods must meet world-class standards. Since the United States can't compete with Asian countries on wages, it, like Germany, Switzerland, or Japan, must compete on productivity. Hence, export related jobs will pay well on average, and as exports continue to grow, they will increase in numbers. More and more firms are now looking to foreign markets for growth, small as well as big. The CEO of U.S. bicycle maker Cannondale has a map in his office on which he has marked the forty countries to which the company now exports its state-of-the-art creations.

How to Predict Job Loss or Gain: A Tale of Two Industries

Which manufacturing jobs will stay in the United States, and which will leave? The answer comes down not just to wage levels or even skills but to cycle time. A short product life cycle, not to mention product fulfillment cycle, allows less time for transportation.

The longer the product life and the lower the weight-to-value ratio of a manufactured product, the greater the likelihood that production and jobs will move offshore.

Consider two sectors, clothing and computers. In the clothing business, there are two regular seasons, spring and fall, that dictate cycle times and product lives. Clothing firms usually send designs out to be manufactured six months ahead of delivery. This provides enough time to manufacture them overseas and ship them back. Offshore manufacturing is common. In the PC business, in contrast, cycle times have dropped to several months, which means that manufacturers have little time to spare for transportation, which also adds cost for both transport and carrying inventory. If they can supply a market locally, they gain an advantage. U.S. PC makers are doing less and less manufacturing for the American market overseas and most of the manufacturing for the overseas market locally. During the month or two it takes a ship to sail from Asia to North America, the cost of a Pentium processor or a megabyte of memory may drop by a quarter. Acer, a Taiwanese firm, has begun building PCs in California rather than Taiwan, despite higher wages here, to be close to its customers. In high-end computers such as workstations, a local presence is even more important. Silicon Graphics makes computers in the United States, Japan, and Switzerland. The weight-to-value ratio is also critical. Laptop computers for the U.S. market can be made overseas, notably in Taiwan, due to their lower weight-to-value ratio. More expensive models are even shipped by air.

In the conventional metal hardware industry—the manufacture of locks and wrenches—cycles are endless and the weight-to-value ratio is moderate. As a result, imports have taken over the market. In contrast, plasterboard and nails are made domestically due to their high weight-to-value ratio.

But while products with short cycle times lend themselves to local production, that doesn't guarantee jobs. If labor costs are high, companies may automate production. Also, bear in mind that Mexico is closer to the United States than to Asia. Offshore manufacturing that doesn't make economic sense in Asia may make sense in Mexico.

In shopping around for a sector in which to work, anyone from an executive to a would-be welder or assembler should not make the mistake of trying to identify companies that are insulated from foreign competition. Professions, yes; companies, no.

The industries that will boom in the future are not the ones that are insulated from foreign competition; they are the ones in which U.S. firms have taken the lead in going international. Only global standards of excellence, honed through fierce competition in overseas markets combined with global economies of scale, can ensure domestic success in years ahead. Protected sectors are weak sectors. Sectors in which American firms are competing and winning throughout the world are strong ones.

Conclusion

Manufacturing is back in America and will remain strong in coming decades, not as an employer of assembly-line workers but as an employer of engineers and designers and as a driver of growth. America's large manufacturing firms will be important locomotives pulling the train of the U.S. economy in coming years just as they were in the past. They won't be the only ones; software and services firms will pull harder. Still, the capitulation of American manufacturers to foreign competitors—a real possibility only a few years ago—would have spelled disaster for the country. Their resurgence means a brighter future.

In the early days of American manufacturing, anyone with a bit of capital could rent a brick building near a mill and pay immigrants to make shoes or shirts. Well into the 1980s, an entrepreneur with only average skills and a bit of capital could make money at cottage manufacturing. Cheap labor and the high quality standards created by international trade have brought that era to an end. Even second-tier manufacturers will be under pressure to upgrade equipment, find skilled workers able to operate it, pursue top-notch quality standards, and form partnerships with customers and suppliers. But numerous entrepreneurs will make fortunes in American manufacturing in coming decades. They will do so by getting hold of a standard, better serving customers, speeding up cycle times, creating global economies of scale, and practicing "instant manufacturing."

Manufacturing is again a viable home for capital in America, domestic as well as foreign. And once more U.S. manufacturing is a place where owners, designers, managers, engineers, and well-trained American workers can build a career, earn a good salary, and build innovative products.

Chapter 5

The Continuing Boom

in Services

Vinod Gupta, today a multimillionaire living in Maui, Hawaii, enjoyed few services in the village in India where he grew up.[1] His small hamlet outside New Delhi had no cars, electricity, televisions, or roads. But Gupta, the son of the village doctor, managed to attend college in India and then, on scholarship, secure an M.B.A. at the University of Nebraska at Lincoln. Although on the fast track by the standards of his village, he got his first job not with McKinsey or Goldman Sachs or IBM, like his counterparts from Stanford or Harvard, but with a local maker of mobile homes. Nor was one of his first assignments glamorous: compiling a list of mobile-home dealers around the country. But he set out to make the most of it.

Gupta ordered a full set of Yellow Pages from AT&T, free because the company had a WATS line. But no sooner did the 4,800 books arrive than Gupta's boss told him bluntly to get them out of the office by five P.M. or else be fired. Unfazed, Gupta hired a mover to haul the books to his garage and received permission to build the list himself. Once it was complete, he offered it for sale to other mobile-home manufacturers. Within a year, Gupta had made $18,000 in profit and quit his job.

Gupta then turned to other industries—boats, motorcycles, and tractors—and soon was compiling data on dozens of businesses. It took over a decade, but eventually AT&T's Yellow Pages from all over the country were in his computers. Today, he sells the data on CD-ROM and other up-to-date formats. His company, American Business Information, has sales of $75 million and services 400,000 customers. When it went public in 1994, Gupta's net worth surpassed $100 million, far more than that of most M.B.A.'s who went to work for McKinsey. Today, he relaxes by cruising on his yacht and visiting India, where his relatives marvel at his good fortune.

Gupta's success illustrates an important principle about the new service economy: people will pay a surprising amount for the service or information they need if it is well packaged and delivered.

Value added in services often comes not from the product itself—which may be free—but from how conveniently it's packaged and delivered.

Services: The Mainstay of the American Economy

Services today account for two thirds of the U.S. economy. In coming years, more Americans will work in them, invest in them, start businesses in them, and build their future around them than in any other sector. And services will grow faster than other sectors. While overall growth is tapering off, a revolution in services, themselves, will revolutionize American business. Electronic services for the information highway will grow sharply over the next quarter century as the United States moves from a manual service economy of retail outlets and pizza delivery to an electronic one in which the movement of electrons substitutes for that of things. The U.S. Labor Department estimates that services will create 20 million jobs in the next ten years; after home health care, information services will grow fastest, by 5.3 percent per year. In contrast, manufacturing will shed about 40,000 jobs per year over the next decade.

The Global Competition in Services

Services never experienced the assault by foreign competition in the 1980s that manufacturing did, in part because they are still less easily traded across borders. U.S. imports of services currently equal about 2 percent of GDP, while imports of goods make up about 10 percent of GDP. The high dollar in the 1980s did not cut into the U.S. service sector. But a more important reason that U.S. service businesses fared well is their high productivity.

U.S. services companies were more productive than their competitors in the 1980s and are more competitive today.

As discussed in Chapter 3, U.S. productivity in services outstrips that in Germany by margins of 4 to 92 percent and that in Japan by margins of 30 to 127 percent.[2] True, Japanese services get a boost from the country's manufacturing prowess. For example, in the 1980s, Japanese banks began to dominate the top ten list, due to the strength of the yen and success of their industrial customers.

On balance, however, the main competitors of U.S. service companies are other American firms. In software and networks, for example, the main players are American, and throughout the 1980s U.S. firms generated trade surpluses in insurance and television. The story here is not one of American comeback but of leadership. Nowhere is this more true than in the services of the future, in particular services for the information highway (see Chapter 7).

Giving People What They Want

While services are changing and becoming more high-tech, the principles of success are remarkably simple. The keys to Vinod Gupta's business, for example—standardization, value, branding, giving customers what they want, and delivering it in the way they want—apply to almost any service you can name. Think about other successes. McDonald's grew in the 1960s, 1970s, and 1980s not because its hamburgers were particularly good but because they were dependably alike and sold where people wanted them: by the side of the road. McDonald's branded and practically copyrighted an American institution, the burger. (In France today, companies are competing to brand nothing less than the centuries-old croissant.) Domino's Pizza soared like a rocket in the 1980s not because its pizza was fantastic but because the company guaranteed to get a pie to your home in thirty minutes.[3] In 1982, Bob Pittman put cable TV on the map not by spending money on programming but by getting music videos free from record companies and putting them out on a network: MTV. A few years later, he turned an ailing network around not with new, innovative programming but by discovering that people liked old programs that he could buy up cheaply, shows such as *The Partridge Family, The Twilight Zone,* and *Alfred Hitchcock Presents* that lay gathering dust in vaults. These shows occasionally popped up elsewhere but without any buildup, fanfare, or theme. Pittman repackaged them in a standardized format to create a branded product: Nick at Nite.

In 1992, Steven Brill, publisher of *The American Lawyer,* went one better. He created today's hottest cable channel not by dreaming up anything new but by finding something—courtroom proceedings—available for the price of setting up cameras. Its name: Court TV. His success has led other would-be cable entrepreneurs to experiment with ideas such as funeral TV, marriage TV, church service TV, and other "free" programming they hope to package. The Home Shopping Network may be the shrewdest venture of all. It's made advertising itself the programming and has managed to brand it.

Not all services you might wish to sell cost nothing to acquire, like Gupta's data or Court TV. The National Football League, for example, is TV's biggest and costliest supplier; networks fight for the chance to broadcast its games. Running an airline is also expensive; there's no getting around the cost of planes and fuel. With financial services, too, you have to deliver the goods.

Still, the basic principles of a successful service business are surprisingly simple. Why has Virgin Atlantic thrived while Pan Am went out of business and most airlines lose money? Virgin, by offering door-to-door transportation and "upper-class" service on a single profitable route, packaged the idea of flying as a door-to-door luxury experience. Why has Visa stolen share from American Express? It has provided its two sets of customers—retailers and consumers—with more for less, taking an old product, the credit card, and adding features without adding cost.

Or why has independent America Online soared while Prodigy, run by IBM and Sears, has floundered? Because AOL gives its customers more of what they want—services, graphics, ease of use, and a choice among various services provided by vendors, at a fixed hourly rate. (AOL, too, gets some of the services it supplies to customers for nothing.)

Whether you're in an older service or a new one such as America Online, the trick is to acquire a dependable product—preferably one that's free—and then package and deliver it in the configuration people desire. The key is to give them options—either ones they pay for, as Gupta has done, or free ones as part of the package, America Online's approach. Sears, for example, has dropped its historic all-things-to-all-people catalog for a portfolio of specialty catalogs servicing niches. The secret of success is rarely the data, programming, food, or goods per se but rather how well and efficiently you delivered them. That, after all, is the meaning of service.

The Sector That Gets No Respect

Yet despite making up close to two thirds of the U.S. economy, services still get no respect. People realize that providing a service may enable some entrepreneurs to get rich. But they question what value services provide. Goods such as steel or cars are something real, that you can see and feel. Services are elusive, evanescent, and hard to measure. And while many people have gotten rich owning a McDonald's, no one has gotten rich working in one.[4] Many people still think of services as the creator of "McJobs," half jobs that keep you in poverty.

But some service jobs can be very lucrative. Critics of services rarely talk about the huge salaries paid investment bankers in the same breath with those paid workers at McDonald's, but both are in service businesses. The difference is that investment banking is highly productive: the large sums and fees thrown around require just a few highly trained people to do the work. Flipping burgers, on the other hand, is unproductive: it takes several people to fill an order, and they don't require much training.

Both investment banking and McDonald's are services.

Nevertheless, both occupations are part of the service sector and figure into service productivity. The main reason that some service jobs paid so little in the 1980s was not that they inherently don't pay but that a surplus of unskilled workers entered the market, driving down wages and creating an opportunity for entrepreneurs to exploit the "factor resource" of low-cost labor through businesses such as fast food. Capital investment shifted to labor-intensive service businesses.

But that has changed. In Flint, Michigan, the rebound of auto manufacturing in the last four years has created an acute shortage of low-wage workers. In 1995, fast-food outlets there were paying $6 an hour, or almost 50 percent above the minimum wage. Why? Supply and demand. Demand for labor rose as the auto business recovered; supply tightened in the absence of new baby boomers and women entering the lower levels of the workforce and, in Flint's case, because people had simply left town. This proves there's nothing inherently low-paying about service work, no matter how mundane, that an excess of demand over supply can't cure. Over the long run, in such conditions, owners of fast-food outlets have no choice but to improve productivity or go into a different, more productive business.

Baumol's Disease

In the 1960s, an American economist by the name of William Baumol made an intriguing if Malthusian argument that services, unlike manufacturing and other sectors, have built-in limits to productivity. Since personal services involve one-on-one activities that can't be measured, said Baumol, output per worker is inherently constrained. As a result, the cost of services is bound to increase since, as other types of work grow more efficient, the productivity of service work will stay the same. He called this phenomenon "cost disease." Its corollary is that individual workers' wages must stay low due to their low productivity. If you can serve only one person at a time, how much salary can you command? In short, Baumol made two interesting points. One: personal service sectors are subject to cost disease; two: they will tend to pay low wages. During the 1993 health care debate, his argument was used to explain the rising costs of the health care sector.

Baumol points out, for example, that it takes just as many people today to play a Mozart quartet as it did a few centuries ago: four. While manufacturing products now requires far less labor, playing a Mozart quartet is as labor-intensive as ever. Sure enough, it's expensive to hear a live performance of Mozart compared with other entertainment. But meanwhile, because of their low productivity, musicians who play Mozart don't make a lot of money.

The cost of putting on a Shakespeare play has also risen. It takes about as many people to stage *Romeo and Juliet* today as it did centuries ago. Consequently, it's usually expensive to see a Shakespeare play, or any live play, for that matter. Likewise, the average doctor's appointment still takes about as much time as ever. And the cost of health care has certainly risen.

At first glance, therefore, it might appear that Baumol's argument condemns America, as a service economy, to low productivity growth and stagnant wages. But upon closer examination, it turns out that the above examples are incomplete. For Mozart is now available on CD, and one performance can be replayed thousands, even millions, of times. Thanks to amplification, even live musical performances (of rock, if not Mozart) can now be seen by 50,000 or more in a stadium instead of several hundred in a concert hall. Movies based on Shakespeare, such as Kenneth Branagh's *Henry V* and *Much Ado About Nothing*, now reach millions, reducing the cost per view to several dollars and making Branagh a multi-millionaire. If Baumol is taken at face value, music and acting should be very-low-paying occupations. In fact, successful musicians and actors today make far more money than ever before thanks to the invention of CDs, films, and television. Technology has dramatically improved the productivity of performing artists.

By the same token, doctors have learned to spend less and less time with a given patient; in hospital emergency rooms, through the use of nurses, assistants, and technology, they spread themselves thinner than before. Nor are they low-paid. In fact, they make a good living, and sometimes more than that.[5]

In short, Baumol has left us a loophole. Other examples:

• Office work, a major component of the service sector, has grown vastly more productive due to improvements in information technology.

• Stock market firms now clear far more trades per day than ever before.

• Warehouse stores are far more efficient than the mom-and-pop stores they have replaced (or else they wouldn't have replaced them).

• Self-service gas stations featuring convenience stores can now be run by one person at a register.

Even airlines have improved productivity. Is Baumol, therefore, wrong? No, he's right in situations where a service defies productivity improvement. Live, unamplified Mozart is one example. So is repair work. Most people are familiar with how expensive things are to repair. In our disposable society, buying a new manufactured good is often cheaper than having an old one repaired. Making repairs involves taking something apart, tinkering with it, testing it, fixing it with a part or parts that may have been made in several countries, and putting the whole thing back together. There are no economies of scale, no advantages of mechanization, no opportunities to use cheap labor overseas. Construction is also susceptible to cost disease. But other service businesses, particularly since the invention of the computer, are quite susceptible to productivity improvements.

Service businesses are just as susceptible to automation and productivity improvements through work design as manufacturing.

The catch is that labor costs must be high enough to justify an investment in productivity tools. Until recently, in fast-food businesses and nursing homes, for example, a plentiful supply of unskilled labor kept wages down. That has changed. With labor in short supply, many service businesses are raising productivity. Higher productivity permits real higher wages, as opposed to inflationary ones. As a result, the service sector will create many high-paying jobs in the future.

Cost disease, however, is having an important effect on our economy by driving the trend to do-it-yourself. To improve their own productivity, companies are finding it advantageous to let customers do it themselves, in effect, outsourcing part of the job to the customer.

For example, fast-food restaurants from day one asked you to bus your own tray, then let you apply your own fixings, and now have you serve your own coffee and soda, reducing their need for labor. Self-service gas stations let you pump your own gas.

But it turns out that Americans like to do it themselves to keep costs down and to see that the job is done right. They're investing in power tools, home computers, and other capital equipment for the new American homestead, as discussed in Chapter 7. They're also learning more skills to be competitive in the workplace. Cost disease and the falling cost of technology are driving Americans to rely on themselves more and on professionals or experts less, as discussed in Chapter 8.

America is becoming a nation of generalists rather than specialists.

The Future Language of the World

The German writer Günter Grass once wrote that the future language of the world will be broken English. He was right. In coming years, English will gain even greater acceptance around the world as the global media and global economy promote a common language. While other languages will, of course, remain important in certain regions, English has emerged as the global language, used in international finance, flight, and even hijackings. It's the language used by Germans and Scandinavians in Italy and by Japanese and Koreans in Hong Kong. This fact will greatly aid American businesses, entertainers, entrepreneurs, and even workers in years to come.

America owes much of its leadership position in services to the control of a single standard: the English language.

One service industry in which America unquestionably leads the world is entertainment. The English language has been invaluable to the success of Hollywood films and American music abroad. French and Italian filmmakers have been all but shut out of the global market unless they make films in English. Likewise, only Ireland (a country of 3.5 million people) and the United Kingdom have been able to challenge the United States in popular music. Few German or French groups are famous. Their problem is not talent but language. German and Scandinavian groups that have made it, such as Ace of Base or Abba, usually perform in English.

For years, first-rate movie directors already famous in Europe have gone to Hollywood to reach a wider audience. The reason is not just Hollywood's weather or fancy studios but the wider potential audience for movies in English. Because the French government frowns on subsidizing movies made in anything other than French, French moviemakers have long had to disguise their involvement in English-language films through joint French/Canadian productions. To combat the dreaded language from over the Channel or across the sea, French Culture Minister Jacques Toubon recently imposed a regulation that fines anyone using an English word in a commercial title or slogan $3,500. Unfortunately for Francophones, Anglophones far outnumber them.

The battle over the language standard resembles battles waged over computer standards.

While English enjoys an enviable position comparable to that of Microsoft Windows, France's expensive effort to promote French resembles IBM's effort to promote OS/2.

As a result of its language advantage and size, the United States will continue to dominate global entertainment. U.S.-based networks such as CNN that use the English language will serve as a pipeline for American products, services, and symbols overseas. Multimedia, virtual reality, and other coming forms of entertainment will all sell best in English.

The English language is also helping other countries that use it. It is no accident that many of the biggest media moguls are from English-speaking countries. Rupert Murdoch, now a U.S. citizen but originally Australian and for a while a resident of England, owns the Star Broadcasting System in Asia, Sky TV in Europe, and, of course, the Fox network in the United States. Sky broadcasts in English, Star TV in English, Mandarin, and Hindi. While Bertelsmann, a German-owned firm, is no slouch as a media conglomerate, nor is Matra-Hachette, the French concern, in foreign countries these firms cannot use their native language to gain economies of scale. If anything, like CNN, MTV, Sky TV, *The Economist* magazine and Star TV, they must use English, the international standard, to stay in the game. This helps the companies make money but moves jobs to English-speaking countries (or forces non–native speakers to learn English).

At first glance, it might seem absurd to broadcast or publish in English instead of the local language. Doesn't such arrogance leave an opening for firms able to tailor their services to the local market? What are these arrogant giants thinking? Naturally, it's cheaper for CNN, for example, to broadcast in just one language, English, but there's more to it than that. By broadcasting in English, U.S. broadcasters have created a standard, analogous to a standard in software, that, by virtue of their market and competencies, they control. If enough broadcasting is in English, programmers, like firms that write software, will have no choice but to produce programming in English. And if all the programming is in English, broadcasters who adhere to this standard gain a proprietary advantage over competitors.

That's exactly what has happened. If programming sources were unlimited and programmers willing to produce programming in every language, the English-language broadcasters' strategy would backfire. But since resources are limited, TV programmers, like computer programmers, program in the language with the widest market, namely English, leaving competitors to scramble for content. (Networks such as CNN and MTV now produce much of their own programming.) All this programming in English creates large economies of scale and competence that programmers in German or French would be hard pressed to duplicate.

Of course, there's plenty of money to be made in languages other than English; given the chance, people prefer to watch programming in their native language. Most news around the world is broadcast in the local language, as are weather reports and game shows. But world-class drama, like world-class software, is difficult and expensive to make. Whereas it's easy to send out a camera crew to report news or interview celebrities, world-class drama is a cluster business that requires a highly developed infrastructure of film editors, actors, sound studios, and writers—all of which cannot easily be duplicated (see Chapter 7). Thus, the vast majority of such drama is made in the United States and exported overseas. No wonder Hollywood continues to tempt overseas investors.

Over time, it's inevitable that world-class programmers will devise ways to tailor first-rate programming to local markets without adding much to their cost. Dubbing is a primitive but widely used method.

Joint ventures between established networks and local firms offer the promise of creating more high-quality local programming.

The English-language advantage extends to more than media programming. It has enabled U.S. firms to dominate financial services worldwide, and it affects computers and software as well. Bangalore, India, has emerged as an important software center, one of the largest in Asia, in part due to the fact that local workers speak English, a fact that helped lure U.S. investment. Because of the common language, an unusual number of graduates of India's demanding Institutes of Technology go to MIT, Harvard, or Stanford to get their Ph.D.s in computer science and then return to India. Texas Instruments and other firms have invested heavily in Bangalore. Because of time zone differences, but also because English is the language of computer programming, many European firms go off-line in the early morning, giving engineers in Bangalore the opportunity to fix problems, dump data, or otherwise maintain European networks.

The largest computer center in Europe is located not in Germany or in France but in Ireland.

Ireland (and also Scotland) has the benefit of using the English language and has fashioned attractive incentives to lure U.S. firms to its shores. Again because of time differences, many American companies go off-line at night, giving Irish engineers the chance to troubleshoot problems, back up data, and perform network maintenance on U.S. networks. England has already emerged as the beachhead of choice for Japanese firms investing in Europe, primarily because of its language—Japanese students study English beginning in first grade.[6] England has accounted for over half of Japanese foreign investment in Europe.

Retail and Distribution

The largest segment of the service sector is trade, both retail and wholesale. Conventional retail will not disappear in coming years even though cyberretail will grow.

Increased development outside cities, thanks to the information highway, will increase the demand for conventional retail, too.

However, retailing will undergo important changes that will reflect new patterns of settlement and evolving information technology, including ever more sophisticated means of tracking inventories and customer needs.

Warehouse Stores

The biggest change, and one that will only accelerate, is the flourishing of warehouse stores such as Wal-Mart. Warehouse stores need space, which in congested areas is expensive (although cheap for them compared with ordinary retail stores). Other than that, they have a huge advantage over traditional retailers. Situated outside cities for the most part, they can easily undercut prices in traditional shopping centers. (Even in suburban malls, they pay anchor rates that are far below those charged smaller stores.) In effect, a warehouse, or category-killer, store resembles a wholesale operation where customers are allowed onto the floor to shop. The huge volumes they purchase let firms such as Wal-Mart virtually dictate to suppliers what they want to pay. It's a far cry from the days when large suppliers told retailers what to buy and what to charge.

But the monster stores have an advantage beyond low cost and high volume: they keep a constantly updated database of consumer needs and preferences. Storekeepers used to have to close their stores one or more times a year for inventory. Now scanners enable stores such as Wal-Mart to update their stock information instantaneously. As inventories change, Wal-Mart's computers quickly determine what to reorder, what not to reorder, what to raise prices on, and, more frequently, what to cut them on. This information then goes back to the chain's suppliers and manufacturers, many of which are on line. Indeed, Wal-Mart is moving toward real-time reordering.

Home Depot is a Wal-Mart spin-off started by a former executive,

Bernard Marcus. Inspired by Wal-Mart's success, office-supply stores such as Office Depot have also appeared. Bookstore chains such as Barnes & Noble and Borders have begun to experiment with megastores. Barnes & Noble has launched 200,000-square-foot monster stores in Manhattan that feature cafés, reading rooms with overstuffed armchairs, and CD departments where customers can preview music over headphones. Record stores such as Tower Records and Virgin Records are also expanding to generate economies of scale. Baby-supply stores, sports stores, and furniture stores have all proven susceptible to the category-killer format.

While the monster stores started out in exurban areas, their economies of scale are so large that they can compete in urban areas too. Zoning laws are the major impediment. When New York City finally allowed a variance, Kmart set up shop in Manhattan.

Warehouse stores have advantages in cities as well as exurbs since they can expand upward from the street into cheaper space.

They also have the advantage of volume. Opening a megastore is not merely good business, it can be a weapon to eliminate competition. Barnes & Noble is using urban megastores offensively to drive out smaller operators. Kmart and Wal-Mart open stores to scare off each other. (Wal-Mart's been winning at this game.)

That said, it's still easier for megastores to operate outside of cities, where regulations tend to be less strict and there is less traffic and congestion. Trucks can easily pull up to deliver goods, ample parking lets customers make larger purchases, and costs are lower. The availability of this form of distribution will give exurban areas a competitive advantage over cities in years ahead (see Chapter 7). Further, the success of monster, category-killer stores has given rise to a new variant on the shopping mall, the power center. Power centers are groups of one or more "big boxes," which may have a few smaller stores or restaurants on "outparcels" of land around their perimeters. These power centers are forcing conventional malls to add amenities such as health clubs, skating rinks, and even amusement parks to draw customers.

Even car dealerships are proving susceptible to the principles of warehouse selling. Car dealerships have been one of the last retail sectors to remain independent, and, composed for the most part of mom-and-pop operations, they have resisted consolidation. However, as the older generation of car dealers bows out, it is increasingly selling to chains. Large auto chains promise the same economies of scale, common discount and service programs, and other standardized practices that have transformed conventional retailing.[7]

One advocate of consolidation in this business is Carl Spielvogel, better known as a former principal of the advertising giant Backer Spielvogel. In his new role, Spielvogel heads United Auto Group, a chain of thirty-nine car dealerships, and is actively buying up more to generate greater economies of scale. If Spielvogel has guessed right, J. D. Power and Associates may be correct in its prediction that, over the next ten years, America's 22,000 car dealerships may shrink by two thirds.

U.S. firms are also using their experience in the world's most competitive retail market to make major pushes into foreign markets. Wal-Mart, Kmart, Pier 1 Imports, and J. C. Penney are all opening stores in Mexico. Toys "R" Us has opened thirty-seven stores in Japan, which is now its second largest market. Tower Records has opened twenty-two stores in Japan since 1979 and, unlike many would-be investors in Japan, has held on to 100 percent equity in its ventures. Its 1994 sales in Japan were $240 million, or one quarter of its global total.[8]

Large stores are so successful that some producers are fighting a full-fledged battle against being pushed around. GE and Whirlpool, for example, have both yanked their products out of the Circuit City and Best Buy chains. Kenwood and Hitachi no longer sell through Best Buy, and Mitsubishi products can no longer be found in Circuit City.[9] As chains grow more powerful, they start dictating price and services to their producers and stop educating their customers about specific products. This has sparked the producer rebellion, but, in the long run, developments favor the megastores. Producers that withdraw from the large chains can't exactly sell through mom-and-pop outfits. Their only alternative to national chains is regional chains that are trying to become national.

Fast Food

A special category of retail stores, fast-food outlets, has exploded in number over the last few decades. In the 1970s and 1980s, fast food boomed as roads grew and women entered the workforce.

Fast food represents the outsourcing of food preparation from the home.

While fast food's salad days may be over, it will further expand in years ahead as development continues into exurbia. Specialty and new health-conscious chains are broadening the market. For example, Rubio's Home of the Fish Taco has grown from a single stand in San Diego a decade ago to seventeen restaurants in San Diego. Proprietor Rafael Rubio, born in Durango, Mexico, is now expanding nationally. His tacos, flavored with chilies, garlic, and cilantro, appeal to health-conscious customers.[10] Similarly, Taco Bell has launched a low-fat Mexican line it calls "Border Lights." And from out of nowhere, specialty coffee bars have become a $2 billion business. Starbucks, the industry leader, has expanded from six Seattle stores in 1987 to close to five hundred stores nationwide today. To supplement its traditional stores, most of which are located in urban areas, Starbucks is now introducing coffee bars in exurban locations. Another food chain to have struck upmarket gold is Boston Market. The key to its success has been to offer a higher-quality, healthier fast-food option with a focus on vegetables and side dishes. Kenny Rogers Roasters now offers high-quality vegetables as well.

Fast-food outlets, however, are finding they must fight hard to keep down costs, which are rising, among other things, due to a labor shortage. One way to cut costs is to outsource food preparation, as PepsiCo's Taco Bell has done. Another is to franchise more. McDonald's, which franchises 80 percent of its restaurants, has outperformed PepsiCo's Pizza Hut, which owns most of its stores itself. In response, Pizza Hut plans to sell stores to franchisees, yet another example of the power of partnering and its frequent advantage over vertical integration.[11] However, this trend toward outsourcing is creating an opportunity for upscale firms that still do much of the cooking in house to trumpet their "home cooking." Even Subway, which outsources some food products, emphasizes its homemade bread. In effect, cost pressures are driving the market in two directions. Starbucks, for example, has chosen not to avail itself of the franchising option in order to keep control over quality.

Construction and Housing

Another sector likely to do well over the long haul, despite cyclical ups and downs, is construction. Housing costs have steadily risen over the last few decades as a percentage of people's income. Construction costs have gone up, and as the cost of building a new house rises, the price of old houses goes up as well.

In 1950, the median price of a house was $39,900 in 1990 dollars. In 1990, it was $79,100, a 100 percent rise. Why? To some degree, housing has gotten better, although only in relation to 1950s tract houses, not Victorian houses or brownstones. New houses have features such as central air-conditioning, and they have gotten bigger, too (by about 20 percent between 1978 and 1994). But even so, this doesn't account for their rise in price. The real reason housing prices have risen is that construction remains a highly labor-intensive business that has changed little over the years. While modern skyscrapers may take advantage of new technologies, hammering a house together today is much like hammering a house together a century ago. The cost of living today is affected by how much cheaper everything else is. Prices of things such as baseball gloves and Walkmans reflect either savings from mechanization or the low wages of people in Third World countries. But housing must still be built by Americans earning American wages. In comparison to everything else, therefore, it has grown more expensive.

In 1930, a construction worker might have made less than a worker on a radio assembly line. Today, a construction worker can earn $250 per day, including benefits and taxes, while the average radio assembler in Mexico makes only a few dollars per day (or else the radio is made in an automated factory). In 1947, construction was 87 percent unionized. Today it's less than 22 percent unionized.[12] Even so, wages have held their own.

Because housing is a necessity, developers and construction workers do quite well and we have no choice but to fork over ever-higher portions of our income to live somewhere.

The rising cost of housing, however, has left some people unable to afford it. For this reason, government has been forced to play a larger role in housing. When the Reagan administration decided to opt out of the government-subsidized housing business in the 1980s, homelessness exploded nationwide.

New housing will continue to grow more expensive to build and buy in proportion to everything else.

This means that housing will be a good investment over the long haul, although short-term changes can always bring on a bust. It also means that developers will continue to get rich. And construction work is not a bad occupation for men. It can't move overseas, and, because of the physical strength required for many tasks, competition from women is limited. Only immigrants are likely to undercut wages. Not surprisingly, construction workers complain about immigrants.

There are other factors that have made real estate a good investment traditionally and will make it a generally good investment in the future. When a house is bought with a mortgage, the rise in the value of the property due to inflation alone raises equity by a leveraged amount. This is the factor that drove the appreciation that many American homeowners realized after World War II. It can almost be said to have created a new middle class, turning homeowners into wealthy landowners. Millions of Americans have retired on the equity realized on their homes. Of course, when money is devalued like this, the lenders of the money—rentiers or the rich—lose out. Real estate price inflation has also kept younger couples out of the market. But in the wake of the late 1980s real estate bust, prices have tumbled back down to their most affordable levels since the 1970s.

Home construction will continue to suffer from cost disease, a bad thing for those who will want to buy housing in the future but a good thing for those who own or buy housing today. The rising population will further drive up demand and price over the next quarter century. Naturally, it will help to pick the right type of house, the right location, and the right part of the country, based on demographic and economic factors.

Three good ideas for coming years:

1. *The retooling of office towers for residential use.* In the 1980s, developers in many cities retooled loft and other industrial buildings for residential and retail use. Office buildings unsuitable for upgrading to handle computer wiring are the next conversion target. Already, Donald Trump is converting the forty-four-story Paramount/Gulf & Western building on New York's Columbus Circle from office to residential space.

2. *The construction of "smart" homes and buildings.* Office buildings from the 1980s already make provision for the computer wiring and large floor plans that corporate customers demand. But home builders must also now run computer, telephone, and cable lines through new construction to create "smart" homes. As discussed in Chapter 7, new houses should also be designed for telecommuters with ample provision for home offices, electronic terminals throughout the house, and other living/working conveniences. Upscale housing must now be built with at least two home offices, one each for husband and wife. For this reason even childless couples are buying three- and four-bedroom houses.

3. *The nanny suite.* Real estate professionals recommend that home buyers (or builders) make a nanny suite a priority.

Such suites can be converted to in-law suites as boomers retire, or used as home offices.[13]

Power Generation and Natural Gas

Just as growth in population alone and the development of regions outside the suburbs will fuel growth in retail and construction, it will also increase demand for electricity and natural gas. And while telecommunications deregulation is drawing more attention than the old-fashioned electric power industry is, it too will deregulate over the next few decades. For a number of years, electric whole-salers have operated around the margin of regulated utilities, buy-ing power where it's cheapest—taking advantage of a national grid—and selling to customers in need. So far, most local utilities still have a monopoly. But they won't forever.

In 2002, according to a new schedule proposed by California's public utility commission, residential customers in California will have the right to shop for power anywhere in the country; Califor-nia small-business owners will be able to shop around for power providers by 1999. Already, big corporate users are allowed to buy directly from small, independent providers, and in 1997 large firms will be allowed to buy energy from any electric utility in the country.[14]

Deregulation of power utilities will make local utilities a conduit for power much as local phone companies now provide access to long-distance lines.

What this means is that local utilities will face pressure to cut costs to compete with cream skimmers, freewheeling firms able to buy power cheaply and sell to the rich, without having to service the poor. California's Pacific Gas & Electric (PG&E), for example, estimates it will have to cut its costs by more than two cents per kilowatt-hour; in the next five years, it hopes to slash costs by $750 million. As billing grows more "intelligent," the utilities plan to charge different rates at different hours (as telephone companies do today), offer customers energy management services, and even provide access to the information superhighway. Natural gas firms are likewise undergoing deregulation through a process known as unbundling that forces utilities to provide access to third-party gas suppliers.

Cream Skimming

As a result, new cream-skimming opportunities abound. Cream skimming of upper-tier customers from sectors served by public or quasi-public entities is a time-honored way of making money. Although it has recently fueled complaints that the rich are seceding from America, cream skimming is an old American tradition. Practitioners have included Fred Smith, founder of Federal Express, William McGowan, founder of MCI, and even Neal Rudenstine, president of Harvard.

Cream skimming is the other side of the coin of government intervention in the economy. When the government required AT&T to provide universal service, it created an opportunity for MCI to skim cream by serving large corporate customers. Federal Express, UPS, Airborne Express, and others skimmed cream from the post office, letting it handle unprofitable rural and inner-city delivery. The post office responded with similar upmarket products and today is quasi-private. Deregulation of local telephone service and cable television is creating another opportunity for cream skimming, this time in local markets where firms are making money hooking up office buildings with satellite dishes. The deregulation of local telephone and cable service will create as many new opportunities as the deregulation of long distance service created. To a degree, private schools skim cream while public schools provide universal education. The creation of a voucher system for schools would create a huge new opportunity to skim cream.

Like its close relative, free riding—which AccuWeather does on the National Weather Service, DRI/McGraw Hill does on the Bureau of Economic Analysis, and any number of biotech firms do on federal support of research—cream skimming is merely the flip side of government support and regulation of the economy. At times it can get out of hand, as happened during the S&L crisis, when savings-and-loan institutions free rode on the government insurance of their deposits. However, government efforts to serve the public good often create opportunities for business.

Other Service Businesses

All sorts of services will adapt and expand in coming years, including the following.

Shipping

Federal Express is branching out from the old-fashioned delivery of packages, in which it will face more and more competition from fax and E-mail, into helping companies manage the shipping process. Its FedEx Ship software product lets companies tie into FedEx's computers to schedule pickups, confirm delivery of packages, and even print out mailing labels on the firm's own computers.

Meanwhile, the new trend toward just-in-time "instant manufacturing" is driving a boom in sophisticated shipping of parts, also known as logistics. As companies have put their operations on line to manufacture to order and service customers better, many have chosen to outsource the complicated business of getting millions of parts where they are needed when. The beneficiaries are companies such as Roadway Express, which recently jettisoned its old-fashioned, unionized trucking business to concentrate on performing full-service logistics for corporate clients. Using computerized methods of tracking inventory, Roadway is able to do a better job moving parts around than the companies themselves.

Filling Stations

Even the oldest, most traditional services are trying to improve their service. Mobil is winning market share at the pump by killing the competition with service. After determining through in-depth market research that only about 20 percent of buyers buy on the basis of price, Mobil is changing how it packages what it sells—gas and groceries.[15] New convenience stores at filling stations sell cappuccino. Helpful attendants check oil and even run into the store to buy Cokes for customers at self-service pumps. The new strategy has driven sales up by 15 percent at trial stations.

Banking

This age-old industry will undergo major changes in years ahead as a result of two regulatory reforms: interstate banking, scheduled to come on line in 1997, and the modification of the 1932 and 1933 Glass-Steagal Acts, to allow banks to deal in securities. With the rise of interstate banking, large banks will expand across state lines, gobbling up their weaker competitors. Already, a few superregional banks, such as North Carolina's First Union, have begun to dominate their local areas by using complicated subsidiary structures. A shakeout lies ahead.

Banking will be one of the most dynamic and turbulent industries of the next ten years. But even though modification of the Glass-Steagal Act will soon let banks sell securities on a limited basis, banking is one service industry that will probably lose many jobs in the years ahead. The reason: competition from securities firms and other financial firms. The tool: information technology. Through home banking, higher productivity, and other means, the banking industry may shed up to a quarter of its workers over the next decade.

Health Care

The aging of America will increase demand for health care and, therefore, doctors, nurses, and other health care workers.

For demographic reasons, health care will be one of the largest businesses of the next half century. The dramatic rise in the cost of health care seems to have tapered off as a result of the growth of health maintenance organizations (HMOs). Nevertheless, an increase in the number of old people means a growing market.

Of course, not all service jobs in the future will be knowledge-intensive, high-tech, or in any way glamorous. There will also be a growing need for low-skill service jobs. And because of limits to productivity improvement in health care, it may become a large employer of low-wage, unskilled workers.

Conclusion

In sum, services will be a large creator of wealth over the next few years, with information technology driving much of the growth. Existing firms from NYNEX to Wal-Mart to Microsoft will benefit from the growth of the information highway, but so will new ones. Remember, the economy of the future will favor businesses based on knowledge as cheap labor disappears.

Job hunters will find high-paying jobs available, providing they possess the necessary skills, notably in the technical area. Without skills, job seekers will find the going tough due to the educational demands of new technology and competition from computers themselves. Industries that will boom include nursing homes, data processing services, management and public relations, health care, equipment leasing and rental, equipment servicing, software, and auto rental. Service industries that will decline include petroleum refining, domestic help, and traditional communications (such as being a telephone operator).

Compared with other countries, America is well ahead of the curve in the evolution of services. The tightening of the labor market will lead services to evolve further toward more productive activities based on knowledge, the leading edge of the twenty-first-century economy.

Chapter 6

Cyberspace and the Information Superhighway

James Gleick, author of the best-seller *Chaos: Making a New Science,* became aware of the Internet earlier than most. As a science reporter for *The New York Times,* he learned about the Internet in the early 1990s, when it was still largely a preserve of government and universities, accessible primarily by mainframe computers running Unix. Despite its complexity, Gleick was intrigued by what he saw as the immense untapped potential of the Internet. He saw a business opportunity in making the Internet accessible to the average personal-computer owner.

Discussing the idea with a New York bridge partner, Uday Ivatury, a seasoned computer programmer, Gleick discovered a common interest. In 1992, the two embarked on a venture to create a software interface to open up the Internet. In December 1993, they launched the results of their efforts, Pipeline USA, an Internet service that didn't require a degree in programming to use. The service took off, winning a *PC Magazine* Editor's Choice award and mention in *Business Week,* and traveling on word of mouth. Little more than a year later, the service had 10,000 subscribers. Besides convenient graphical Internet access, Pipeline USA featured AP and Dow Jones news and stock quotes, restaurant menus and reviews, and a cybermall. In February 1995, Gleick and Ivatury sold the firm to PSINet, a nationwide Internet service provider, for a figure in the millions.

Pipeline USA is only one of countless firms that are appearing from nowhere and growing explosively as the information superhighway unfolds. For all the ink and bandwidth consumed in discussions of the information highway, existing projections do not fully convey the extent to which it is changing the U.S. (and the global) economy.

The Second Services Revolution

In one sense, information services are just another form of services, which are already the mainstay of the U.S. economy. But the speed and breadth of the network revolution make them more than that. The shift from conventional services to electronic services represents nothing less than a second services revolution, equal in importance to the first one. Remember that new sectors do not appear overnight but grow out of what preceded them. Industry grew out of agriculture; the first uses of the steam engine were on farms and in mines. Services grew out of industry, which drove the development of railroads, banking, and stores. Just as industry soon outstripped agriculture, services grew while manufacturing automated. In 1956, the number of white-collar employees surpassed that of blue-collar ones, prompting Daniel Bell to announce the arrival of the "postindustrial revolution" and Alvin Toffler to proclaim services the "third wave" of human development. Had industry disappeared? No, but something profound had occurred: the first services revolution. Now a new type of information service is growing out of conventional services and threatening to eclipse them in turn in an equally important change.

Just as industry gave birth to services, so services are giving birth to information services.

In place of conventional retail, electronic retail is emerging as a major industry. From sales over the Internet of just $100 million in 1995, Killen & Associates, a market research firm, estimates that sales will increase to $300 billion by the year 2000.[1] In place of the sale of videocassettes or CDs in stores, we are seeing more electronic transfer of entertainment into the home. Instead of the sale of shrink-wrapped software in stores, we are seeing a migration toward metered software that is distributed free but requires you to pay a toll down the road!

As with the development of services out of manufacturing, the change from manual services to electronic services is occurring gradually, yet its consequences will be profound. The second services revolution is also the third industrial revolution and spells good news for productivity and wages.

If services in the 1970s and 1980s were characterized by an explosion of retail franchises along America's highways that utilized low-paid, surplus labor, services in the 1990s will be characterized by an explosion of jobs along the information highway that require education and pay far better. The new jobs will require workers to use their brains. They are capital- and knowledge-intensive instead of labor-intensive. And since they take advantage of automated networks, they will enable one person to do and earn more.

The advance edge of this wave was growth in the financial services sector in the 1980s, when networks made their first major headway, linking up markets and traders and equipping them with huge amounts of real-time data. The explosion of capability and productivity in this single sector created hundreds of thousands of well-paying jobs. The most money went to managers, but even computer programmers, secretaries, and others earned more in financial services than elsewhere.

In the 1990s, the advance edge of networks moved from servicing the financial community to serving the home, providing consumers with entertainment and shopping. If Bloomberg was the network success story of the 1980s, America Online (AOL), with more than 5 million subscribers, is emblematic of the growth of networks in the 1990s. In 1994, AOL transmitted 50,000 pieces of E-mail a day; only a year later, it was handling 1.5 million pieces daily, a thirtyfold increase. Cellular-telephone networks have also been huge successes.

The success of network services in coming decades will surpass that of financial services in the 1980s.

Since the entire business of network services is new, entrepreneurs will have an unprecedented opportunity to enter it. Retail services have always had comparatively low barriers to entry. Electronic retail sales and services will be even cheaper to enter, and those who can figure out how to do it best will have as good a shot as Wal-Mart, Sears, Bell Atlantic, or any other company. In fact, entrepreneurs who enter the business soon may become the Wal-Marts of the future.

The Information Highway Versus Cyberspace

This new world of networks has earned the moniker "information superhighway." But anyone who has navigated computer networks can testify that using them doesn't feel like traveling on a highway. Logging onto the Internet, AOL, or other services feels more like entering a glorified library than a car. You're stationary, and when you "move," it's effortless. Even when there's "traffic" on the 'Net, all you see on your monitor is an hourglass. On the World Wide Web, travel literally means jumping among computers all over the world, but the data moving across wires is something you hardly notice.

As people spend more time in cyberspace and experience more on-line services in their homes, they have already begun to talk less about the information superhighway and more about cyberspace. Terms such as "information highway" and "infobahn," like the term "iron horse" for the railroad or "horseless carriage" for a car, reflect the present's attempt to envision the future in familiar terms. Cyberspace promises to unite libraries of books, movie archives, TV Land, and famous figures from these media—rock musicians, actors, and newscasters—in one interactive arena.

In their earliest incarnation, networks were just a means of moving data between point A and point B. Western Union's network enabled someone in New York, for example, to send a cable or money to someone in Chicago, while telephone networks let people talk to one another. Networks took a step forward when they allowed more than two people to talk at once and added computers and a software interface. Wide-area networks, such as American Airlines' SABRE reservations system, let travel agents all over the country book flights simultaneously by putting them on line with a central computer. Financial networks, such as Bloomberg and Quotron, furnished traders with the latest data. Local-area networks (LANs) enabled people in offices to use software or edit documents stored on a central server.

The idea was still for point A to communicate with point B, the center, but now there were many point A's. As more people logged on and access reached a critical mass, networks became a place, as well as method of meeting, creating an entirely new, parallel universe. It's as if a set of narrow corridors linking people together had widened into a giant plaza. No wonder Bill Gates called cyberspace and the information highway the greatest business opportunity in history. And this change has profound implications for productivity.

Cyberspace: The New Electronic Frontier

Long ago, wise men noticed that knowledge or information is somehow different from objects such as grain or wine. It's a so-called nonconsumable resource. As the Bible says, it's better to teach people to fish than to give them a fish to eat. The fish disappears when you eat it; the ability to fish persists. Networks take advantage of the fact that information—the description of a thing as opposed to the thing—does not disappear with use. Like libraries, they multiply the value of a commodity—information—by giving more people access to it. And, increasingly, they also allow you to use the processing capability of others' computers.

Networks multiply knowledge and power as though a man in the industrial age had had access to all the mills and turbines and cotton gins in the world.

Imagine what a capitalist at the beginning of the Industrial Revolution would have said if you told him he could use the machinery of everyone else in the world for free. This multiplication factor is unprecedented in human history.

But cyberspace is not only a place to obtain information. It's also a place, like the American West, to make money and accordingly, people have already begun to fight over it. Like previous frontiers, it's a blank canvas on which entrepreneurs seeking profits and others seeking less clear-cut goals from religious salvation to political revolution will paint their destinies and the future. And it's not totally disembodied from the real world. Just as buccaneers took their fortunes gained in the West Indies back to Europe to buy mansions, so entrepreneurs will swap the E-cash they make on the Internet for homes and cars in the real world. Americans have a head start on the rest of the world in exploiting this new frontier for a number of reasons: more advanced networks, the size of the U.S. market, and an entrepreneurial tradition. The basic building block of wealth on this frontier will be what I call cyberestate.

Cyberestate is simply cyberspace viewed as property. It's real estate out in the void. Those who control this real estate are the people who control how you get there, integrated service providers such as AOL and Microsoft, vendors offering services such as Sabre and Westlaw, and lesser-known companies such as Pipeline USA and Panix, which provide telephone links to the Internet. Just as railroads turned vast stretches of America's frontier into valuable real estate, so these providers are creating valuable cyberestate out of interchangeable bandwidth. During the railroad era, moving passengers and freight around was never a particularly good business. What made railroads attractive investments was the developable land they created from nothing. Even today, owners of

Japanese private commuter rail lines outside Tokyo make money not from running cars but from developing and managing property around the stations.

U.S. railroads got an additional boost from free land provided by the government. To raise money on Wall Street for the Union Pacific, for example, Thomas Clark Durant bribed members of Congress, which granted him ten acres of free land for every mile of track. Unable to get the backing he needed to build the railroad, he returned to Congress, which duly doubled his grant to twenty acres per mile of track. He got his funding, and the transcontinental railroad was built. In a similar vein, during the Reagan years, the federal government gave away cellular-telephone licenses for free. A resource that few knew existed, a thin stretch of the broadcast spectrum, became an asset thanks to new technology. In coming years, new networks, by opening new paths through cyberspace, will create valuable cyberestate out of the void.

A Map of Cyberspace

Unlike conventional real estate, no maps yet exist for cyberspace. Nevertheless, it's possible to describe the three basic communications channels that can be used to get there: telephone systems, cable systems, and the wireless spectrum.

Telephone Systems

Telephone systems will play a major role in supporting cyberspace. They can be used for a lot more than talking and are no longer synonymous with telephony, which will run over cable as well. Nor is it correct just to speak of telephone wires, since large chunks of the system are now wireless. But the telephone system—consisting of fiber-optic and copper wires owned by local phone companies; fiber-optic wires, satellite links, and microwave links owned by firms such as AT&T and MCI; and wireless cellular service supplied by firms such as McCaw Cellular Communications—will carry a good share of traffic in the future.

The phone network is one that other companies can easily piggyback on, since it was designed from the outset to support two-way conversations between subscribers.

Telephone networks have a tremendous amount of switching capacity, allowing users to direct calls wherever they want. They were never designed as a conduit for the government or a central authority to broadcast over, like traditional television or even cable. The phone network is, of course, the basis of the Internet (although Internet traffic may also soon move over cable networks). It's also the basis for AOL, CompuServe, and other on-line services. And it's the basis for many cyberspace bulletin boards. Because phones were designed to let anyone use the network for a small payment, they are the most wide-open route to cyberspace.

CABLE SYSTEMS

Cable systems will also play a large role in delivering services, but they are not as wide open as phone networks. They were designed as captive networks to carry an operator's programming to subscribers, not to let subscribers communicate among themselves. But that too will change. Cable companies such as John Malone's Tele-Communications Inc. (TCI) and Time Warner plan to offer phone service soon. In its choice of acquisitions, Time Warner has pursued a strategy of "clustering" so that it can provide telephone as well as cable service. It now has thirty-three clusters, each of which has 100,000 or more subscribers.

Because they were designed on the model of broadcasting, cable systems are quite vertically integrated. The two large cable firms, TCI and Time Warner, have extensive programming holdings: Time Warner owns parts of Warner Bros., Home Box Office (HBO), and other programming sources, while TCI owns chunks of Time Warner, Home Shopping Network, and Discovery Communications, owner of the Discovery Channel. They are closed networks at the moment, accessible only to the cable firms themselves.

But cable's connection with Hollywood and other programming gives it a leg up on phones as an entertainment medium.

THE WIRELESS SPECTRUM

Wireless systems other than cellular-telephone service will also play a large role in sustaining cyberspace. Personal communications systems (PDAs) will communicate via a new set of frequencies auctioned off by the FCC. Other wireless networks already exist, including Motorola's Ardis network, which supports messaging and E-mail in America's four hundred largest metropolitan areas. Since a handheld device doesn't have the broadcasting power needed to reach the nearest TV tower, wireless networks usually use the cellular concept.

Also included in the wireless category are traditional broadcasting systems. Traditional broadcasting from the TV tower to your home has been entirely one-way. But all that may change with the advent of digital TV, which will let broadcasters cram more channels into a limited number of frequencies. Promised an additional channel for high-definition television (HDTV) by the FCC, broadcasters want to use it for two-way paging, high-speed data transfer, and other services in lieu of broadcasting HDTV.[2]

These are the main channels that will open up the world of cyberspace. But fiber-optic lines and coaxial cable do not a cyberworld make. That world will come into being only when networks carrying data begin to travel over physical wires and frequencies. And more than communication is needed. Computers are also required, both to provide an interface to others and to store data, whether shopping software, a movie, a newspaper or magazine, or some other interactive service.

Value-added Networks (VANs)

If hard-wired networks such as telephone, cable, and wireless are the rivers and roads of cyberspace, value-added networks are the truckers and shipping firms that ply them for business. VANs run over the wires owned by phone companies, but where exactly they go and what customers they serve change from day to day. Examples of VANs are AOL, Prodigy, and CompuServe. The World Wide Web on the Internet is also a VAN, and each of them adds value through software and computer processing. They don't just send Morse code back and forth, as the original Western Union wires did. They don't just transmit sound over wires, as a telephone does. They let you transfer photos, access information, write notes, and otherwise add value. As computer processing speeds increase and memory grows cheaper, they will add more and more value.

Consumer Versus Producer or Wholesale Nets

While consumer nets such as AOL are getting much of the publicity right now, it is a mistake to think that the information superhighway is devoted just to the final user. Banks and brokerage firms are already using it to transmit information in house and from one to another through what's known as electronic data interchange (EDI). Federal Express markets a VAN that handles logistics for other companies. American Airlines' SABRE reservation system services business customers. Many of the services crossing cyberspace will be intracompany, infrastructural, or wholesale with large wide-area private networks accessing the public "highway" at specified junctures. Companies are creating internal Intranets modeled on the Internet protocol.

Just as trucking companies, large distributors, and even corporations have made fortunes moving goods on the auto highway, so many firms will make money on the information highway without ever servicing the retail customer.

IBM, for example, hopes to get a piece of this business with its IBM Global Network. The network already provides service to some 2 million subscribers at 25,000 businesses in more than ninety countries. But IBM expects it to grow far larger and hopes that businesses will handle everything from inventory management to videoconferencing to supply requisitions to communications on its network. The network will also offer users convenient access to IBM software applications and additional services. To succeed with these plans, IBM hopes to build on the knowledge it has obtained from Prodigy, the consumer network it co-owns with Sears.

Creating Your Own Cyberestate

Wheeling and dealing in cyberestate will be a huge industry in the future, equivalent to wheeling and dealing in real estate today.

How to get your piece of the rock? The best method at the moment is the Internet. To create your own cyberestate on the Internet, you need only five things:

1. A server, which is to say a computer with server software.

2. A router to handle calls.

3. A fat phone line to permit faster throughput of data. Options include an integrated services digital network (ISDN) or T1 line.

4. Software to process the incoming calls and sell your product or spread your message.

5. A connection to the Internet through a service provider.

Once you have your server, you need to develop the graphics for your Web site. At the moment, the language you must use is hypertext markup language, an easy language to learn. Through hypertext you can link yourself up with the rest of the Web, increasing the odds that someone will find you. And you can get listed in Web directories. With the purchase of some additional equipment, you can become a full-fledged Internet service provider.

In lieu of a Web site, some people set up a bulletin board service (BBS). These range from venerable services such as San Francisco's The WELL to small boards run by high school students. Most BBS owners are now hooking their boards up to the Internet.

As bandwidth continues to expand, distinguishing your cyberestate from what surrounds it will be critical to enhancing or even preserving its value.

The keys to creating valuable cyberestate are content and connectivity.

If you offer sufficiently interesting content, the world may beat a path to your door. If you have many doors open to many key locations and business partners, the world is more likely to find your door.

Time Warner has set up a giant Web site called Pathfinder that offers the company's magazines, movies, and other properties. To make the site even more glamorous, Time Warner has struck deals with blue-chip retailers, including The Sharper Image and Williams-Sonoma, to offer their wares in adjacent rooms. In contrast, Clark Internet Services, an Internet service provider headquartered near Baltimore, lets companies rent space in its Lighthouse mall for a modest price. Companies as diverse as National Public Radio and Atomic Books, a Baltimore bookstore, have set up shop there. While not as upmarket as the Time Warner site, Lighthouse has found a profitable niche. Other cyberestate malls are being created that cater to various price points, themes, and regions.

In cyberestate, as in real estate, what counts is location, location, location.

However, in cyberspace, location is not fixed but can change as a store owner forges alliances with various sites. Cyberestate developers able to create local networks will be able to charge rent to local services such as grocery stores, locksmiths, lunch delivery services, movie theaters, and other businesses. They will be the cyberequivalent of today's neighborhood shopping centers.

Special-interest networks will do well too. Malls oriented toward the outdoors, boating, hunting, gourmet living, and antiques will attract customers interested in those activities.

Steven Brill, founder of *The American Lawyer* and Court TV, has created a BBS for lawyers called Lexis Counsel Connect.[3] Marketed to *The American Lawyer*'s readers, it permits them to chat, post questions about legal matters, and peruse legal documents. Originally, Brill priced the service at $975 a month plus 65 cents per minute. The service didn't sell at that price, but since cutting the price, he has racked up 16,000 subscribers, creating a multimillion-dollar business. His service benefits from a partnership with Nexis Lexis, which gives his BBS access to the Lexis database.

Entrepreneurs anxious to address niche markets will have to compete with AOL and Microsoft in a business where it will be easier and easier for the "big guys" to service niches through a central doorway. But like any specialists, they should be able to make up in content what they lack in size. In fact, the on-line services are recruiting content just as television networks pay for programming. AOL pays participants in its Greenhouse program up to 20 percent of revenues for running sites on subjects such as personal financial investment.

Not every merchant will want to own, however; far more will rent. Larger firms are making deals with networks such as AOL and Prodigy to hawk their wares. Sears and IBM are advertising on Prodigy, which they own. Countless smaller merchants, selling everything from flowers to videos to software, are renting space in smaller malls. Cyberestate options will be as wide and varied as real estate options today.

Security and Payment on the 'Net

The big hangup about Internet commerce at first was security, and providing security has emerged as a business in and of itself. A programmer named Phil Zimmerman waged a one-man war against the Clipper standard (an encryption method with a key that would have enabled feds to snoop on suspected criminals) with his Pretty Good Protection (PGP) system. MasterCard and Visa have also been developing secure standards, as have banks and start-ups such as CyberCash, based in Reston, Virginia.[4]

Credit cards won't be the only payment method for on-line shopping, however. Other firms are developing E-cash— cyberscrip, as it were—that can be used in cyberspace. Think of what cash is: it's an IOU issued by the Federal Reserve Bank that was once redeemable for gold or silver but that today merely says it's worth a certain amount. It's not that different from a check. The difference is that it's issued by a central authority whose credit and "full faith" are particularly strong.

Electronic cash will simply be an electronic IOU issued by an entity whose credit and faith are strong. For the paper to function as genuine cash, it will have to be fully encrypted, uncounterfeitable, and untraceable. Companies such as DigiCash, a Dutch firm founded by a former Berkeley professor, are working on the technical side of this. DigiCash's E-cash is encrypted code issued in a certain amount that cannot be traced to its holder. To obtain cash in the future, you will probably make a draft on a bank account or credit line or run your "smart card" or credit card through a computer. In exchange, the issuer of the cash—for example, DigiCash or a bank—will give you cash that you can use in cyberspace for whatever you want. *Wired* magazine has created a system of electronic chits, or "poker chips," that can be used within its network.

The U.S. Treasury is currently exploring creating E-cash of its own, to be backed by the full faith and credit of the U.S. government.

The situation for E-cash is not unlike that for cash in the middle of the nineteenth century, when state and local currencies proliferated before the passage of the National Bank Act in 1863. Short-term notes issued by states and private banks proliferated until the federal government created a common currency. This time around, however, the government may well pass on issuing E-cash, given the proliferation of credit cards and other money instruments and the declining popularity of paper cash itself.

Software in the Twenty-first Century

If computer memory is the equivalent of real estate in cyberspace, software is the way to develop it.

Software can turn desert into farmland, a vacant lot into a building, or swampland into a golf course by activating inert memory. It will grow in importance in coming years, creating more jobs and economic opportunities. And it's an area of U.S. strength.

The United States sells about 75 percent of the prepackaged software in the world. And as the twenty-first century unfolds, U.S. firms are likely to retain their dominance over its development, both because software is technology-intensive and because it involves minimal manufacturing. However, there are other important reasons why the U.S. software industry has grown so dominant and will remain so.

- The United States has far and away the largest installed base of computers, making it the world's largest market for software.

- U.S. customers are the world's most demanding; software's cultural dimension gives local developers an insider's advantage.

- Software and hardware design are linked; software developers benefit from proximity to hardware innovators, most of which are in the United States.

- U.S. graduate schools are the best in the world, and software is highly knowledge-intensive.

- The United States has adopted an open PC standard.

The last point is noteworthy. To a degree, U.S. dominance of software, like personal computers themselves, is a result of IBM's decision to outsource its operating system to Microsoft and go with open systems, which had the effect of splitting operating systems from the hardware. (The Apple, Commodore, and Atari systems had bundled these together.) This kept Japanese firms first from gaining PC hardware market share with lower costs and then from imposing proprietary software standards to knock their competitors out of the box, as they managed to do in video games.[5]

Further, Japanese firms at first were incapable of creating software for the U.S. market due to the language barrier and the American head start; only manufacturing hegemony might have overcome those disadvantages. (A proliferation of incompatible standards in Japan retarded later software development.) European firms possessed neither the hardware nor the software lead to challenge U.S. firms. As a result, American firms, today as a decade ago, dominate the global market in software. And while some functions are being outsourced to places such as Bangalore, India, they are likely to continue to dominate the industry in coming decades.

Metered Software

But the software that will change the future won't be the kind sold today: single programs packaged in shrink-wrapped paper boxes.

Software is becoming a utility business.

While traditional software won't go away, most of the growth in the industry will occur in metered or tolled, as opposed to stand-alone, software. The new software will increasingly be distributed for free. Revenue will come from renting it, not from selling it.

Microsoft CEO Bill Gates recently told stock analysts that if Microsoft sticks to writing conventional software, it can at best grow by 10 to 15 percent per year. Not bad—but a far cry from Microsoft's 30 to 50 percent growth up until now. His remedy: Microsoft must shift from conventional software to new kinds of software for the information superhighway, where he's now spending "ninety percent of his IQ" and one fourth of Microsoft's R&D.

Gates has made it clear that he wants to turn Microsoft into a cyberutility that makes money on rents and tolls, not on sales in the traditional sense. Consider the company's attempt to acquire Intuit, maker of Quicken, the world's best-selling personal money management program, a plan that the Justice Department finally vetoed. Quicken is not just a tool for balancing your checkbook; it also lets users do home banking and conduct financial business on line. In the case of Quicken, Gates wanted to collect a charge from banks every time a Quicken user paid a bill, moved money from one account to another, checked a balance, or completed an on-line transaction. The banks would have been happy to pay the toll since on-line banking is far cheaper than bricks and mortar.

While Gates gave up on acquiring Intuit, his strategy is simple enough: to make money every time something moves in the electronic marketplace of the future. For example, Windows 95 comes bundled with the Microsoft Network and built-in Internet protocols. (A rumor persists that when you log onto its on-line service, Microsoft's computers scan your hard drive to see what programs, including unlicensed ones, you have and which you might need.)

Freeware and Shareware

But Microsoft isn't the only company to see ongoing revenues, as opposed to onetime sales, as the key to growth. The most spectacular IPO of 1995 and most successful Internet company to date, Netscape, gives away its popular browser free. On-line services such as AOL and CompuServe distribute their software free as well; they make money from usage fees. They also distribute a good deal of third-party software for free and sell software over their networks. On-line services are an ideal venue for selling software, since it can be downloaded immediately.

The new Java programming language from Sun Microsystems will let servers on the Internet do your processing for you and will permit companies to rent out use of a program rather than selling it to you outright. Software developers are also using the Internet to distribute software in lieu of selling it through stores. For years, small companies such as PKWare, the inventor of the PKZIP and PKUNZIP data compression and decompression programs, distributed programs by the shareware method. Shareware is software distributed on the honor system. Developers post a program to computer bulletin boards and then ask users to send in a check and register if they like using the program. (Registration entitles them to mailings and future upgrades.) Some shareware programs automatically delete themselves if a user fails to pay a fee within a certain period of time. Shareware cuts out the middleman and gives small firms a way of distributing their product cheaply. But it's also a way to get people hooked and then bill them for upgrades and other services down the road.

Even large companies have begun experimenting with shareware. Oracle was the first large maker to try distributing programs on the Internet; a Menlo Park, California, start-up, CyberSource, has created a site offering numerous third-party programs, including Symantec's Norton Utilities.[6] If a customer doesn't pay for a program, the program deletes itself in thirty days.

Microsoft considered trying a variant of this method using CD-ROMs. In what it called its "Ali Baba" project, it planned to encode programs such as Word and Excel on CD-ROMs containing Windows. Users would only have had to authorize a charge to get the code to make the program "open sesame"—i.e., activate, hence the name "Ali Baba." The concept was a way of getting free shelf space in computer stores and further decimating the competition. Microsoft backed off from this killer strategy only when confronted by cries of outrage from other software companies. But while it retreated from its Ali Baba plan, Microsoft has loaded its new operating system with smaller programs that used to be separate applications.

The Importance of Standards—
Now and in the Future

One of the main reasons to give out copies of your software—or to slash its price—is to make that software into a standard.

It's not that different from the old razor and razor blade gambit: you give away the razors for next to nothing and make your money on blades. Gillette invented this method during World War I, when it gave away millions of razors to soldiers, thus creating a mass market for blades.

Looking back on the history of software and looking ahead to the twenty-first century, it's clear that standards play the crucial role in success. By dominating the standard for personal computers, Microsoft bankrupted numerous competing software firms. How? Microsoft's applications, such as Excel, Word, and PowerPoint, work seamlessly with Windows. In contrast, WordPerfect, Lotus 1-2-3, and other programs have glitches. Microsoft claims it's because the developers haven't done their homework. Rivals claim that Microsoft puts "back doors" into Windows, secrets it doesn't tell others, that allow for fancy features that competitors have to jump through hoops to duplicate. Whatever the reason, once-great firms are in shambles. Lotus, for example, now a subsidiary of IBM, has pretty much given up on conventional programs such as spreadsheets, which it pioneered.

Not surprisingly, IBM spent billions trying to make OS/2 Warp a standard, but with limited success. Apple tried licensing out the Macintosh operating system to widen its standard.[7] In the workstation area, the principal users of UNIX—Hewlett-Packard, Sun Microsystems, IBM, and Novell—adopted a new common UNIX standard in 1995, giving the serviceable program a common look and feel in an effort to slow the Microsoft juggernaut.[8] Ironically, only months earlier, the same companies had been trying to differentiate their versions of UNIX to put a proprietary stamp on their programs. The release of Microsoft's Windows NT and Windows 95 forced them to work together.

Now Netscape is feverishly forming alliances in competition with Microsoft to try to make its browser software an industry standard. The ability to strike alliances can play a key role in establishing a standard. Whoever controls standards in the future will likewise call the shots. When General Magic, an Apple spin-off with AT&T, Sony, Motorola, and other giants as investors, went public in 1995, its stock shot through the roof. Why? General Magic had devised an operating system for PDAs that many believe would become the next Microsoft Windows. But with the success of the Web, General Magic has been retooling its program Telescript to compete with Java, as discussed below.

If a Japanese or European firm were to get control of a critical operating system standard, it could spell disaster for the U.S. software industry. (The logical way for a Japanese firm to get control of a standard would be either by acquiring a firm like General Magic or by using hardware skill to take over a market, as Nintendo and Sega managed to do with video games; an area in which they might try to do this is TV set–top boxes.) Sony has held talks with Apple. However, U.S. firms realize the stakes, and unless they fall asleep at the switch, should be in a position to prevent this from happening. The Apple standard, for its part, is a minority one.

While operating system standards and browser standards are software choke points, other standards also determine the success or failure of products. Adobe Systems prospered because it managed to make PostScript a standard for printing. Adobe followed a slightly different model than Microsoft did; it made its standard open but bet it could write applications for it faster and better than anyone else. It has been less successful making something called "Acrobat" the standard for electronic documents.

Perhaps the boldest attempt to impose a standard by getting around others' standards and in the process to transform computing is Sun Microsystems' Java programming language. Java can enable network servers from Internet servers to the mainframes in your cable company's office to do the computer processing for you. In effect, Java ships out software that emulates a computer for whomever logs on. This virtual computer can then run "applets," or small applications written in Java, which are also shipped out via the server, on whatever computer you happen to have, whether a "dumb" terminal, a PC, or a mainframe. Applets shipped out over wires won't substitute for complex word processing and spreadsheet programs that run on your desktop, but it will let "dumb" terminals such as your TV's set-top box or a so-called Net computer (stripped-down PC) act like more robust machines. In Sun's vision, "the network is the computer." Java is already livening up pages on the World Wide Web. While Java has won many converts, including Microsoft, other firms may well begin to offer competitive products.

Software Services of the Future

Despite all the hype about the information superhighway, most of the services that will run on it already exist.

For example, telephones, E-mail, videoconferencing, television, home shopping, and electronic news are already in wide use. In law, Westlaw lets users perform complex searches using English sentences rather than complex codes. The system can even display the page of a given case that is most applicable to a given situation. Nexis Lexis lets users search law documents and a mind-numbing number of periodicals. Other systems provide access to airline schedules, articles, books, and even software. Rough versions of future services can be seen on AOL and Prodigy. While TV viewers may soon use voice commands to jump around in new, imaginative hierarchies of videos, games, shopping, and news, they can already do some of that with a clicker. The main difference between current and future services will be in degree and special features. MTV's offering on AOL originally had only text; now it has pictures and sound. Eventually, it will have virtual reality and three-dimensional graphics. Chat boards will include audio and video.

The demand for conventional network television has remained constant through the introduction of many alternatives in recent years.

Broadcast television, with its continuous programming, will not go away. The home interface to the information highway will simply give users additional options if they wish to use them.

In that respect, things will not change as much as some people might expect. Even the fanciest applications have already been envisioned in science fiction. Computer personalities that talk are less than a decade away, but HAL, the computer in *2001: A Space Odyssey,* was imagined decades ago. Recreational, virtual reality computing was imagined in the movie *Total Recall,* based on a story by Philip K. Dick. What will change is the sophistication and features of these services. For although they exist today, their progeny a quarter century from now will be as different as McDonald's is different from yesterday's mom-and-pop diner. Future versions of the services will incorporate new technologies such as virtual reality and artificial intelligence to make them more enticing.

Of course, some entirely new services are sure to appear. Yet in this area, as in most things in human history, there is nothing new under the sun; rather, people improve on basic ideas such as theater, talk, food, and commerce. Principal services will include the following:

Telephony

Everyone from cable firms to gas and electric companies to thruway authorities wants to enter the telephone business. The big firms will run fiber-optic cables. Smaller ones will resell service, wire offices and factories, or put satellite dishes on top of buildings to bypass regional phone companies. For example, New York–based Teleport, a Merrill Lynch spin-off owned by four cable firms, Tele-Communications Inc., Cox Cable, Comcast, and Continental Cablevision, started out wiring buildings in New York and linking them by satellite with long-distance carriers, thus bypassing the local phone company, NYNEX. It now owns four thousand miles of fiber optics and services twenty-four cities. Traditional phone service will also acquire new "bells and whistles." NYNEX has already built speech recognition into its network that will let customers say "mother" into the phone to dial their mother, "wife" to dial home, or "pizza" to call a pizza delivery store.

It's now possible to talk for an indefinite period of time for free or next to nothing on the Internet through telephone software.

It's only a matter of time until free videoconferencing also becomes possible over the 'Net. But if the 'Net can handle phone calls for nothing, won't it put telephone companies out of business? The answer is no, since the 'Net runs over the telephone network and just uses excess switching capacity. One day, the telephone companies, if they go into direct competition with the Internet, may try to kill it off or take it over. For the time being, however, the Internet is an arrangement that benefits everyone.

Videophony

Videophony is just an extension of telephony, and it's already widely available. AT&T marketed a videophone that failed only because of its price. Like fax machines, videophones will take off when a critical mass of people can afford them. Corporations already use teleconferencing extensively. Sun Microsystems workstations come standard with videophony. Firms such as C-Phone already offer "TV-quality" video that runs on your PC. Any way you cut it, widespread videophony is just around the corner.

E-Mail and Document Transfer

Numerous corporations already use the Internet to shuttle messages and memos around. Corporations have long been players on Usenet newsgroups, File-Transfer Protocol (FTP), and E-mail and are expanding their use of networks in place of faxes and parcel post. For example, Smith Barney sends out research reports to customers over the 'Net to save on paper and postage, and the SEC began allowing distribution of prospectuses by Internet in 1995.

Video on Demand

True video on demand is the killer application that everyone is waiting for. Yet it represents only an incremental improvement over existing pay per view. Video on demand is part of a process that will obliterate time constraints as information services become available on the user's schedule, not the producer's.

News

AOL and Dow Jones already offer custom electronic newspapers that check wires for stories of interest to a given client and serve them up as a personalized newspaper. Future versions of interactive news will include less text and more video clips, hypertext capability, virtual reality effects, and other features already found on multimedia CD-ROM.

Multicasting

Until quite recently, broadcasting or the distribution of video or moving pictures was a controlled activity. The ability to send video out to others lay in the hands of TV stations and cable companies, all of them highly regulated. But thanks to the World Wide Web, that has changed. The Mbone network, which is superimposed on the Web, now permits multicasting or broadcasting by individuals to others. The Rolling Stones have used it to broadcast a concert, NASA has used it to broadcast images from the Russian space station, and the House of Blues, a Cambridge, Massachusetts, restaurant, has used it to broadcast blues music. Unlike traditional broadcasting, which is top down, allowing a broadcaster to send video to passive consumers, multicasting lets anyone on the network broadcast to everyone else the way people make phone calls. It's therefore different from either broadcasting or teleconferencing, which just lets people videocommunicate one on one.

The Mbone network was developed by scientists at Xerox's Palo Alto Research Center (PARC) facility and other engineers. Its principal drawback is video's huge appetite for bandwidth. Since too much multicasting could eat up the capacity of the Internet, its proliferation remains controlled by a core group of scientists. As the available broadcasting bandwidth increases, multicasting is sure to increase as well.[9]

Interactive Entertainment

Video games will get better and better, adding realistic graphics, virtual reality effects, and greater activity within narratives. It's unlikely that interactive movies, during which the watcher can change the plot, will ever replace conventional start-to-finish stories. What's more likely is that movies will be released in various forms. They will continue to come out as full-length features, but studios will also release interactive CD-ROM versions, whose plots can be changed and during which viewers can interact with actors; they will also use the characters to sell things, to increase revenues, and to leverage copyrights. Games involving many players are a natural for the Internet.

On-line services such as AOL have found that chatting, often between members of the opposite sex, is one of their most profitable offerings. In the future, virtual reality may be used for high-tech chatting.

Shopping

One of the most widespread activities in real life, shopping is sure to be one of the most widespread activities in cyberspace. Home shopping will benefit from the addition of virtual reality. Future home shoppers will be able, using a joystick, trackball, or verbal command, to enter a virtual mall. From there they will be able to enter a store and pause before different products. A voice command might instruct a salesman to lift a pair of shoes into view or provide a list of product characteristics. While existing virtual reality requires goggles, goggle-free technology is under development.

Banking and Financial Services

Home banking is well under way. Future software will let people integrate their banking with their personal finance management. Already it's possible to trade stocks on AOL and the World Wide Web.

Other Services

Many other services await. Videophones will let doctors perform some tests by wire. In certain situations, such as on a battlefield, doctors may eventually even perform operations by wire using virtual reality, through a technology called "telepresence." By manipulating controls in a laboratory, a doctor would be able to manipulate instruments in faraway places, such as battlefields. Already, technology developed by Ameritech lets doctors in urban areas study ultrasound images of babies in rural areas. In fact, some local hospitals fear telemedicine will shift business to famous clinics. Service providers such as plumbers and architects will also be able to look at work in progress and give instructions to those on the spot.

Genies, Wizards, and Agents

Perhaps the biggest development in information services of all will be their increasing automation. Say good-bye to laborious trekking around in search of information or, indeed, many of the labor-intensive parts of using a computer. Web Crawlers are automated. General Magic has designed software agents that can scan the 'Net for information, buy things, pay bills, apply for loans, find business partners, do taxes, screen calls, answer letters, and handle other chores. These software "agents," "genies," or "supersecretaries" will perform many of the tasks users now perform themselves.

Long before physical robots become part of daily life, virtual robots, free of the confinements of gravity, will roam the 'Net on various missions.

These computer-generated entities will be able to answer phones, take messages, place calls, file incoming E-mail, search databases for information, and even shop for the best prices on a list of goods. They may even be able to do higher-level management tasks involving expert decision making, freeing their masters for more rewarding work. Thus, the new electronic services technology will threaten certain classes of jobs. Just as the Industrial Revolution forced the masses to compete with machines, so the Information Revolution will force them to compete with "virtual employees."

Portals to Cyberspace:
Living Room, Office—Or Anywhere

One confusing thing about the future of cyberspace is that since it will be accessible by phone, cable, or wireless, which lines will handle what? Bill Gates's partner in Microsoft, Paul Allen, has underwritten an R&D lab near Seattle to research just this question. Researchers equipped with PDAs, laptops, clickers, and other devices wander around model homes and offices trying to divine where consumers will want to do what. They practice ordering groceries on their Newton MessagePads in imaginary beauty parlors, leafing through electronic catalogs in mock living rooms, and balancing their checkbooks in different settings.

Traditional considerations such as the arrangement of furniture and rooms will play a decisive role in how and where data enter the home.

Services people prefer to do from a couch in the living room will enter the home through a TV set–top box. Services people prefer to do at a desk will enter via the PC interface. Services they prefer to do on the go will run through their souped-up telephone or PDA. For example, recreational services such as watching video on demand and sports will be offered primarily via a set-top box and TV in the living room; better graphics, including 3-D virtual reality effects, will enhance video games and traditional home shopping. Set-top boxes will perform some processing, network host computers in the cable companies' offices—or on the Internet—the remainder. Video on demand, for example, will probably be run by supercomputers or a group of centralized servers. Anything that people would rather do from a couch will probably be carried via coaxial cable to their TVs.

Meanwhile, demanding, more user-active applications, such as word processing, designing a house using virtual reality, planning a trip, or paying bills, will be offered via a desktop computer, whose microprocessor will do much of the work. CD-ROM encyclopedias, CD-ROM games involving lots of processing, and other processing-heavy applications will run on personal computers rather than the living room TV. Midway between the TV and the traditional desktop, stripped down 'Net computers may also offer affordable access to the Internet.

Of course, certain services such as telephony, teleconferencing, and even radio and television reception will be available in both formats. And while consumers will probably do most of their at-home shopping in the living room, rest assured they will still be able to order a book off the Internet, download a movie, or buy groceries via their desktop PC as well. Cable firms, for their part, will offer access to the Internet.

New Players in Cyberspace

Who will deliver all these fantastic new space-age services? Whereas a few years ago the big question was who would win the battle between cable and telephone, it's now clear that the industries are likely to converge. Cable firms will start offering telephone service, while telephone companies will offer television service. The big firms would just as soon eliminate the competition implicit in having two wires into the home, and they have found sympathetic lawmakers to press their cause. They may also get help from consumers, who will tend to order everything from a single company rather than run accounts with both a telephone and cable firm. While it's hard to predict the degree of concentration lawmakers will ultimately permit, it's probable that everyone will offer everything. Both telephone and cable firms are expanding overseas.[10] And driven by the quest for monopolies on that single wire that will enter most homes, creators of content, such as movie studios and publishing firms, are merging with owners of wires and pieces of the electromagnetic spectrum to form integrated information superhighway conglomerates.

The furthest along the road in the marriage of delivery and content are cable firms. They were not barred from delivering services, as telephone companies were. And they were built on the model of broadcast television, which is vertically integrated. Meanwhile, phone companies are eyeing the glamorous world of entertainment. Starstruck executives of regulated utilities see an opportunity to join the high-stakes worlds of publishing, movies, and retail. It remains to be seen whether stodgy telephone firms can make the transition to entertainment juggernauts. But their vast telephone franchises ensure that they will be players.

Killer Copyrights

At the level of content for the information highway, the name of the game today is intellectual property, the ability to build blockbuster copyrights.

The idea is to take a book, movie, or character and to devise innovative merchandising and distribution deals that turn the property into a piece of the culture. Explains Scott Sassa, the thirty-five-year-old head of the Turner Entertainment Group, "It's all about creating ways to make a good copyright and then leverage the hell out of it."[11] The democratization of media and information has splintered the old-fashioned entertainment channels. As a result, Sassa says, "there are going to be lots of smaller movies and projects and then there'll be one or two giant hits that become part of pop culture." Sassa explains that "the 'middle class' of movie" is extinct. "So, first, any company has got to have the capital to build those big *Jurassic Park* copyrights. And second, it's got to have the wherewithal to get all the value out of them because the entry cost is so incredibly high."

This highlights the fact that the big players—Bell Atlantic, TCI, Time Warner, Walt Disney, Viacom, and others—are obsessed with getting big hits and providing comprehensive service. Combinations of phone companies such as BellSouth and AT&T, cable companies such as TCI, and media firms such as Viacom will furnish blockbuster movies on demand, TV, and other heavy-duty services and mainline them into the home. The big bucks will surround properties that can be fed into the popular-culture-creating machine. No wonder Disney is spending so much on a New York presence by buying Rockefeller Center, with its Radio City Music Hall, and constructing a new Disney building. Ditto Time Warner, which is expanding its already large New York presence and is opening retail stores. How better to build up and capitalize on those killer copyrights?

However, the giants can't create all the programming or services themselves. In electronic malls of the future, while movies on demand, NFL football, the Yellow Pages, and other blockbuster properties will serve as anchors, as Sears does at the conventional mall, there will be plenty of room for specialty services and stores, the equivalent of Radio Shack, Victoria's Secret, the Food Court, and other tenants. So while Turner may build and distribute blockbuster copyrights, the explosion of distribution channels will also create opportunities for the "little guy."

Video on Demand will anchor cyber-malls offering pizza delivery.

More channels and greater transmission capacity into the home mean that it will become easier than ever for creative people to distribute their work, for individuals to offer services, and for small

shops to sell their goods. Some of tomorrow's blockbuster properties will cut their teeth on the World Wide Web or elsewhere on the
Internet. And it is here that entrepreneurs can enter the game.

Cyberspace is so open at the moment that even relative un-
knowns have a shot at even bigger prey. Numerous entrepreneurs
are fighting to get a piece of video on demand, for example. Forty-
three-year-old Gordon F. Lee, an oil-and-gas speculator, has bought
into a company, USA Video, to provide video on demand; the firm
raised $1 million from Rochester Telephone and has secured rights
to films from Paramount Communications. Whether Lee will succeed or flop is anyone's guess, but for now he's being taken seri-
ously by the big guys. Likewise, Ken Williams of Sierra On-Line
struck a deal with AT&T to provide video games on line and later
sold the business to AT&T. The big players are shelling out big
bucks to unknown entrepreneurs to solve their problems.

How the "Little Guy" Can Win

In fact, the evidence so far suggests that networks that leverage off
the capabilities of suppliers will outperform those that try to do
everything themselves. The more the conglomerates try to control
all the services they provide, the worse they may do. So far, service
providers that leverage off the capabilities of vendors—magazines,
movies, and shopping services—are succeeding where the big conglomerates are failing.

AOL and CompuServe, for example, have been growing explosively, whereas Prodigy has floundered and is losing money.
Why? Because both AOL and CompuServe believe in serving as
doorways to vendors that provide the content. AOL lets you log on
and flip to *The New York Times, Business Week, Car and Driver,* and
other newspapers and magazines that provide their own content. In
contrast, Prodigy was initially organized as an old-fashioned TV
network. A team of journalists and editors edited the news, and
advertisements were cycled across the screen at intervals. But in
light of its problems, Prodigy switched gears and decided to copy

AOL. It's another case of command and control no longer working as well as a strategy of relying on the skills of suppliers. No dummy, Microsoft decided that with its new MSN network, "We want information providers to set their own price, manage their own business and get the lion's share of the revenue," according to Russ Siegelman, the former general manager of on-line services.[12]

Understanding the Early Failures of Interactive Cable

This principle helps explain the sorry track record of interactive cable ventures to date. Cable TV runs over coaxial cable, which can carry a great deal more information than copper wire. With its pipeline straight into your living room, cable should be winning the cyberspace race. Instead, interactive cable experiments have failed—expensively so (with the exception of a few educational applications and a sports venture in Canada). While they have solved some of the early technical problems, such as a lack of switching in older cable networks built on the top-down broadcast model, other problems remain. For example, in a test Time Warner ran in Orlando, engineers incurred major problems with the computer processing part of the job. Cable's centralized computing model means that one control room had responsibility for processing data for thousands of customers at once. Unaccustomed to a challenge of this magnitude, the cable firm had to hire engineers with NASA and military backgrounds.

The failure of interactive cable also reflects a shortage of content for interactive viewing and the difficulty of enticing TV viewers to interact in the first place. Because each cable experiment has been a one-off, cable operators can't piggyback off the work of suppliers or build on a standard such as the World Wide Web. Perhaps more ominously, it turns out that people sitting on a couch do not necessarily *want* to interact with their TV, which gives rise to a basic principle that will distinguish the living-room interface from the desktop interface.

The desktop, or Internet, is user-active, the living room, or cable, is user-passive.

Silicon Graphics has held three years of trials to compare viewers' response to desktop computers to their response to television. Explains CEO Ed McCracken, "We found that if a TV image stays the same for more than two seconds, people change channels." (It is probably for this reason that home shopping programs that focus a camera on something for sale have someone's hand or finger in the picture moving the item.) TV viewers expect the program to act on them. In contrast, computer users have no problem with a static screen, since they expect to act on it. In fact, says McCracken, computer users and TV watchers have remarkably different characteristics.

Interactive cable will not take off until two things happen:

- The market grows, costs fall, and standards evolve sufficiently for third-party suppliers to create a body of interactive programming and perhaps offer them on decentralized servers.

- Cable operators recognize that people sitting on their couches are in a passive state of mind.

QVC's Home Shopping Network was one of the big success stories of the 1990s. Leased infotainment such as Susan Powter's diet shows came into their own in the 1980s. Religious shows that include appeals for money proved successful. Interactive home shopping flopped. Why? First, the traditional programs treated "couch potatoes" as the passive creatures they are. Selling over a conventional TV show or even out of a paper catalog using a toll-free number is a two-step process. First, the program or catalog inspires you to call. Then an operator closes the sale. Time pressure is a helpful factor in the case of TV that forces you to call immediately.

In contrast, interactive shopping leaves you with too many outs. Absent a pitchperson urging you to buy or someone at the other end of the line ready to close the sale, there's no pressure to force you to click. Low sales volumes have also precluded bargain pricing.

Drama, time pressure, and discounts will be the keys to interactive selling.

Once these problems are solved, interactive shopping will have the advantage of multiplexing shopping options. Moreover, almost everyone in the United States has a TV in the home, while computer penetration is only about 40 percent. Television experts point out that toll-free numbers took time to catch on as well.

Current problems with cable ventures are shifting action to the World Wide Web. When a Time Warner–Spiegel cable venture, Catalog 1, an upscale cable TV mall, failed to deliver as planned, managers decided to begin selling the wares of its ten upmarket catalog sellers through a site on the World Wide Web.[13] The Web format permits complex, interactive shopping for a fraction of the cost of a complicated, dedicated at-home shopping service on cable. The computing challenges are vastly simplified, since the Web is a decentralized system in which processing is divided over thousands of servers. Computer firms hope inexpensive Net computers will bring the 'Net to the remaining 60 percent of Americans.

The New Freedom of Information

One final consequence of the network revolution: as a result of "Moore's law" (named for Gordon Moore, one of the founders of Intel), that processing power doubles every eighteen months, and cheaper information technology, information has grown vastly more democratic—with both good and bad consequences.

Two decades ago, to compute, you needed capital, a bunch of white-coated technicians, and a clean, air-conditioned room.

At best, an individual could gain access to the temple of computing through time sharing. Appropriately enough, a leading computer company in the 1970s was named Control Data. In the arena of television, the three networks enjoyed an FCC-licensed monopoly on the national distribution of information. Even long-distance telephone calls were restricted by virtue of their cost until 1984. Moguls and top government officials could talk freely on phones labeled "New York," "Los Angeles," and "Chicago"; the rest of us waited until rates went down after five, or better yet, eleven P.M.

A parade of new information technologies has chipped away at control of information. In the 1960s, the solid-state amplifier made possible rock concerts where thousands of participants could hear alternative points of view. The spread of cold type in the 1970s led to niche magazines that put mass-circulation ones such as *Life* and *Collier's* out of business. In the early 1980s, new direct-mail technology made it easier to tailor products and messages to narrow groups, and fax, low-cost photocopying, and E-mail technologies have created more ways for people to sidestep the centralized media. The "ten-thousand-dimensional web in heaven and net on earth," or World Wide Web, lets Chinese activists talk with one another and Americans pursue specialized interests.

While democratic, "narrowcasting" represents the multiplexing of America's view of the truth.

Wider access to information once restricted to those at the top has led to a decline in respect for America's experts and elites. Polls show respect for the press down from 51 percent in 1979 to 29 percent today, confidence in banks and schools down 25 percentage points over the last twenty years, and confidence in the Supreme Court and churches down 10 points.[14] In effect, information technology has drawn back the curtain on many economic, political, and cultural establishments, and Americans are not impressed. This phenomenon is contributing to uncertainty about the future but has a positive consequence that is often missed. For in withdrawing their respect for elites, Americans are increasing their self-reliance; in withdrawing a measure of their trust from so-called experts, they are increasing their trust in themselves. And armed with new technologies and knowledge, they are right to trust their own instincts and capability.

In coming years, no citizenry will have better access to information than the people of the United States. Politically, it can be fractious, just as democracy is often fractious; but economically, access to information will empower individuals to do themselves what once only a priesthood of rarefied experts could do. We are still exploring cyberspace; the information superhighway is far from complete. But in both the economic and cultural dimensions of this venture, singular in the history of the world, the United States has a commanding lead.

Chapter 7

Where the
Renaissance
Will Occur

Six years ago, at the beginning of the last decade of the second millennium, the town of Telluride, Colorado, on the western edge of the Rockies, was little changed from the way the last Ice Age had left it. Sometime around the year 70,000 B.C., retreating glaciers carved out a valley in the midst of mountains. Around 1000 B.C., Indians entered the region, but the mountainous terrain kept their numbers low. In the 1870s, gold was struck and a gold rush began. In 1887, the town adopted the name Telluride, after another mineral found in the mountains. But while thousands of miners made the difficult trek into the valley to work in its mines, most left when the mines closed, leaving a wooden ghost town and holes in the mountain as the main evidence of their presence. In the 1960s, a number of hippies settled in the town. By the 1980s, a ski resort and tiny airport had been built. Seasonal visitors were attracted to the spot. But apart from that, Telluride remained a small town and a few outlying houses in the midst of wilderness.

Beginning in about 1990, however, drawn by skiing and the

beauty of the valley, people began to arrive. The first arrivals were often Coloradans, but soon Californians began to buy houses, some of them movie people. Attracted by the Hollywood buzz, lawyers, doctors, and others followed. Restaurants, cappuccino bars, and boutiques opened their doors. A summer film festival was launched. But while the town had become glamorous, it still lacked industry. The only people to live there were old-timers, the relatively wealthy, and those catering to tourists.

Then everything changed. The sheer beauty of the region, its favorable climate, and the low cost of living, combined with its new and glamorous associations, began to attract a new group of people that the locals called "modem cowboys." Many drew their income from California but through telecommunications were able not just to vacation but to work in Telluride. When the town expanded its Internet hub, it reached takeoff velocity.

Older arrivals, those who have been in the town five years now, say that Telluride has been ruined. One thing is clear: the population has jumped dramatically, incomes have risen, and the cost of an acre near town has exploded.

Telluride's San Miguel County is an example of what have been called "amenity counties." Distinguished by physical beauty, lack of crowding, activities such as skiing, sailing, or other recreational attractions, and a desirable climate, they are growing up all around the country. While older parts of the country struggle with problems from crime to pollution to homelessness, towns such as Telluride, Old Fork on Flathead Lake in Montana, and Jackson Hole, Wyoming, are booming. Resort towns are becoming year-round economies.

These remote amenity counties are not the only areas in the country on the move. Exurban areas located outside older suburbs but within an hour or two of cities such as Douglas County, Colorado, south of Denver, and Summit County, Utah, east of Salt Lake City, are growing by leaps and bounds while older cities and suburbs retrench. University towns are also emerging as technology centers and the nodes of future growth.

The coming American renaissance will occur throughout the

country, but in these places more than others. Knowing which areas will do what, where jobs will appear, and where they will vanish, as well as the living costs and characteristics of different regions, will provide important advantages in years to come.

Playing the Population Trends

The single best indicator of what will happen culturally and economically in America over the next quarter century is population growth. In general, economic indicators are unreliable. Interest rates rise and fall almost hourly. Exchange-rate moves confound the instincts of even seasoned traders. GDP growth is not only hard to predict but hard to measure. In contrast, identifying which areas of the country are growing or shrinking is easy.

Unlike monetary indicators, which jump up and down, population trends are relatively stable, reflecting the difficulty of moving a family compared with money over a network.

Population trends are also robust, meaning that they hold up over time and withstand short-term changes.[1] As a result, they are excellent markers for changes in the economy and culture. When combined with historic data on factors such as income changes, education levels, housing preferences, age, and ethnicity, they reveal a great deal about what will happen and where. Quite simply, population growth translates into more demand for services, products, and homes. The process of development itself creates huge numbers of jobs and economic activity to the point where growth can appear to feed on itself with no underlying cause or reason.

New areas of the country are usually easier places to do business in than old ones, giving them an advantage in competing for capital.

In general, new regions of the country feature new houses and office buildings built to a higher standard than those of older areas. Newer regions have more fiber-optic telephone lines, buried power lines rather than wires strung on poles, and cheaper systems of distribution, such as warehouse stores instead of crowded malls or small stores. New people mean new sources of tax revenues, which can be used to build better roads, airports, schools, and public projects, which in turn tend to attract new businesses.

The bottom line is that Americans have always moved to where opportunities are. But few people approach the matter scientifically. They go where their jobs take them or just stay put. By being open to new opportunities and new locations, and staying slightly ahead of the curve, individuals and companies gain an advantage.

Of course, to make a reasoned judgment, one needs solid data.[2] Businesses and shopping center developers, which must think ahead in five- to ten-year cycles, use such data profitably all the time. So do companies selling new soft drinks or potato chips and their advertising firms. The government collects and projects tremendous amounts of data, but they are hard to locate and use. And while a number of companies compile demographic data in specialized formats, they are extremely expensive and not readily available to the layman.

A Fairfax, Virginia, company, Urban Decision Systems is one of a number of highly specialized firms that provide demographic data to real estate firms, *Fortune* 500 companies, and others. It compiles census data, matching categories across different years, does annual projections, and makes the data available in a standard format. It also projects growth to the year 2005. Using this database on population, income, education, home ownership, and other variables for America's 3,500 counties and certain metropolitan areas and zip codes, I have performed extensive analyses of growth patterns throughout the country. The results are extremely revealing.

America's Fastest-growing Counties

The following is a list of the ten fastest-growing counties from 1990 to the year 2000:

COUNTY	GROWTH (%)
Douglas County, Colo.	107.0
Summit County, Utah	92.9
Camden County, Ga.	87.8
Washington County, Utah	86.7
Elbert County, Colo.	80.7
Flagler County, Fla.	79.1
Henry County, Ga.	78.3
Paulding County, Ga.	77.7
Park County, Colo.	72.9
San Miguel County, Colo.	71.9

Source: Urban Decision Systems

What do these counties have in common? They are all in the South and West, for one. Four lie in Colorado, three in Georgia, two in Utah, and one in Florida. And while none contains a major city, all lie within an hour or two of a city. They also contain amenities, and most contain a large number of college-educated people. It is further worth noting that the counties on this list have been growing for some time. That's one thing about population trends: they don't change overnight.

The long-term pattern of population and income growth in the United States is a robust one that is continuing through temporary changes.

Let's look at each of the ten counties in turn.

COLORADO DREAMS

Douglas County, Colorado, America's fastest-growing county, is located south of Denver on the way to Colorado Springs. Besides being the country's fastest-growing county, it is number twelve (out of 3,500) in per capita income, which is no small achievement. And it has been growing larger and richer for some time. In the 1970s, its population tripled, and in the 1980s it grew by a factor of 2.4.

It's easy to see why Douglas County is booming. It's near Denver, a relatively new city, which itself is continuing to grow. As Denver grows, however, it has begun to experience crowding and the social and quality-of-life problems typical of large cities. And, as in many metropolitan areas, the most dynamic region today lies outside the city.

Denver's economy boomed on oil and shale in the 1970s and early 1980s before hitting a rough patch. During the boom years, energy firms grew up in Arapahoe County's Tech Center, a business district between the city and Douglas County. In the late 1980s, as the Denver region emerged from its doldrums, energy firms gave way to companies in high-tech fields. Today the Tech Center has spread into Douglas and employs almost as many people as downtown Denver, many of whom are settling in Douglas. Mission Viejo, a developer of megasuburbs, has built 22,000 homes in the county, primarily in a sprawling area called Highlands Ranch.

On either side of Douglas lie Elbert and Park Counties. Roughly aligned in a row, the three counties form a 150-by-50-mile band of exurbs that is the country's fastest-growing region of its size. While Park and Elbert Counties are almost as large as Douglas in area, they are a fraction of its size in population. Park has about one tenth the number of people Douglas has, but is growing almost as fast. Park contains much national parkland and, though not known for skiing, mountain peaks of 12,000 feet and higher. Both Park and Elbert lie a good distance away from Denver but are capturing people who prefer a more exurban as opposed to a suburban environment.

San Miguel County, the fourth Colorado county on the list, sits in the southwestern part of the state on the Utah border and contains the town of Telluride. Like Park and Elbert Counties, it is small, with fewer than 4,000 people. Unlike them, it is nowhere near a large metropolitan area. Its economy consists of tourism and modem cowboys.

Accordingly, San Miguel is an amenity county rather than an

exurb, connected to the rest of the world not by commuter buses but by wire and wireless. It remains mountain country but has been discovered by people who have left Aspen or California to seek a more relaxed pace of life. Its large number of educated people reflects Telluride's appeal to the most mobile people in our society, those who are able to telecommute.

In fact, all four of these Colorado counties have a highly educated population. Despite San Miguel's remote location and small population, it has one of the highest percentages of college-educated people of any county in America: 28.1 percent. In Douglas County, 25.8 percent of the population hold either bachelor's or advanced degrees, and Park and Elbert Counties are well above the national average with higher education rates of 15.4 percent and 12.8 percent, respectively.

GEORGIA ON MY MIND

On the opposite side of the country, a look at the growth in Georgia reveals a surprisingly similar story. Henry and Paulding Counties lie outside Atlanta, just as Douglas, Park, and Elbert Counties lie outside Denver. Neither is contiguous with Atlanta, but both are fast-growing exurbs.

Like Denver, Atlanta was one of the growth capitals of the 1980s. And like Denver, it flourished thanks to services as opposed to industry. But beginning in the mid-1980s, boomers with children faced the same pressures to leave the city for the suburbs as their counterparts in Denver, namely, a desire for more space, lower taxes, less crime, and better schools at an affordable price. At first, they moved to De Kalb, Cobb, and other traditional suburbs, or to Buckhead and the new edge cities north of Atlanta. Increasingly, however, both white and black families are settling beyond Cobb and De Kalb in farmland to the south and west of the city, sometimes on what used to be the "wrong side of the tracks." The educational levels in Henry and Paulding Counties are lower than those in and around Denver, but this reflects the educational levels in their respective states. The pattern is clear. Throughout the country, the fastest-growing places are exurban regions outside growing cities.

The other Georgian county in the top ten is Camden at the southeastern corner of the state about 40 miles from Jacksonville, Florida. Camden's growth is largely attributable to the presence of the King's Bay naval submarine base.

FLORIDA REAL ESTATE

The only Florida county in the top ten, Flagler, is also located about an hour from Jacksonville, this time about 60 miles south along the Atlantic coast, north of Daytona Beach. Significantly, it lies not immediately adjacent to Jacksonville but an hour or so away; and while it benefits from its proximity to Jacksonville and Daytona, Flagler has its own exurban economy. With a population averaging 47.1 years of age, it is a favored retirement community. It also has a high average per capita income of more than $40,000. Growth has been bolstered by an ITT development known as the Palm Coast Area.

THE MORMON STATE

Utah also boasts two of the country's top ten fastest-growing counties: Summit and Washington. These are amenity counties, as opposed to exurban counties; their link with established centers of commerce is electronic, not by road. Both of these counties lie long distances away from the Ogden–Salt Lake City–Orem corridor along Route 15 that has historically been the focus of Utah's growth (and that continues to grow at a respectable rate). Like other exurban counties, they are neither rural nor urban and do not depend on a downtown area for jobs.

The Exurban Boom

The biggest demographic trend of all over the next quarter century will be the move of people ever further into the regions beyond suburbs.

In the 1980s, no fewer than seven satellite cities grew up in northern Virginia, outside Washington, D.C. Throughout the country, people are moving out of aging cities. There are two distinct routes of escape. Some people will move to true amenity counties, such as San Miguel County, Colorado, and Summit County, Utah, which are separated from developed areas by tracts of wilderness. They will either have to work in the comparatively small local economies or connect by wire to economies elsewhere. At the moment, this group tends to be wealthy, interested in real estate or tourism (the two standby businesses in amenity counties), or creative. For example, Telluride can count movie people, writers, scientists, artists, and management consultants among its residents. As working over wires becomes more common, however, more and more people will be able to move to amenity counties. Some who intend to work by wire, however, may end up working in the local economy by opening a shop serving local clients, working as a waiter or doing construction, or hiring on with a high-tech business as amenity counties grow more populated.

A larger group of people will move out of aging cities and their immediate suburbs to contiguous exurban areas that offer more land and space for less money. Some of these people are moving into town houses and high-rises on the immediate edge of cities and suburbs. Others are moving further out, into more rural stretches of exurbia. In most cases, once out of the city, they are leaving it for good and working either in the suburbs or at home.

Letting Electrons Commute

At the heart of this new way of living is electronic commuting. Currently, modems and faxes, operating over phone lines, make it possible for certain people to work away from the office. Those who do a lot of writing and talking on the phone can do much of their work at home. (By using voice mail and call forwarding, a person can already disguise his or her true location.) However, telecommuting is still imperfect. The low bandwidth of conventional phone lines has been a bottleneck to videoconferencing, the transmission of video images, and other technologies that will truly annihilate distance. As a result, most of the people who now telecommute have been creative types or the member of a family who takes care of the children. Telecommuting, while growing rapidly, has not yet become a dominant way of working.

But that will change. The problem of bandwidth choke points will be eliminated within the next ten years. Soon videophones and videoconferencing, as well as networked virtual reality, will enable people to do more and more work at home, and a huge number of people will begin to telecommute.

Telecommuting will encourage people to leave the cities.

The decrease in commuting time alone is a powerful incentive. There is even an environmental rationale. In California, the state is actually encouraging telecommuting to help reduce pollution from cars.

However, don't be fooled into thinking that electronic networking will eliminate the automobile. The main beneficiaries of networking will be the exurbs and other areas in which an automobile is essential. Because almost everyone will need a car, development will be marked to the scale of the automobile. Highways, byways, and driveways will be just as important to exurbanization in years ahead as they were to suburbanization.

The number of autos on the road from 1950 up to the present has grown steadily. Since the nation's population will increase by a quarter over the next twenty-five years, traffic will get worse, not better. Some argue that environmental problems will limit the use of cars. If we don't run out of gas, this argument runs, the smog is sure to kill us. But it is not widely recognized that auto companies have made huge strides in the reduction of emissions in response to government regulations. Emissions today are just one-tenth of what they were in 1968.[3] State regulations such as California's as well as federal corporate average fuel economy (CAFE) standards will further slash emissions. Total smog will go down despite the increase in the number of cars.

But will we run out of oil? During the oil crisis of the 1970s, people made much of the idea that we would. As the liquefied remains of plants and dinosaurs, oil appeared to be a finite resource that we would soon exhaust. In the 1980s, scientist Thomas Gold argued an alternative view that oil is a natural substance in the earth rather than the remains of earlier life. While his theory is highly speculative, it is clear that proven oil reserves have gradually increased as new fields are found. And there is evidence that old oil fields, if left vacant, replenish themselves from below, through the same process that brought oil into underground chambers in the first place from deeper down in the crust.

The earth has large untapped reserves of oil. We won't run out for the foreseeable future, and if oil grows too expensive to retrieve, alternative fuels such as natural gas, electricity, or fuel cells may replace it. But nothing will replace the car for the foreseeable future.

Exurbs as Opposed to Suburbs

Note that the growth of exurbs will be a totally different thing from that of suburbs. In the old model of suburbanization, residents commuted downtown to work. In the new model of exurbanization, a handful will still commute, far more will work nearby in the exurbs themselves, while an increasing number will work at home by wire. Often one spouse will work outside the home, while the other will take care of the children and telecommute.

Exurbanization, although it is only now beginning to accelerate, has actually been a robust trend for many years. Around older cities such as New York, the development of exurbs began in the 1970s. America's fastest-growing county in the 1970s was Ulster County, New York. Not far behind was Litchfield County, Connecticut. But while exurban counties around the country are beginning to explode, suburban counties have stayed the same or actually shrunk.

In the New York area, mature suburbs such as Westchester County, New York; Bergen County, New Jersey; and Fairfield County, Connecticut, are shrinking or growing only slowly. In contrast, Putnam County, a rural area north of Westchester, is growing by 14.2 percent. Putnam County is also the ninth wealthiest county in the country.

In the Boston area, where inner counties such as Suffolk and Middlesex are losing population (by −13.3 percent and −1.6 percent, respectively, between 1990 and 2000), exurban amenity counties such as Nantucket Island and Barnstable on Cape Cod are growing rapidly (by 30 percent and 10.1 percent). Exurban Worcester County, an old industrial area reanimated by high-tech businesses, will grow 27.5 percent over the decade. In the Chicago area, it is the same story. While Cook County will stay even in population, exurban McHenry County will grow 43.5 percent and Lake County to the north will grow 19.9 percent. In Pennsylvania, however, the state's fastest-growing counties lie far from its larger cities. They are amenity counties: Pike, Monroe, and Wayne Counties along the Delaware River, far from Pittsburgh or Philadelphia.

The main reason that conventional suburbs have ceased to grow are their high costs and stringent zoning laws. Large minimum lot sizes, high prices, and bans on office buildings, wider roads, and sprawl are limiting their growth, a good thing for those who live there but one that is pushing growth further outward. In contrast, exurbs are open canvases on which developers can often paint as they please. This gives rise to the paradox of town houses, office parks, and sprawl in satellite cities lying outside older, leafy suburbs.

Exurban counties retain ties to cities since they grow by recruiting city dwellers who retain connections with the city. However, unlike traditional suburban bedroom communities, exurban counties have important economic identities of their own. The principal difference between both exurban and amenity counties and traditional suburbs is precisely this fact: exurban and amenity counties do not depend on a city for their livelihood; suburbs do.

The words themselves describe the difference: the Latin prefix *sub* means "under"; the prefix *ex* means "out of." Exurbs and amenity counties, in turn, differ from the rural and resource economies they replace by their dependence on local trade, services, and construction and, increasingly, on residents' telecommuting over wires.

Edge Cities

In places such as Schaumburg, Illinois; Fairfax, Virginia; and Alewife, Massachusetts, some suburbs have become "downtowns" in their own right to which exurbanites commute. This particular brand of suburb, known as an "edge city," often boasts more office space than the downtown area of a midsized city. Joel Garreau, author of the book *Edge City: Life on the New Frontier,* defines an edge city as having 5 million square feet of office space or more.

Today, developers are building more office space in suburbs than in cities.

Edge cities are essentially suburbs that have gone commercial, and they are typically located in a county that is adjacent to a city. In addition to normal suburban housing and a handful of malls, they have a significant core of office space and may also boast hospitals and other citylike institutions. Suburbs at this stage have already reached their peak. They're not where the action will be in the future. They are where the action was a few years ago, however, and are a new model of growth.

In coming years, the action will move further out as exurbs develop beyond suburban office towers and, in some cases, give birth to a new generation of satellite cities. Already, in some parts of the country, there are no rural areas left at all. Coastal Florida, for example, is one huge stretch of sprawl. California also has large stretches of sprawl that surround various satellite cities or nodes of economic activity.

The Air Plant Model of Growth

Sprawl is a peculiarly American phenomenon that has left its mark all over the country. I call it the "air-plant" model of growth because it appears to feed on itself with no apparent source of water or nutrition. To many it's simply ugly. It's easy to write off suburban or even exurban development as something unpleasant and peripheral to the main attraction, the cities. Some hope that sprawl will simply go away. But increasingly, such development is the main event. It's where the jobs are. It's the future of America. And it doesn't have to be ugly.

Sprawl does, in fact, have economic underpinnings that underscore America's shift to a service economy. Virtually nothing is grown or manufactured in a patch of sprawl as in agricultural and industrial economies. In a typical patch, almost everything is trucked in and nothing visible except for garbage is trucked out. Residents work building houses, lending money, running stores, selling gas, or delivering pizza to their neighbors. At first glance, it can be hard to understand how such an enterprise stays aloft. There is, however, an answer.

Food and gas in the United States are relatively cheap. So are goods imported from Third World countries, thanks to minimal barriers of trade and America's superior system of distribution. As a result, an extremely high percentage of what economists call "value added" occurs locally within the service economy of a patch of sprawl. Wal-Mart may charge $3.87 for a basketball but pay only a fraction of that to the company that made it in China. Because of the comparatively low price of things coming into the sprawl, i.e., pizza dough and the goods at Wal-Mart, the local economy has to "export" only a small number of higher-value-added goods or services to pay for what it imports. It needs only a thin stream of income from the outside to pay its bills. This is how the air-plant model of development works.

The stream of income can come from proximity to an older

economy, such as a city from which people draw salaries, from local manufacturing, from large companies that pay employees' and executives' salaries, from the federal larder (through a military base or, in retirement communities, Social Security checks) or from credit from banks, at least for a while. Without this continuing stream of income, overbuilding can lead to a bust. One should never underestimate the ability of development to continue well past what seems sustainable, but eventually the air plant must grow roots.

A good example of air plant growth is northern Virginia, outside Washington, D.C. During the 1980s, developers converted mile after mile of farmland in Fairfax County, Virginia, into tract houses, town-house developments, and malls. As the cycle progressed, they squeezed office and apartment towers in between the malls. Eventually they threw up entire satellite cities. How did they do it?

At first, the developers targeted refugees from Washington and built housing and malls following a traditional suburban model. Development led industry by a significant margin. Developers dominated local business organizations and local chambers of commerce. Most of the people moving into the houses worked in Washington or immediately outside it in places such as Crystal City. The rest provided basic services to residents at stores, restaurants, and gas stations.

Gradually, however, lured by the potential workforce and spurred, no doubt, by the proximity of the Pentagon (the world's largest office building) and the 1980s military buildup, genuine local industry arose. Today, a raft of businesses, many but not all supplying the Pentagon, have sprung up in the region. Many specialize in software and networks, and high-tech entrepreneurs have eclipsed the developers in local business organizations while Virginia businesses have replaced Washington businesses as the main employers. The air plant has taken root.

The Effect of the Information Highway on Air-Plant Growth

Enter the information highway. Increasingly, it's possible for people to live in one place but draw income from somewhere else. This new source of sustenance for air-plant economies will let them pop up even further outside of cities. Galena, Illinois, a resort town known for its Victorian architecture located 150 miles northwest of Chicago, is growing quickly as visitors who might have wanted to live there in the past now discover they can, explains Mayor Gary Bartell.

Old patches of sprawl, however, are themselves undergoing change. An important trend in coming years will be the conversion of unplanned sprawl into more traditional communities as the air plants put down roots. In Cape Cod, Massachusetts, for example, the New Seabury shopping center has been redeveloped in the shape of a New England town. Developer Douglas Storrs laid new streets in the parking lot, moved parking to the street, so that customers now pass shops on the way to their cars, and built "downtown" buildings within the mall, including a church, a library, a home for senior citizens, and office space. And in Landover, Maryland, architect James Wagman is turning an aging mall into a city center. The mall's interior corridors have become the beginnings of streets that now extend outward in a grid, and a city hall in the middle of the mall will become the nucleus of a new town center.

The Big Picture: Moving West

While exurbanization and telecommuting from amenity regions will occur everywhere in America, one huge trend will dominate population growth: the continuing migration of people west.

The following are the twelve fastest-growing and fastest-shrinking (as a percentage of the country) states from 1990 to the year 2000, based on their projected ten-year percentage change in population:

FASTEST-GROWING STATES	GROWTH (%)
Nevada	40.4
Idaho	27.8
Alaska	26.8
Washington	24.4
Utah	24.4
Colorado	22.9
Arizona	20.8
New Mexico	20.0
Oregon	19.5
Hawaii	19.4
Florida	18.1
Texas	17.7

SHRINKING OR SLOWEST-GROWING STATES	GROWTH (%)
District of Columbia	−11.7
Massachusetts	− 1.4
Rhode Island	− 0.8
Connecticut	− 0.7
North Dakota	0.4
Maine	0.7
New York	1.1
West Virginia	2.3
Pennsylvania	3.2
Michigan	4.7
New Hampshire	4.8
Vermont	4.9

Source: Urban Decision Systems

As a yardstick for comparison, keep in mind that the average growth for states as a whole is 8.7 percent. The twelve fastest-growing states far exceed this, and the twelve shrinking or slowest-growing states fail to match it. The list reveals unmistakably that the West is growing while the Northeast is shrinking as a percentage of the country. Literally every single New England state is on the list of population laggards. Also lagging the national average are nearby New York and Pennsylvania. (New Jersey is thirteenth on the list of laggards.) The only western state on the laggard list is North Dakota.

Now look at the list of fastest-growing states. With the exception of Florida, every one lies in the West. Nevada takes the crown. Las Vegas, within Clark County, is the fastest-growing city in the country. Granted, a large state such as New York can grow at a meager rate and still add 88,000 people per year as it did between 1992 and 1993, a larger numerical gain than Montana's increase of 17,000 people. The point is that New York's population is shrinking as a percentage of the country's population, while Montana's is rising. In 1994, Texas passed New York in population to become the country's second largest state, behind California. And in the year 2020, Florida will pass New York to leave the Empire State, once the nation's largest state, in fourth place.[4]

What's notable about the westward sweep of the American population, as much as anything else, is its longevity. The American West has been growing for two hundred years. Indeed, the list of fastest-growing states today is virtually identical to that two decades ago during the 1970s. The only states not on the list two decades ago were Hawaii and Oregon, which were thirteenth and fourteenth then and have nudged up to tenth and ninth today.

Other measures bear out the country's relentless westward shift. Three western states—Arizona, Nevada, and Idaho—lead the country in the formation of new businesses. In 1993, Arizona witnessed a 22.1 percent gain in new businesses, Nevada a 20.8 percent gain, and Idaho a 18.1 percent gain, according to Dun & Bradstreet, seizing win, place, and show among the fifty states.[5]

As another indication of this trend, California had 45 electoral

votes in 1970, compared with 41 in New York. Both states had
similar populations: California, 20 million and New York, 18 million. Today California has 32 million people and New York has 18
million people. It now has fifty-four electoral votes and fifty-two
representatives, compared to thirty-three and thirty-one in New
York.

While California's growth has begun to slow, its huge size means
that even moderate growth of 1 percent a year will add 300,000
Californians annually in coming years, increasing its lead over all
other states. Moreover, California's growth is expected to speed up
again in the year 2000 after a cooling-off period following the end
of the Cold War. What's particularly interesting today is that the
migration west has bounced off the Pacific Ocean and people are
now settling in Colorado, Nevada, Utah, and inland states. But
easterners and foreigners will continue to go to California, which
demographers predict will capture 39 percent of immigrants over
the next quarter century, barring immigration reform.[6]

To understand the future, one must understand the growth of
the West. The country is changing from a young, east-leaning country to an older, west-leaning country. This has implications in everything from the country's view of the old eastern elite to the
distribution of political and economic power.

Going South

While less pronounced than the migration west, Americans are still
moving south. While western states have locked up the top ten
places, the eleventh through twenty-first fastest-growing states are
Florida, Texas, Georgia, California, Montana, Wyoming, North
Carolina, Delaware, Virginia, Tennessee, and South Carolina. The
move south is important, too, because of the spectacular changes
that are occurring in Dixie.

The South is older than the West. In fact, some states, such as
Virginia and Georgia, are older than some northern states. After
the Civil War, the South settled into a pattern of living based on
agriculture and scattered manufacturing that persisted, little

changed, for more than a century. But it is now undergoing an economic revival that will continue for many years and will dramatically alter its institutions and culture.

Credit must be given to the invention that enabled the South to rise again: central air-conditioning.

Before air-conditioning, many areas of the South were simply too hot to be productive. The area's economy languished, with many regions relying on federal money from military bases, agricultural programs, and road and bridge construction projects. It's no accident that southern Democratic politicians favored programs that brought federal money down home. But air-conditioning has changed all that, and malls, offices, and other businesses have sprung up all over the South.

America's Southern Manufacturing Belts

Many people still think of North Carolina as a land of tobacco and farms, but a higher percentage of North Carolinians now work in manufacturing than do New Yorkers. North and South Carolina, Kentucky, Alabama, and Tennessee have all become important manufacturing regions.

The South is emerging as America's manufacturing center.

One of the most dynamic of these regions is the corridor along Route 85 from Atlanta, Georgia, through Greenville and Spartanburg, South Carolina, to Charlotte, North Carolina. It is here that BMW recently decided to make cars. BMW and Mercedes-Benz chose southern states for their new factories not only because they offered the best incentives but because there is little tradition of union organizing in the South (both factories are nonunion). Many executives also equate the agricultural tradition with a strong work ethic. But automobile manufacturing is only one of a number of industries represented on the Route 85 corridor. There, companies as diverse as Nucor, Benetton, and Freightliner make everything from steel to clothing to trucks.

CHARLOTTE, NORTH CAROLINA: A GLOBAL BANKING CENTER

Not only is the South emerging as an important manufacturing area, it is also becoming a financial center. That's not surprising: when other businesses thrive, so do banks. Nevertheless, the rise of southern banks is impressive. For years, the top ten banks in the country were based in New York and California.

Two Charlotte, North Carolina, banks now number among the top ten U.S. banks.

The two banks are headquartered on opposite sides of town. NationsBank, the country's third or fourth largest, depending on daily variations, with assets of $185 billion, is the baby of Hugh McColl. It is now bigger than such New York institutions as Bankers Trust. Across town, Ed Crutchfield, a country music lover and onetime football tackle, runs First Union, the country's sixth largest bank since its acquisition of First Fidelity, an old Boston concern.

Charlotte went down the road to international banking when North Carolina, ahead of most other states, decided to allow statewide banking. Then, in 1985, thirteen southern states agreed to liberalize cross-state banking, and NationsBank and First Union began to buy up southern banks. Some states opposed interstate banking out of a fear that New York banks would gobble up local institutions and take over a national banking market. In Charlotte's case, however, local banks are gobbling up northern ones.

THE TEXAS TURNAROUND

One southern state deserves special mention: Texas. For years, Texas languished in recession, unable to overcome its dependence on oil. Finally, it has revived. With NAFTA, proximity to Mexico and

Latin America will prove a further advantage for Texas, which continues to gain population.

Not Taxes but Space

The westward and southward shift of the country has nothing to do with taxes. It can't be explained by simplistic free-market rhetoric. Connecticut, with almost no income tax, is a population loser. New Hampshire, a conservative state with minimal taxes, will grow more slowly than its liberal neighbor Vermont. New Jersey, which had no income tax until 1976 and has historically resisted taxation, places thirteenth on the shrinking or slow-growing list, immediately behind Vermont. Washington, Oregon, and Florida, three of the fastest-growing states in the country, are all comparatively high-tax states.

Nor can the shift be explained by race. True, some prime-destination western states are overwhelmingly white, but so are population laggards such as Vermont and New Hampshire, while southern states with above-average percentages of African Americans are gaining, not losing, people. Nor does it have to do with zoning. It is harder to build in much of California than in New Hampshire, but look at what's happening to each. The desertion of the Northeast for the West and South is a long-term regional phenomenon that has to do with lower costs, better job opportunities, and, perhaps most important, the desire for space and sun.

The Role of Clusters in Future Growth

In the old America, industry clusters encouraged by natural resources were America's engines of growth, creating jobs and building cities. Pittsburgh, a center of glassmaking in colonial days, became the City of Steel thanks to nearby deposits of coal and iron as well as available transportation by water and rail. Detroit, founded by Antoine de la Mothe, better known as Lord Cadillac, in 1701 and besieged by an Indian named Pontiac in 1763, became Motor Town thanks again to iron but also to Lake Erie, which had made it an industrial center in the nineteenth century and hence a good place for Henry Ford to make cars. New York became a trading capital due to its superior port and access to the West—via the Erie Canal after 1825 and via railroads by the middle of the century; as a result, it became a center for the financing of trade and then for the trading of paper on Wall Street. Hollywood became a center of filmmaking thanks to its bone-dry climate, which let the cameras roll every day. All these cities turned a small natural advantage into a towering source of dominance by achieving system economies of scale.

As documented by Michael Porter in *The Competitive Advantage of Nations,* a cluster takes hold when the growth of support services makes it decisively easier to do business in one place. A critical mass of suppliers, friendly bankers, distributors, and other support services creates an infrastructure that gives one region a leg up on others.[7] From then on that region rules—unless of course it fails to adapt or is overtaken by some other cluster (such as one overseas), or the product loses its market, all three of which struck America's steel belt, for example, in the 1980s.

Clusters are alive and well and will remain so for the foreseeable future. Silicon Valley is a cluster economy in computer hardware and software. So, too, is Provo, Utah, in software. However, there is one major difference between new clusters and old ones.

In the industrial economy, clusters typically rose up around some natural endowment such as iron or a natural port; in the information economy, clusters are growing up around seeds of knowledge.

And since knowledge can move faster than deposits of, say, oil or iron, clusters will rise and fall more rapidly in the future.

The Role of Education in Economic Growth: The Mountain Comes to Mohammed

Education and knowledge have always played a role in industry. Today they are becoming the reason for industry in the first place. In the industrial economy, educated people had to go to industrial areas to ply their trade because capital was tethered to those areas. Many university towns such as Kyoto in Japan, Oxford in England, and Princeton in New Jersey evolved as unspoiled scholars' paradises. But graduates faced the same classic dilemma as Mohammed: since industry wouldn't come to them, they had no choice but to go to industry. They left Oxford for London, Kyoto for Tokyo, and Princeton for New York.

No more. In the knowledge age, education is proving to be the single most important determinant of wealth. With mobile capital able to chase opportunity, and with opportunity defined as knowledge, the mountain of capital is coming to Mohammed.

The Correlation of Higher Education and Income

Today, higher education correlates so well with income that comparisons are eerie. A century ago, there was a correlation because only the wealthy could afford an education. Today, however, the poor have access to higher education and, once they get it, they stop being poor. This demonstrates that education has begun to lead to wealth, rather than just the other way around.

The following are the counties with the highest household incomes and the highest numbers of postgraduate degrees:

COUNTIES WITH THE HIGHEST ANNUAL HOUSEHOLD INCOME (1990)

Fairfax County, Va.	$59,381
Morris County, N.J.	56,415
Somerset County, N.J.	55,543
Los Alamos County, N.M.	54,900
Hunterdon County, N.J.	54,752
Nassau County, N.Y.	54,486
Howard County, Md.	54,395
Montgomery County, Md.	54,154
Putnam County, N.Y.	53,744
Rockland County, N.Y.	53,034

COUNTIES WITH THE MOST ADVANCED DEGREES (1990)*

Los Alamos County, N.M.	20.5%
Falls Church County, Va.	18.8
Arlington County, Va.	17.6
Montgomery County, Md.	15.7
New York County, N.Y.	14.7
Alexandria County, Va.	14.2
Orange County, N.C.[8]	13.8
Fairfax County, Va.	13.4
Tompkins County, N.Y.[9]	12.6
Howard County, Md.	12.5

* Percentage of population holding postgraduate degrees.
Source: Urban Decision Systems

No fewer than four counties appear on both lists: Los Alamos, New Mexico (home of the Los Alamos Scientific Laboratory); Fairfax, Virginia; Montgomery, Maryland; and Howard, Maryland. Considering that there are more than 3,500 counties in

America, that's a high level of correlation between income and higher education.

At the very top levels of both lists, suburbs and exurbs of Washington, D.C., account for a large percentage of the leading counties. Much of the money and growth around Washington is recent and attributable to the new information economy. And in many cities and counties around the country, the presence of universities and a high level of education has triggered outright booms.

The New Mill Towns: University Cities

Just as rivers in New England created the mill towns that were centers of industry in an earlier era, in the Information Age universities are becoming the new magnets for capital. This represents a major change in the relationship between education and industry. Traditionally, most colleges, especially religious ones, had little to do with commerce. Those that did, principally land-grant colleges, were primarily concerned with agriculture. When industry did interact with colleges, it was usually in the form of financial support. For example, as Rochester, New York, grew rich from the success of Eastman Kodak, Bausch & Lomb, and Xerox, Kodak chief George Eastman led the drive to endow the University of Rochester.[10] Businessmen or cities funded universities as they might opera houses or museums. Today, however, the process works in the other direction: instead of businesses endowing universities, universities are creating business and industry.

Early models for university-led industrial development were Cambridge, Massachusetts, which benefited from the presence of MIT and Harvard; the Research Triangle in Raleigh-Durham, North Carolina; and Stanford University's Palo Alto Research Center. Stanford and the Research Triangle actually set aside land and provided incentives for companies to locate in their research centers. This first generation of knowledge clusters surrounded America's research universities, the prime beneficiaries of Cold War military research contracts.

But as a result of their success, other schools in other regions have begun to create industrial centers of their own. They are turning cities such as Bozeman, Montana, the site of Montana State University, into budding high-tech centers. This second generation of clusters is often centered on land-grant schools, rather than research universities.[11]

People doing business in these new, high-tech towns and cities find they have almost all the services of more crowded areas without their disadvantages and costs. The universities provide knowledge and educated employees as well as federal money, which often irrigates the new communities. Universities are principal conduits for state and federal grants to high-tech business.[12]

Education has played *the* critical role in the growth of many high-tech corridors. These corridors are notable not only because they pay high wages but because they represent the future of the country's economy. Today, high technology is the prime mover of the economy. Universities that furnish new technologies are, in a real sense, guarantors of future prosperity.

Those older cities fortunate enough to have many universities, such as New York, Boston, and Chicago, will possess an important advantage in years to come. Their universities will go a long way to keep them perennially young and in tune with the future. Smaller cities with state universities will benefit as well. But old cities without first-rate universities will have a tough row to hoe.

SILICON VALLEY

Silicon Valley is the textbook case of a knowledge-economy cluster. Younger than Route 128 near Boston, the region began to transform itself into a high-tech enclave in the 1950s, thanks to Cold War government contracts doled out to Stanford and the creation of the Stanford Industrial Park, the dream of Frederick Terman, a professor at and later provost of the University. By the early 1960s, the park already employed 11,000 people at about twenty-five companies spread over more than six hundred acres of land.[13] A decade later, the enclave had outgrown the park and nearby Silicon

Valley employed more than 100,000 people. Since then, it has grown so fast that today it is the nation's premier technology center with more than 4,000 companies employing more than 200,000 people. The region went through its most severe crisis in 1985, when Japanese firms hijacked the memory chip business, but later reemerged stronger than ever. The valley has now produced several generations of firms, championing new technologies.

Given its size, the region has become susceptible to the vicissitudes any economy faces. Nevertheless, Silicon Valley will remain an important industrial center for years to come. Indeed, it has become the mother ship to other high-tech communities popping up in towns and cities throughout the West.

BOSTON AND ROUTE 128

Route 128 near Boston is the granddaddy of high-tech clusters, with roots going back to nineteenth-century New England manufacturing. MIT, located in nearby Cambridge, as one of the first land-grant colleges, had an early mission to provide service to industry. After World War II, Cold War–era government contracts pumped money into the region through both MIT and companies such as Raytheon. Soon Route 128 evolved into the country's preeminent center of high-tech defense. In the 1960s, Cambridge emerged as the center of the advanced hi-fi industry, and firms such as KLH and Bose, founded by MIT professors, were synonymous with excellence. A large number of consulting firms with expertise in technology, such as Arthur D. Little, further aided the cluster. With the invention of the computer, Digital Equipment and Wang Laboratories grew up nearby, started by Harvard graduates. Minicomputer firms such as Prime Computer and Data General also grew up in the region.

Route 128 has been through several waves of expansion and contraction. It experienced a downturn after the Vietnam War but took off again like a rocket, powered by the rise of the minicomputer in the 1970s. In the late 1980s, it tanked again when personal computers brought the minicomputer business to a crashing halt.

In recent years, however, biotechnology and software have pumped new blood into the area. MIT and Massachusetts General Hospital are important players in biotechnology development. MIT has an aggressive policy to let professors or others capitalize on its patents and intellectual property. Genzyme, Biogen, and Immunogen are all headquartered in Cambridge; in software, Lotus, later acquired by IBM, is a local success story.

While much of the rapid growth around Boston as a consequence of the development of Route 128 has probably already occurred, the cluster is the country's third largest high-tech area, with about 1,200 high-tech firms. But as biotechnology moves into its own, the region is likely to grow again.

THE RESEARCH TRIANGLE

North Carolina's research triangle, the 7,000-acre region between Raleigh, Durham, and Chapel Hill, contains only several hundred companies. It is world famous, however, because of its size and the depth of its research facilities. Unlike some high-tech areas, which specialize in one or two industries, the research triangle covers the waterfront. Companies as diverse as Du Pont, Ciba-Geiby, and Data General have facilities in the area. The three main universities in the area—Duke, the University of North Carolina, and North Carolina State University—all have different specialties, with Duke excelling in biology and medicine, the University of North Carolina in health services, and North Carolina State in engineering and computer science.

The region benefits both from the 15,000 graduates its universities turn out annually and from its low cost of living. While the ability to tap scientific and engineering talent from its universities is important to the region's success, it is also significant that Raleigh is the state capital. State capitals often feature a higher standard of living than other areas of a state, since government services and largesse help to insulate them from economic downturns and support amenities. The success of the region has transformed eastern North Carolina, which now boasts excellent French restaurants, first-rate bookstores, theater, opera, and public television—amenities that attract educated people.

New University Enclaves

Many other high-tech corridors are hoping to copy or surpass Silicon Valley, and some are close to doing so. The following are some of the leading new high-tech clusters around the country. Inevitably, one or more universities lie at their center. Capital, usually at the coaxing of local university and government officials, has sought out these regions to take advantage of the brains of the local inhabitants as well as the university facilities.

AUSTIN, TEXAS

The country's second largest silicon cluster, after Silicon Valley, is Silicon Hills, located in and around Austin. The region is home to Dell Computer and CompuAdd, as well as to facilities of their Texan competitors, Texas Instruments and Compaq. About 100,000 students live in the Austin area, distributed across the University of Texas, Southwest Texas State University, and Austin Community College. Michael Dell attended school at the University of Texas at Austin, and the cluster has drawn sustenance both from Austin's university and from the high quality of life in the town.

As a state capital, Austin has numerous amenities and a floor to its economy thanks to government spending. It is also hilly and green for Texas and within a short distance of several lakes.

About 450 high-tech firms are located in Silicon Hills and employ 55,000 people. The presence of large computer firms, along with consortia such as the Microelectronics and Computer Technologies Corp. (MCC), has contributed to the growth of a critical mass of suppliers, raised local banks' understanding about lending to high-tech firms, and helped create the infrastructure for a successful cluster. IBM, Motorola, and Apple Computer, none of which is headquartered in Austin, paid it the ultimate compliment when they chose to design the PowerPC chip here.

The Washington, D.C., Area

The greater Washington, D.C., area, just a decade or two ago still
farmland only lightly colonized by bureaucrats, has turned into a
major high-tech economic center focused on networks despite the
inner city's problems. After Silicon Valley, the Washington area—in
particular, northern Virginia—has the highest concentration of
high-tech firms in the country, in part, thanks to the presence of
the federal government. Numerous companies compete on a daily
basis to sell software and systems to the government and closely
follow publications such as *Washington Technology: The Business Newspaper for Federal Systems Integrators.* MCI has its headquarters in the
District of Columbia, a legacy of its long battle to enter long-
distance service. PSINet, an Internet service provider, is located
near Herndon, Virginia. A few large firms, such as America Online
in Vienna, Virginia, have no direct connection with the government but have leveraged off the high level of support services for
high-tech firms in northern Virginia.

It is fitting that key players on the information superhighway are
located near Washington, given the government's role in the early
stages of computer networks. ARPA, formerly DARPA, the Defense
Advanced Research Projects Agency, funded the linkup of the first
four computers on the Internet in California and Utah in 1969. For
many years, the National Science Foundation paid for the cost of
the Internet's transcontinental backbone. Washington has long
been at the forefront of satellite communications. It's also where
frequencies are auctioned off, where local and long-distance firms
slugged it out in Judge Harold Greene's courtroom for many years
(Greene having issued the judgment that broke up the old Bell
system), and where lobbyists fought over the 1996 bill to deregulate
cable television and telecommunications.

Businesses related to the Internet dot the road to Dulles Airport,
and the concentration of network-related businesses in northern
Virginia has led to cross-fertilization similar to that in Silicon Valley.
With more than 1,200 high-tech firms, many in networks, the Wash-

ington area will be increasingly important for decades. In Maryland, the National Institutes of Health (NIH) are spawning a respectable biotech cluster.

SEATTLE, WASHINGTON

While Silicon Valley was gaining most of the spotlight in the 1980s along the Pacific coast, Seattle, Washington, was quietly becoming a major player in high-tech industry in its own right. As home to Microsoft and billionaires Bill Gates and Paul Allen as well as Aldus, the region is famous for software. However, Seattle and its suburbs of Redmond, Kirkland, Bellevue, and Bothell also boast a significant biotech industry.

The region's success was typical of that of many other high-tech centers. The presence of Boeing created a market for some high-tech services. However, the success of a few bellwether firms, such as Microsoft and Aldus, later purchased by Adobe, opened the gates to success by others. In part, alumni of successful firms started successful spin-offs of their own. At the same time, a network of support services and a favorable attitude toward high-tech businesses on the part of everyone from banks to local government made entrepreneurship easier. Located on the Pacific coast, Seattle has a strong international orientation.

While the region lacks a research facility on the order of Stanford or MIT, it boasts the University of Washington, which has served as a conduit for government funds. The university has also emerged as a major player in advanced software applications, including virtual reality, at its Human Interface Laboratory, which is headed up by an air force VR pioneer. The region has been so successful that its major constraint may be a shortage of additional labor.

PROVO, UTAH

In 1977, Provo, the home of Brigham Young University, gained prominence as the backdrop for the crimes and execution of murderer Gary Gilmore. What a difference a few years can make. In the last decade, Provo has become internationally known as one of the country's largest high-tech centers. Today this dry college town, populated mainly by Mormons, and nearby Orem have become home to close to 300 software firms. The best known are Word-Perfect and the neighbor that later acquired it, Novell.

Brains trained at Brigham Young have been the magnet that has drawn international capital to this small desert town and the strip along Route 15. A strong religious culture persists in the region, and the city fathers, most of them Mormons, discourage businesses that might pollute or that pay low wages from coming to town while encouraging software companies.[14]

ORLANDO, FLORIDA

Orlando is famous to most people as the home of Goofy, Mickey Mouse, and the other characters of Disney World. But beyond that reputation, the city has emerged as an important high-tech cluster. Specifically, it has become the country's third largest city for film production, behind New York and Los Angeles. And in and around Orlando's Laser Lane, a burgeoning laser industry has taken root. Centered on the University of Central Florida, Laser Lane now includes hundreds of companies and employs more than 10,000 workers. Why the University of Central Florida? Because originally, the university had a solid optics department. A conscious decision by the university and local planners to strive for critical mass in lasers paid off. The university helped attract companies, and the companies have helped make the university's laser department one of the best in the world.

PHILADELPHIA, PENNSYLVANIA

In the Philadelphia suburbs along the Delaware River valley, a number of new companies are sprouting up in the field of bio-technology and medical devices. So many new companies are taking root along the Route 202 corridor, linking Chester, Montgomery, and Bucks Counties, that locals have begun to call the area "Medical Mile." Helped by the presence of universities that graduate one fifth of the nation's doctors and by the University City Science Center, a giant incubator, the cluster already employs 160,000 people. The area has become a shopping center for European pharmaceutical firms looking to invest in or acquire U.S. biotechnology companies. And it's not far from central New Jersey, home to such U.S. drug companies as Bristol-Myers Squibb and Johnson & Johnson.

SAN FRANCISCO, CALIFORNIA

Although an hour's drive from Silicon Valley, San Francisco has always been close enough to benefit from its success. Recently, however, the city has won a new name, Multimedia Gulch, due to the large number of multimedia firms that have taken root here, not in Silicon Valley or in the suburbs. The diverse skills needed in producing multimedia—art, music, and video, as well as computers—make a city a logical place to find them.

BOISE, IDAHO

Boise, Idaho, is emerging as a fledgling hardware center. Like Seattle, Portland, Missoula, Salt Lake City, Boulder, and other large western towns, it is basking in the reflected glow of Silicon Valley. Tired of California's costs and hassles, many firms are looking to nearby states as places in which to expand. The home of the potato, Boise got a break in the 1970s when potato kingpin John R. Simplot put money into Micron Technology, a home-grown start-up that proved successful. Hewlett-Packard was another early investor when it placed a division in the area in the 1970s.

Today, more than twenty-five high-tech firms in Boise employ close to 15,000 people. The city benefits from the presence of the University of Idaho and, like other western cities, from its proximity to California and advantageous costs. Boise offers Californian transplants cappuccinos, lattes, and other familiar amenities.

Portland, Oregon

Portland's Silicon Forest has emerged as a genuine high-tech center. In Portland and its suburbs of Beaverton, Wilsonville, and Hillsboro, hardware firms such as Mentor Graphics and Sequent Computer Systems have put the region on the high-technology map. More than twenty-five firms employ more than 14,000 people in Portland, a city of half a million.

Down the Road

Some clusters are still gelling but may become important in the future. They include the following.

Bozeman and Missoula, Montana

The home of Montana State University, a land-grant school with an active technology extension program, Bozeman has a small but energetic technology community focused on lasers and computers. The scene of the movie *A River Runs Through It*, it is a true amenity town. Missoula, home of MSU's rival, the University of Montana, has also spawned a fledgling high-tech community. And a number of local firms have cooperated with a nearby NIH facility in Hamilton, Montana.

Baltimore

A somewhat depressed city for many decades, Baltimore is trying to find itself. The city does have one ace in the hole that may help it mount a comeback. That ace is Johns Hopkins University. Robert Gallo, formerly head of the National Cancer Institute at NIH and a codiscoverer of the AIDS virus, chose Baltimore from among a long list of contenders for a new center for AIDS research he has begun. Baltimore also recently inaugurated a new facility for biotechnology firms. And Johns Hopkins has altered its rules on how it handles its intellectual property to encourage the commercial exploitation of discoveries it makes. While it's too early to tell precisely what will happen to Baltimore, it has the potential to participate in biotechnology's growth in the twenty-first century. Suburban Howard County (on the way to Washington) is already one of the richest in the country.

Still other ascending high-tech enclaves include San Diego, California, the home of the University of San Diego, a large student population, and a burgeoning biotech and communications community; Minneapolis, Minnesota, the home of Medical Alley, a group of five hundred firms employing 40,000 people; and Tucson, Arizona, the site of Optics Valley, a group of forty companies employing 1,000 people. All these areas share the presence of a university, an educated workforce, and prospects for healthy growth.

High-tech clusters are not only founts of knowledge but founts of money.

What makes high-tech industries attractive to regions and investors is their potential for future growth. As computers, software, and biotechnology flower and develop, the regions that monopolize them will outstrip regions wedded to older industries or devoid of industry at all. High-tech industries foreshadow the future. They may never make as much money as air-plant businesses such as McDonald's or Jiffy Lube. However, they are genuine industries that can provide the outside income needed to keep air-plant economies in flower.

Geographic Versus Virtual Clusters

All the budding high-tech areas around the country show unmistakably that clusters are here to stay. While the new ones have universities and knowledge at their core, there is no substitute for physical proximity. Just-in-time delivery is predicated on the proximity of suppliers and purchasers. So is design-in manufacturing. Computer makers benefit from having a disk drive supplier down the road, just as biotech firms benefit from having suppliers of bacteria nearby.

But it goes even further than that. Product development works better when R&D people work closely with people in manufacturing and sales. Failure to unite these functions crippled U.S. consumer electronics firms in the 1980s. Keeping them together is now standard operating procedure at cutting-edge firms.

Even software firms benefit from proximity to one another; hence the cluster in Provo, Utah. While the physical transport of parts is not an issue, the presence of a large computer-literate workforce is. Just as northern Italian clothing manufacturers benefit from the depth of knowledge about how to make clothes that is embedded in the northern Italian workforce after hundreds of years, so software makers benefit from having a high level of computer expertise in one place.

However, the next quarter century will also see the appearance of virtual clusters; that is, networks of firms or people linked together by wire instead of geography. Teams of designers can easily work together over wires, and more and more financial activity is conducted long distance, not only big deals but small ones. It used to be that businessmen would cultivate a relationship with the vice president of their local bank, confident that when it came time to borrow he would approve their loan. Today, most branch managers have no say whatsoever about loans, which are approved by experts on the other end of a phone or by software, sometimes in another state.

Software development also lends itself to virtual clustering. In certain niche specialties, such as software security, experts are dispersed around the country, but all know one another via the 'Net. A software designer might put out a call on the 'Net to recruit programmers and then let them work together by modem. For reasons of security, comfort, and productivity, however, most software firms still like to hire people the old-fashioned way and have them come in house to work.

Virtual clusters can be formed and disbanded far faster than geographic clusters.

A geographic cluster such as the infrastructure for making computers in Silicon Valley gives firms there a major advantage over firms trying to make computers in, say, Topeka, Kansas. Since the advantage is based on something that took a long time to create and cannot easily be duplicated, it is likely to last for a while. However, a virtual cluster—whether of designers, manufacturers, or distributors—that comes together in cyberspace on a network has fewer sunk costs or other reasons to stay intact after a project is finished. Its great virtue is speed of formation and agility. As a result, relationships and clusters in cyberspace will be inherently fluid and fleeting. People will secure competitive advantage in cyberspace by being agile—being able to form and disband alliances quickly—not by building up a bulky cluster over time that others would be hard pressed to reproduce.

Strategies for the Future

These sea changes in American life—the move further out into the exurbs, the shift west, and increased telecommuting—will permit a whole new group of strategies, both for individuals and for businesses.

Arbitraging Places

Differences in living costs combined with the new ability to work long distance over wires will create one of the single greatest opportunities for Americans in many years: the opportunity to arbitrage places. Wall Street arbitrageurs make fortunes buying on one market and selling on another to take advantage of price differences. Now any worker can do something similar.

Arbitraging places—living in a low-cost area and making money in a high-paying one—is a great new opportunity.

Traditionally, to make a high salary it has been necessary to work in a high-wage area. Anyone who has moved from Texas to New York is familiar with the huge jump in salary that such a move can entail, offset by a corresponding jump in the cost of living. Increasingly, however, it will be possible to make a salary in a high-wage area and live where costs are low. Typically, inexpensive regions are also less crowded and more beautiful than developed areas. The opportunity to arbitrage places will not be limited to freelance writers and artists. Examples of people who, by telecommuting, are already arbitraging places include chief financial officers, accountants, lawyers, and other highly skilled managers and consultants. Further improvements in the information superhighway will make leveraging places even easier in the years ahead.

Enterprise Mobility

People aren't the only ones who will move or alter their working arrangements to take advantage of the powerful tool of arbitraging places; companies will use it as well.

While few companies are yet comfortable assembling an entire workforce of telecommuters in scattered locations, few hesitate to put whole divisions in far-flung places and hook up those divisions to headquarters by wire.

Only five years ago, for example, most Wall Street firms had their back offices literally in back of their front offices in New York's financial district. Now almost all have moved their back offices to low-cost areas around the country.

Or consider the story of tiny Polygon Network, an on-line service company that links up independent jewelers.[15] Jacques Voorhees ran the company in New York until costs and the call of the West led him to move to tiny Dillon, Colorado, elevation 11,000 feet, on the edge of the Continental Divide. Polygon enables jewelers' suppliers to exchange information and conduct business on an electronic bulletin board system without going through wholesalers.

To link up its clients, Voorhees has yoked together two Digital Equipment VAX computers and a Sun Microcomputers workstation and hooked them up to the world at large with seventeen modems and twenty-five phone lines. The whole operation sits in a loft in one of the town's only two-story buildings. But Voorhees can service customers just as easily from Colorado as New York and at a fraction of the cost. The ability of small businesses such as Polygon to relocate not only enables their proprietors to relocate but will also create unusual jobs in amenity regions.

Choosing Between Crowded and Empty

Many areas of the country are growing, while others are shrinking or staying the same. Some of the fastest-growing places, such as Telluride, are still remote. Despite rapid growth, the mountainous terrain alone will keep a check on change. But other fast-growing regions, such as Douglas County in Colorado, will not remain rural for long. They lie directly in the path of progress, which will lead to another opportunity to pursue a business strategy. Those looking to open a retail business, make money in real estate, or otherwise exploit the local economy will do well to locate in the path of growth. And, in general, that path is to the west and south, around universities, and out of the cities and suburbs into exurbs.

The following is a list of how many people the fastest- and most slowly growing states (in terms of absolute numbers) will gain or lose between now and the year 2020, according to the Bureau of the Census.

Western and southern states, with California in the lead, will gain the most new people. However, those able to make money long distance over wires may well have no desire to subject themselves to the downside of growth. If so, remote amenity towns in Vermont or Maine may prove more appealing. Those selling over the Internet can operate as easily from Montana as from Chicago. Some may prefer a stable, mature area of the country where change will occur slowly, such as New England. There is no better place to start a high tech business than in a knowledge cluster around a university town.

Finally, many inveterate urbanites will choose to live in cities or their suburbs. Why? For all their problems, cities will continue to offer things that exurbia can't. In coming years, the information highway will bring more and more citylike services to rural and

MOST NEW PEOPLE 1995–2020
(PROJECTED NET INCREASE IN POPULATION IN MILLIONS)

California	15.6
Texas	7.0
Florida	5.2
Washington	2.5
Georgia	2.3
North Carolina	1.9
Virginia	1.7
Arizona	1.6
Illinois	1.4
Oregon	1.2

LEAST NEW PEOPLE 1995–2020
(PROJECTED NET INCREASE IN POPULATION IN THOUSANDS)

West Virginia	28
District of Columbia	77
Vermont	79
North Dakota	82
Rhode Island	89
South Dakota	128
Delaware	153
Maine	164
Wyoming	171
Iowa	177

Source: U.S. Department of Commerce

exurban America, but cities will still provide job opportunities, markets, and cultural amenities that small towns cannot. The big leagues will still be the big leagues. The bottom line is that whether you choose to move or stay put, you should be aware of the patterns of growth that are transforming America.

The Return of the American Homestead

The changing nature of work in the future means that new American homes will be far different places from those built in the 1950s, the 1960s, or even the 1980s. To make the most of the future, you should build or live in a home equipped for the future.

New homes must be "smart" and equipped for telecommuting.

Contractors are already running more telephone, cable, and other wires into new houses to cover the need for data transmission, electronic gadgetry, and home entertainment. At one extreme, Bill Gates has programmed his multimillion-dollar house near Seattle to draw a bath when he calls from the car and to project art onto the walls according to his mood. But even smaller houses should have space for one or more home offices and be wired for data. Indeed, the house is evolving in such a way that it is becoming a new American homestead.

The original American homestead, idealized by Thomas Jefferson, was a self-contained economy. Likewise, the White House, designed by James Hoban, an Irishman, after a mansion in Ireland, was built as a living/working environment. The new American homestead will be similarly living/working- and family-oriented, a change from the apartment housing of the 1970s and 1980s built for boomers. Although not self-sufficient, the new American homestead will have everything its residents need to do their work and will permit at least one spouse to look after children while working at home.

While telecommuting will promote the use of home offices and the new American homestead, it will also reduce the demand for older office buildings. Today any building that cannot be readily wired cannot be rented to blue-chip tenants. Older buildings, already in oversupply following the 1980s boom, have a future principally as living/working residences, as discussed in Chapter 5.

Just as warehouses were converted to loft residences in the 1980s, so older office buildings will be converted to residential apartments in coming years.

In Manhattan's Wall Street district, astonishingly high vacancy rates in the early 1990s led the New York City Council to authorize incentives to convert offices into housing. In the mid-1980s, Wall Street was fully let. But only a few years later, the growth in importance of computers and telecommunications made small or older buildings unrentable and enabled firms to move their back offices out of town. Buildings that once housed banks and brokerages will soon house people, many in living/working spaces. This trend is likely to be repeated throughout the country.

The Future of America's Large Cities

The decline of office space poses a major challenge to large cities, one that will give exurban areas an even larger advantage. Commercial buildings provide space for businesses, which pay taxes and create jobs. Residential buildings create few jobs, generate fewer taxes, and create a need for schools for children. At the same time, the shrinking population in the northeastern cities is putting pressure on the tax base that remains. Why? Because the demand for and cost of services once they are in place does not decline as population declines. Bridges still need to be repaired. Economic drift causes crime to increase. With fewer working people and businesses around to foot the bill, cities face the choice of raising taxes, cutting services, or both, thus accelerating the flight of more affluent residents.

This problem, which has long afflicted older industrial cities from New York to Philadelphia to Gary, has now started to hit some western cities such as Dallas, Houston, and Denver, causing people there to move to the exurbs. But many western and southern cities have found a way out of this problem: they increase their boundaries every year so they can suck in new revenues from the suburbs. Los Angeles has long since engulfed its surrounding regions. Orlando annexes about five square miles of surrounding land per year. Houston now measures more than one hundred square miles.

Older cities are often denied this option by old state laws and stronger nearby municipalities and most are losing population. The District of Columbia is the fastest-shrinking city in the nation. It has been the victim not only of white flight but of black flight, this while Virginia and Maryland at the same time were growing by leaps and bounds. The middle class—both black and white—is moving out of the District for the usual reasons: crime, taxes, the cost of living, and the quality of schools.

New York has held its own in population, but only because it has absorbed millions of immigrants in the last ten years. Boston is losing population. Indeed, nationwide, forty-five of the two hundred cities with more than 100,000 people are losing population. A barometer of the falling fortunes of older cities is their declining political clout. In the early 1960s, John F. Kennedy consulted weekly with the U.S. Conference of Mayors. Presidents Johnson, Nixon, and Ford all treated the organization with respect, and Reagan tried to infiltrate it. However, today the organization has faded from importance.

But look west and south, and the picture changes! Las Vegas, the country's fastest-growing city, has an unusual growth rate of 6 percent, followed closely by Moreno Valley, California; Laredo, Texas; and Chandler, Arizona. Thirteen of the twenty fastest-growing cities with more than 100,000 people are in the West, six are in the South, and one is in the Midwest. By contrast, six of the ten fastest-shrinking cities are in New England.

What this proves is that the city model of living can still work. However, it's working best for new cities which in many ways don't resemble the old cities at all but are built entirely to the scale of the automobile, as, for example, Las Vegas.

New cities (as well as exurbs) have inherent advantages over old cities that translate into a higher standard of living at a lower cost. Take housing: new houses are bigger, on average, than old ones, have more bathrooms and better wiring, and conform to stricter codes. True, the craftsmanship in older houses and apartment buildings in places such as Brooklyn and Baltimore may be better. But it's both cheaper and easier to construct new buildings than to renovate and repair old ones.

Americans have also demonstrated their preference for getting around by car. In cities built to the scale of the car rather than the pedestrian, it's easier to run errands and people feel more secure from crime. This does not necessarily mean that the crime rate is lower. Violent crime is higher in Dallas and Houston than in New York, due primarily to the greater availability of guns. However, new cities feel less threatening because the poor are less visible, as they once were in rural areas, and because the car insulates passengers from their environment.

Does this mean that older cities are finished? Not at all. After declining for decades due to the postwar exodus to the suburbs, cities got a second wind in the 1980s as young, unmarried baby boomers found them more to their liking than the suburbs. During this phase, almost every older industrial city saw its downtown redeveloped. Boston got Faneuil Hall; New York, the South Street Seaport; Atlanta, the Underground; San Francisco, Ghirardelli Square; and Baltimore, the Inner Harbor.

The tide of young white urban professionals who flooded the cities were dubbed "yuppies." They gentrified whole neighborhoods and revitalized businesses from boutiques to bars. But typically, these boomers then got married, and now that many have children and have moved to the suburbs, traditional cities are again experiencing a drain.

The old cities will get a third wind, beginning in about the year 2005, when a baby boomlet will hit its late teens.

Beginning a few years after the turn of the millennium, the children of the baby boomers will come of age, and many will flock to cities in search of fun and experience. There they will frequent the same neighborhoods and patronize many of the same businesses as their parents did before them. Not that cities have emptied out; they will always attract young people. However, young people are not arriving in the numbers they did during the 1980s for the simple reason that there are fewer of them. Gentrification is no longer the significant force it was, and it won't be again for another five to ten years.

Of course, some people are forever young: the rich. The international rich will continue to flock to international cities such as New York and Los Angeles that support rarefied culture and businesses. But in addition to being magnets for the young and the rich, cities have one more ace in the hole: the bigger ones can boast scary concentrations of brains and talent. New York, Boston, Philadelphia, Washington, Chicago, and San Francisco, for example, are all knowledge-rich places.

The combination of talents that continue to seek out cities will be a respectable draw for capital.

Make no mistake. In many businesses the equation has changed. Companies no longer have to do business in cities. But some businesses, such as multimedia publishing, filmmaking, advertising, and television, particularly those in which personal contacts are critical, will require the wide mix of educated, creative people that only a city can bring together. Cities will create a good deal of the content for the Information Age, and many are perfecting the technology to transmit it.

New York, for example, is the single largest, most concentrated site of fiber-optic cable in the entire world. Fiber-optic cable is so omnipresent that the city can support firms such as Petrocelli Communications, a division of Petrocelli Electric Company. Petrocelli's rolling laboratory, a truck specially configured for splicing fiber, patrols Manhattan's streets; when a break occurs, the truck parks next to a manhole and the crew performs an emergency splice. The wires linking New York's major buildings in the financial district are capable of handling massive numbers of transactions, ensuring that Manhattan will remain a major force in financial markets for years to come. Note that Manhattan may thrive while the Bronx and Brooklyn languish.

The Future of Medium-sized Cities

While New York will retain its cachet, smaller cities, particularly those once supported by a business or industry that has moved elsewhere, will have to scramble to attract capital. Some are offering tax breaks and other incentives to new businesses, and some have succeeded. Pittsburgh and Cleveland have done exceptional jobs reinventing their economies after the departure of the steel industry. Both have made high-tech businesses and services a centerpiece of their strategy. But as successful as they have been, they are still losing people to the exurbs. In general, medium-sized cities in the East and Midwest will not experience the economic vitality and growth of cities of similar size in the West and South. Seattle, San Diego, and Santa Fe, to name three, are all gaining population.

The Attractions of Smaller-Town America

Undoubtedly, the smaller towns and amenity counties of America will have a unique opportunity. They offer freedom from the hassles of city life—or even the suburbs. And, increasingly, they also offer all of the services needed to do business.

Over the next quarter century, information technology will revolutionize small-town America.

Perhaps the biggest advantages most small towns have are a lower cost of living and a more relaxed lifestyle. In small towns and exurbs, stores such as Wal-Mart and CostCo that offer warehouse distribution can cut the cost of living to the bone. For that reason, exurban towns and counties—particularly those outside newer western and southern service-oriented as opposed to older industrial cities—will boom. Amenity counties, linked to the rest of the country by wire and airplane, will also flourish. In contrast, older cities that lack a critical knowledge mass will have to struggle while older suburbs will stay the same or decline. The only exception will be the university cities that serve as nodes of growth and further urbanization.

Those pessimists who cite the problems of America's great cities as proof that America itself is in decline fail to note the enormous economic vitality in other regions of the country. Quite simply, the information superhighway is enabling American businesses to take advantage of one of the country's greatest assets: the wide-open spaces. The 60 million new Americans who will appear in the next three decades will continue to spread out from cities in search of those ever-elusive goals: more disposable income, less congestion, and a higher quality of life. Whether pursuing a dream or reacting to a layoff, they will be guided by economic incentives favoring new, more productive modes of work. On a macro level, therefore, Americans will migrate into an ever more productive economic configuration. This geographic flexibility has allowed America to renew itself before and will permit it to continue to do so in the decades ahead.

Chapter 8

Looking at the Twenty-first Century

America's economic renaissance to date and its bright prospects for the future demonstrate that the problems of the 1980s were not part of some inevitable decline but a short-term consequence of the policies and practices of the decade. In banking, manufacturing, finance, and other problem areas, the United States has recovered quickly and dramatically, so that today it is again the world's most dynamic economy. On the eve of the new millennium, the United States has entered a new phase in its history. In coming years, its flexibility and strength, combined with favorable long-term demographic and technological trends, will sustain and intensify economic revival.

These are the main elements of the American Renaissance and the directions of global change:

- Trade of goods will become less global and more local, trade of services the opposite, reversing the current situation and helping the service-oriented U.S. economy to improve its balance of trade.

- Using new network technologies and improved accounting, U.S. companies will continue to reinvent themselves as more efficient organizations, adapting faster than their foreign competitors.

- Work in the United States will become less labor- and more knowledge-intensive as the labor market tightens now that baby boomers and women have been absorbed into the work-force and immigration may soon be constrained, removing a cap on the growth of wages.

- Manufacturing will move from flexible to instant and from long distance to local, decreasing U.S. imports from Asia (while increasing them from Latin America); with the American advantage in networks, "instant manufacturing" will enable the United States to thrive in high-end twenty-first-century manufacturing and continue its export surge.

- In a second services revolution, information technology will become the dominant sector of the U.S. economy, and just as the use of information technology increased productivity and compensation in the financial sector in the 1980s, it will drive wage increases in other sectors.

- Information technology has created a new, parallel world of cyberspace made up of long-distance networks; the United States is well ahead in converting unmapped cyberspace into profitable cyberestate and developing the electronic marketplace.

- Americans will continue to move from cities to exurbs as growth follows electronic lines outward; university towns will be the mill towns of the twenty-first century, nourishing a variety of high-tech clusters.

When one looks at these directions and indeed the direction of electronic technology itself, for example, from mainframes to microcomputers, one overarching trend emerges.

America is moving from a country of centralized intelligence to one of distributed intelligence.

From Centralized to Distributed Intelligence

Centralization is not something that has always existed in the United States or, for that matter, anywhere. The world has been decentralized for most of its history. Centralization occurred only when one power or person was so powerful and skilled in administration that it managed to dominate and organize others. Rome achieved this goal through the exertion of military might, followed up by the building of roads and aqueducts and the imposition of laws. Louis XIV centralized French life by physically assembling the nobility in his court at Versailles and building canals to link up the hinterland. But far more kings and would-be emperors conquered, but never organized, their holdings. Before the Industrial Revolution, economic entities apart from feudal holdings (including the great commercial houses of Florence and Venice, as well as the Antwerp guilds) were, for the most part, small in size. For much of the world's history knowledge was so thinly distributed and communications so difficult to establish that decentralized stupidity, not centralized intelligence, ruled.

This changed with the Industrial Revolution, which led to the emergence of the centralized nation-state and businesses under centralized control. These new, outsized, centralized organizations, whether political or economic, thrived by using the latest, most expensive technologies, which smaller competitors—lesser political powers or entrepreneurs—could not afford. The great banking houses, which arose in the nineteenth century to finance government and industry, owed their growth, in part, to superior communications. The House of Rothschild, for example, made a celebrated killing after the Battle of Waterloo, when its couriers were the first to reach London. And as the Industrial Revolution progressed, industries such as steel, railroads, and cars became more and more capital- and technology-intensive, so that, over time, only the biggest, most centralized players survived.

Government grew larger and more centralized, too, thanks to wars and the Great Depression of the twentieth century. By the 1930s, the Soviet Union, Germany, Italy, and Japan all had totalitarian regimes that controlled production and the lives of their people. In America, democracy granted greater individual freedom, while the telephone and the automobile gave smaller players a better chance. But much technology remained in the hands of business and, in time, the government. World War II provided conclusive proof of the power of centralized government: the atomic bomb. After the war, our national highway system and space travel provided others. During the Industrial Age, size and centralization became the keys to power in every walk of life. In this top-down model of command and control, the city boss in politics, the mogul in business, and "Mr. Big" in crime presided over large centralized organizations.

That era is over. In recent years, the distribution and dissemination of intelligence via information technology has made it possible for smaller organizations to compete effectively with big ones. Today, a state of the-art computer linked to the Internet gives the computer-literate individual powers to obtain information comparable to that of the CEOs of the world's largest companies. Moreover, more and more work is now done on computers; they account for a sizable chunk of our society's so-called means of production. And they are widely distributed: about 40 percent of American households now have a computer at home.

In recent years in America, the trend in both government and business has been toward deregulation and decentralization. The U.S. government still has the best weather data in the country. But whereas it once had a monopoly on satellites, today a consumer of satellite images or communications can buy time on a Soviet, French, Indian, or Chinese satellite or even launch his own. Everywhere today, we see cases of widely distributed capital, technology, and intelligence that further undermine big government's authority.

Does that mean that the federal government's role in the economy is obsolete? Hardly. Advanced science will never be profitable and is now more expensive than ever before. The imminent handoff of space exploration from the federal government to private contrac-tors is a natural evolutionary stage, but other projects await. Only the federal government can afford to finance the Human Genome Proj-ect (which does, however, use the principle of distributed intel-ligence by splitting grants across hundreds of research teams); only the federal government can finance the National Institutes of Health. There is still such a thing as critical mass, and often only large, centralized organizations can muster it. In coming years, the government will still be called upon to explore the next scientific frontier, whatever it may be. Similarly, distributed intelligence does not imply that we should resurrect the nineteenth-century Corn Laws by encouraging a thicket of local regulations in place of na-tional laws, as some states' rights advocates suggest. It does mean, however, that states, towns, and smaller players can now do what once only the federal government had the wherewithal to accom-plish.

The story in business is similar. Once upon a time, IBM had a monopoly on computers, AT&T on telephones, and Xerox on copiers. No more. Even within companies, intelligence gathering and the performance of R&D are breaking up. Today, according to the Industrial Research Institute, 85 percent of R&D performed in many industries is performed by small units rather than centralized labs. Silicon Graphics practices what CEO Edward R. McCracken calls "just-in-time research," securing much of its research exter-nally from universities. No longer must firms establish a huge critical mass at a centralized location to practice R&D. In place of supercomputers, scientists use workstations and communicate with one another over networks.

This trend toward distributed intelligence should lead to a better-informed, more capable citizenry, a more responsive gov-ernment, and smarter, more entrepreneurial businesses. For the following reasons, America is uniquely positioned to take advan-tage of distributed intelligence:

• Its ample area will permit new development outside cities that takes advantage of distributed capital and intelligence. In contrast, Europe has less room available for development and Japan virtually none.

• America is well ahead of its competitors in the creative use of information technology.

• Numerous American universities will serve as nodes of high-tech growth.

• A tradition of entrepreneurship will encourage Americans to make the most of distributed capital and intelligence.

From Established to Agile

A related, overarching direction of the American Renaissance is the evolution of successful organizations from those that are established to those that are agile. When capital, technology, and intelligence were centralized, in particular, during the 1950s and 1960s, an establishment ran the country. As they have become more widely distributed, the establishment's authority in business, politics, and everything else has been undermined. In coming years, agility will be worth more than established position. While in theory an established position gives anyone an advantage, in reality it creates resistance to change. In business, adhesion to an old technology or type of product can spell disaster for a onetime leader. Cases in point:

• U.S. auto companies continued to manufacture larger cars in the 1970s despite customer preferences for small cars, and they paid the price.

• IBM's reluctance to undercut its own sales of mainframes slowed its forays into microcomputers.

• In contrast, Hewlett-Packard's decision to aggressively cannibalize its own sales of printers led to its stellar success in ink-jet printers.

In the continually changing economic environment of the next few decades, agility, not established position, will be the key to success. And time and again, the American people as well as American businesses, albeit with some initial reluctance, have demonstrated their agility.

Change destroys establishments. As a case in point, the so-called Eastern Establishment has been under siege since the 1960s and has steadily lost influence and control so that today, while still significant, it is a ghost of its former self. For example, two Charlotte-based banks are now among America's top ten, and in coming years interstate banking will enable so-called regional banks to challenge further New York's financial institutions. The East is steadily losing population, economic power, and electoral votes to the West, again as a result of the distribution of capital, technology, and intelligence. The failure of the Vietnam War, prosecuted by establishment figures like Robert McNamara, dealt a blow to the establishment's prestige, inflation in the 1970s eroded its assets, and in 1980 after native son George Bush lost the New Hampshire Republican primary, the Eastern Establishment found itself compelled to join forces with western conservatives to elect Ronald Reagan. While the decade that followed enriched individual members of the Eastern Establishment, it undermined it as a group.

In coming years, the millions of people with access to the Internet and the millions moving from the East to the West will further undermine the Eastern Establishment. Yet while its members must now share power with people from other parts of the country, those who worked for them undoubtedly have it harder. Large organizations provided job security to their many employees, but as the organizations have come under siege, so have the people who worked there. They have no choice but to practice agility. As discussed in Chapter 4, as capital grows more mobile, labor's best response is to get hold of capital, which has become easier to obtain.

Regionalism Versus Nationalism

The increasingly borderless nature of world trade in the wake of the Information Revolution, combined with the breakup of the former Soviet Union, has led some writers to proclaim the end of the nation-state. According to them, it is only a matter of time before Scotland separates from the United Kingdom and Quebec leaves Canada. And as countries move to legitimize supranational organizations such as the European Union or the World Trade Organization, these same writers argue that regional identity will become as, if not more, important than national identity.

In the United States, big government is certainly under attack, while some regions of the country are gaining in political and economic power and others are in decline. Upon close examination, however, it is clear that the national principle is stronger today than it has ever been. At one time or another, almost every portion of the United States, with the exception of the Midwest, has tried or been willing to secede. Pennsylvania separatists were put down by George Washington during the Whiskey Rebellion in 1794; the New England states held a convention in Hartford about secession in 1815; Texas and California were willing to go it alone before joining the Union; and the South's secession, of course, caused the Civil War.

But in coming years, the United States, for once in its history, will not have to worry about regional splits. Information technology is pulling the country closer together, not further apart. Economic ties between regions have been strengthened by networks, and more and more Americans are using faxes, phones, and the Internet to make their voices heard and their views known to their government. This pattern is global. Italians, for example, are cleaning up their government and promoting rule by law at the expense of cronyism, family ties, and prenational allegiances.

Other Sources of Identity

But if the trend toward distributed intelligence is engendering a strong sense of national identity, it has also led to a realization among the American people that their government cannot be their long-term provider. What is taking the place of big government and the paternal company? The answer is the very institutions that are replacing them in reality: small businesses, in particular those they own; their homes, which may also be their places of business; their careers, if not their companies; their networks of friends and professional associates; and their churches.

Since the late 1960s, America and the world have been in the midst of a religious awakening that will continue into the next millennium.

Religion has benefited greatly from modern technologies, including direct mail, television programs using toll-free numbers, and now the Internet. Video chat lines will encourage the formation of even larger, more active virtual communities of people around the country, religious and otherwise. The new technologies short-circuit distance and reduce the significance of geography.

Providing ammunition to those who are pessimistic about America's future is the phenomenon of multiculturalism, which has been on the rise in the United States in recent years. We are not one nation, it is said, but rather a collection of minorities. In fact, multiculturalism as a phenomenon has already crested. In coming years, people will think of themselves more as Americans, less as members of a minority group. Why? Again because of distributed capital, technology, and intelligence and because of the proliferation of small businesses in America. As a nation of immigrants, America has been highly polarized by ethnic differences at various times (and, after all, fought the Civil War over slavery). But beginning in the Depression, which leveled Americans economically, and continuing through World War II, in which equalization occurred in the ranks of the military, Americans suppressed their differences. In the 1950s, suburbanization erased differences further, and America was hailed as a melting pot. The invention of television and the proliferation of mass media that celebrated an ideal American family further minimized ethnic differences.

It took the postwar migration of southern blacks to the cities to put the race issue at the top of the political and social agenda, and in 1965 the national origins provisions of the Immigration and Nationality Act, which restricted immigration, were repealed, reopening America's gates. The phenomenon of multiculturalism and diversity closely tracks the entry of diverse groups into the workforce, where they became capable of exerting power. The first germ of multiculturalism was the affirmative action bill President Nixon signed into law in 1972, granting special protection to blacks and women. Later in the decade, protection was extended to Hispanics (who had not experienced legal persecution).[1] White ethnics then applied for and were denied federal coverage, though in some cities such as New York, some groups such as Orthodox (but not Reform) Jews secured special perquisites.

Recast as the Political Correctness movement, the issue of diversity pierced the public consciousness again in the 1990s, as a result of the Judge Clarence Thomas–Anita Hill controversy. In 1993, the Clinton administration adopted many tenets of the PC movement with its policy of quotas on political appointments and intervention in civil rights matters. (President Clinton promptly became the target of a sexual harassment suit himself.) In 1994, white men who had returned to the Democratic Party to elect him president deserted it again over the familiar issue of preferential rights for disadvantaged groups.

The Supreme Court has steadily narrowed the use of affirmative action, but, more important, multiculturalism's fortunes have always been linked to those organizations in which it has most leverage: government, large companies, and universities. And while it will linger there, it is unenforceable and therefore largely irrelevant within smaller companies, the most dynamic and fastest-growing part of the American economy. In fact, the economic strides being made by women, blacks, and ethnic minorities are due far more to their own efforts than to government assistance programs. In Atlanta, blacks have their own paper, the monthly *Tribune*. In Queens, New York, blacks earn as much as whites, and in the District of Columbia, they are leaving the city to move to middle-class suburbs. The unemployment rate among blacks is currently the lowest it has been in decades. Women's wages, adjusted for education, now virtually equal those of men and rose 54 percent between 1967 and 1992, while men's actually dropped 4 percent. The wages of black women rose 57 percent over this period.

Deep divisions along racial lines will continue to exist, sapping America's strength. But ethnicity will become a source of new strength as the American economy globalizes and cultures mingle on the information superhighway. And within our own borders, again through information technology, people will be drawn together by the pursuits and interests they have in common, regardless of their ethnic differences.

Other pessimists have predicted that even though multiculturalism may recede, America will become a nation of economic haves and have-nots depending on their level of knowledge, creating a permanent underclass. There is solid evidence to the contrary. While educated workers will reap greater benefits, information technology is creating jobs in America at all economic levels. It was, in fact, the industrial economy that stratified America into blue-collar and white-collar workers. In the service economy of the Information Age, there will be more opportunities for a greater number of people. Americans, even those working in low-paying jobs, have learned that they must be entrepreneurial and look out for themselves. Ten years from now, as the service economy matures, more people, whatever their race or ethnic origin, will own houses, live in the suburbs instead of the cities, and own businesses. The prognosis is for more economic equality and less class stratification. The spread of capital, technology, and intelligence will cut across geographic, ethnic, and economic lines, bringing people and nations closer together.

Looking Further Ahead

Over the next quarter century, new technologies will continue to favor the smaller player and undermine economies of scale—the principal advantage enjoyed by large organizations. As the price of computing power and bandwidth continues to plummet, more power becomes accessible to more people. Contrary to George Orwell's prediction in *1984*, technology has proved to be the undoing of totalitarianism rather than a tool for suppression, as it has become more readily affordable.

However, as we look further into the future, what if top-of-the-line information technology stops getting cheaper and becomes more capital-intensive? Will it shift power away from the "little guy" back to the big boys? History is full of examples of what happens when advanced technology reaches the hands of individuals. In general, it has been an equalizer: the centralized order has been weakened, and the individual has gained—but not always indefinitely.

In 1836, Samuel Colt introduced his Colt revolver, making the most advanced gun on earth available to almost anyone. God may have created all men, the saying went, but it took Mr. Colt to make them equal. Whereas in the Middle Ages, it took several small farms to fund a knight in shining armor, the technology of the Colt gun put the poor man on a par with the rich man. It let him stake and protect a claim and influenced the development of the West, where capital and power remained widely dispersed until the appearance of the railroads. The technology of rail permitted greater freedom of movement but concentrated capital, technology, and power in the hands of the railroad magnates.[2]

When Henry Ford's inexpensive cars came on line in the 1920s, they bore the same relationship to trains that the personal computer bears to mainframes. Cars democratized transportation, just as personal computers have democratized knowledge. But while car manufacturing started out small, it quickly became capital-intensive, driving out small fry as the Big Three consolidated the industry. In the computer and networks sectors, a scenario could likewise unfold, if not in the near future, sometime later in the twenty-first century, in which large firms consolidate control over the movement of data. Huge cyberconglomerates are already vying for control over the wire into your home, and the history of computing is littered with the corpses of companies ground up under the wheels of IBM, Microsoft, and others. If the pace of software development slows, if economies of scale become decisive, or if the cost of innovation climbs, thus raising stiff barriers to entry, bigness may well become a requirement of survival.

But for the foreseeable future, the Internet will continue to democratize information and "the means of production" as putting up content grows more affordable. The fact that the cost of processing power and bandwidth is shrinking suggests that capital requirements will stay in bounds, encouraging competition, shifting power to the consumer, and providing opportunity for innovators. While cyberconglomerates are emerging, they are finding they must rely on smaller suppliers for content in order to survive. Changing standards and accelerating technology are creating opportunities for some while at the same time reducing them for others. As a result, new companies are emerging as others disappear. In cyberretail and cyberentertainment, there is every reason to think that the "little guy" will have plenty of chances to grow. Thus far, information technology has been an equalizer, decentralizing organizations and encouraging agility.

The fall of communism in Eastern Europe has removed one major barrier to capitalism, the decline of the labor movement another. Does this mean that history is over and that capitalism and the march of technology will face no further challenges? The answer is no. History abhors a vacuum and no status quo can continue unchallenged. The most likely obstacles to unrestrained capitalism in coming years will be religion, tribalism, and environmentalism, with religion the strongest of the three. In Iran, clerics continue to suppress the functioning of the free market; in Algeria, religious fundamentalists oppose democratic capitalism. Where communism lingers, for example in China, one can draw parallels between

Marxist views of the market and those of religious clerics. But, in general, having largely defeated communism, capitalism now finds its greatest threats on the right.

In the United States, religion remains largely allied with capitalism, but this could change. Already, religious leaders and conservative politicians have attacked some functions of the market, such as its toleration of sex and violence on television. The success of Republican presidential candidate Patrick Buchanan in 1996 suggests that some conservatives put religion above free market ideology. Capitalism may soon draw the ire of religious leaders for its role in breaking up the family by putting women to work. Moreover, the emergence of biotechnology as a major industry will pose new ethical questions. At the moment a small industry with total revenues less than that of one good-sized computer firm, biotechnology will come of age in the mid–twenty-first century. The perfection of cloning technologies, for example, could provoke a battle royal between businesses ready to capitalize on the new technology and religious forces sure to oppose it. Religion could well come to challenge and eventually modify capitalism, just as socialism challenged and modified it through the end of the Cold War. For the time being, however, this is mere speculation. Over the next twenty-five years, both capitalism and new technologies will face only limited challenges to their proliferation worldwide and fewer still in the United States.

The America of the next quarter century will be an exciting place to live. Ample room for expansion, favorable demographics, a dynamic labor market, improved links with a more stable Latin America, and an advanced technology infrastructure will enable it to lead change in the global economy. In contrast, Japan, in spite of its superior performance since World War II, has run up against limits that will check its once-stellar growth. It lacks land to improve its standard of housing. There is no reason to expect the yen to decline dramatically in value, which means that Japan will have to continue to shift manufacturing to lower-cost countries. And its people will age dramatically in coming years, leaving fewer of working age to support the old. For almost five years, Japan has experienced very little growth, and when it recovers, its growth will be comparable to that in the United States and other G-7 countries. The wonder years have ended.

Europe, for all its efforts to integrate, will remain a federation rather than a single political entity. Over the next quarter century, it will maintain a high standard of living. It will grow more homogeneous as a Euroculture formed of common clothing, food, and products arises to complement the cultures of its constituent countries. With the exception of the problems it will face from Eastern Europe, it will fare quite well indeed. However, it will lack the dynamism of the United States and Asia due to stronger traditions, heavier regulations, and a multiheaded government.

Economies of scale mean that information technology and information itself will grow cheaper in coming decades, benefiting all those who have access to them and can put them to productive use. In general, Americans will have a far better time of it than their competitors will. With capital and the ability to control the networks and the highest-tech information systems, Americans will be in a powerful negotiating position relative to those who must compete with electronic systems, robots, or, alternatively, low-cost human labor. Thus, the Information Revolution, while in one sense improving the lot of everyone, like the Industrial Revolution, will create fortunes for some and prolong the misfortunes of others. But in America, it will be easier than ever to start a business, due to the distributed nature of capital, technology, and intelligence.

Culturally, dramatic changes lie ahead due to the advance of technology. Virtual reality may become the new opiate of the masses, and temperance groups may urge its severe regulation. But on balance, the United States will be uniquely poised to benefit from the electronic cultural revolution. With its large and diverse population, it will be both a market for new cultural ideas—in music, video, and writing—and a source of them. In contrast, European culture, while it too will benefit from new technologies and from the single European market, will remain somewhat fragmented along lines of language and nationality. Japan will possess the critical mass, as a market, to reward cultural expression. However, its comparative homogeneity and language will limit export potential.

Those best prepared for the coming American Renaissance will reap the greatest rewards. To stay ahead, Americans must continue to educate themselves, locate in low-cost areas, and earn money in higher-cost ones. It will pay to start a business, since job security will continue to diminish. Those who work for a living will face ever-increasing competition from low-wage countries and the evolving skills of computers themselves. Prospering in the future will take work, but those who make the right decisions now will live well, and many will become rich. Indeed, historically, the greatest fortunes have always been made with new technologies in periods of rapid change. Blessed with a legacy of technological advantages and the ability to create and use new technologies, America today and for the foreseeable future will lead the world into the next millennium.

Notes

INTRODUCTION

1. On *Rush Limbaugh* television show, March 10, 1995.
2. On *Meet the Press,* as quoted in "Budget Cuts Spark Bitter Battle," Associated Press, February 26, 1995.

CHAPTER 1:
From Prosperity to Prophecies of Doom in Postwar America

1. For a broad canvas of thirty-two countries during this period (and others) see Angus Madison, *The World Economy in the 20th Century* (Paris: Organization for Economic Cooperation and Development, 1989).
2. Ibid.
3. U.S. Department of Labor, *Monthly Labor Review,* November 1993 (Washington, D.C.: U.S. Government Printing Office, 1993), p. 7.
4. It is also widely believed that the increasing role of services in the economy has skewed overall productivity growth numbers downward. Numbers measuring productivity growth in services appear to fail to reflect quality improvements. For example, supermarkets showed little or no productivity growth during the period when scanners and electronic methods of controlling inventory were introduced, in part due to the introduction of new services such as pharmacies and gourmet delis as supermarkets began to compete on quality. Productivity figures also exclude the role of software. Finally, real growth would be higher if inflation numbers were adjusted downward, as many economists including Federal Reserve Board Chairman Alan Greenspan argue they should be. For a further discussion of difficulties in measuring productivity, see *The Economic Report of the President* 1995 (Washington, D.C.: Government Printing Office, 1995), pp. 110–13.
5. Ronald Reagan's Misery Index (inflation plus unemployment), introduced during the 1980 presidential campaign, was a crude measure of stagflation.

6. Donella H. Meadows, Dennis L. Meadows, Jorgen Randers, and William W. Behrens III, *The Limits to Growth: A Report for the Club of Rome's Project on the Predicament of Mankind* (New York: Universe Books, 1972).

7. The World Bank, *World Development Report, 1991* (New York: Oxford University Press, 1991).

8. An assassination attempt less than two months after the inauguration helped Reagan move his agenda.

9. See Paul Krugman, *Peddling Prosperity: Economic Sense and Nonsense in the Age of Diminished Expectations* (New York: W. W. Norton, 1994), pp. 130–50.

10. Given the proven ability of the Soviet government to force people to tighten their belts, it still surprises many observers that the USSR capitulated to the West. A fairly strong argument can be made that its capitulation owes much to Mikhail Gorbachev's personal interest in market reforms. Alternatively, some argue that the Soviet system would have collapsed without a U.S. military buildup. Regardless, it is clear that the U.S. military buildup, by forcing the Soviet Union to beef up its military spending, added to the strain on the Soviet economy.

11. An alternative, conservative point of view holds that increased social spending starved expenditure on infrastructure. Given that both social spending, primarily on programs for the old, and defense spending increased after 1980, it is only common sense to conclude that both crowded out infrastructure spending.

12. The product life cycle theory of Professor Ray Vernon at Harvard University provided theoretical and academic underpinnings for versions of this thinking that appeared in popular business media.

13. The Japanese sought out product groups with export potential, a steep learning curve such that high production volumes would lead to lower prices, and high demand elasticity so that, as manufacturing volume increased and unit costs dropped, overseas markets would hungrily devour as much or as many of the product as they could make.

14. Rather than subject the world economy to a deep recession, Western countries decided to "monetize" the problem by taking steps to increase the money supply, causing inflation.

15. The G-7 countries did try to stem the dollar's drop with the Louvre Accord in 1987, but the accord proved ineffective.

16. While in theory a cheaper currency will raise exports and de-

crease imports, exceptions to this rule abound. Great Britain, for example, steadily devalued the pound in the 1970s, but its balance of trade showed little improvement.

17. Japanese investment in the United States was an obvious way to combat trade tensions created by the high U.S.–Japanese trade deficit and to cope with the rising yen.

18. Taylor, the first management consultant, was a Phillips Exeter– and Harvard Law–trained engineer who, after falling ill, on the advice of his doctors, left Harvard to become an apprentice in a machine shop. He worked his way up and began experimenting with new ways of production. Because Taylor was an advocate of relentlessly improving efficiency, he became an enemy of unions (though he was admired by Lenin). Congressman William B. Wilson, who would later become America's first Labor Secretary, invited him to testify before Congress. Taylor took great pains to say that his method of "scientific management" was not just the use of time and motion studies. Nevertheless, it involved carefully analyzing processes to improve productivity. Despite the degree to which modern consultants disparage Taylorism, he combined practicality with evangelism and was probably quite similar to modern management gurus.

19. Lester Thurow, *Head to Head* (New York: Morrow, 1992), p. 130.

20. One can make a strong argument from the standpoint of economic development that encouraging capital-intensive facilities such as semiconductor plants in places like Indonesia is a bad idea compared with encouraging labor-intensive facilities there (which give more people jobs and in which poor countries have a competitive advantage). The move of countries such as Indonesia into semiconductors and advanced technologies, nonetheless, offered support for the idea of convergence.

21. George Gilder, *Wealth and Poverty* (New York: Basic Books, 1981).

CHAPTER 2:
America's Core Advantages

1. John Fiske, *American Political Ideas* (New York: Harper & Brothers, 1885).

2. Economists call this problem the Dutch disease after the experience of the Netherlands following the discovery of North Sea oil.

An abundance of one commodity, such as oil or gold, can over-whelm a smaller economy, rendering the rest of its economy non-competitive by raising the exchange rate and lifting wages and the cost of many inputs beyond what other sectors can afford to pay.

3. Joseph Spiers, "The Bright Outlook for Housing Prices," *Fortune,* November 14, 1994, p. 74.

4. While the United States benefited in its early years from its proximity to Europe via the Atlantic, it actually *caused* the develop-ment of the Pacific Rim. All of the Pacific Rim superstars, from Japan to Korea to China, rose up, in part, due to their easy access to the American market via the Pacific.

5. Much of the recent gain by the Japanese GDP on the U.S. GDP in dollar terms has been due to the strength of the yen. Whereas Japanese per capita GDP exceeded the U.S. level by 44 percent in 1994, the U.S. per capita GDP using purchasing power parities exceeded Japan's by 23 percent, according to OECD figures.

6. The historical literature on this subject is rich and conclusive. For example, in his classic work *Religion and the Rise of Capitalism* (1926), Richard Henry Tawney wrote, "Between classes, there must be inequality; for otherwise class cannot perform its function, or—a strange thought to us—enjoy its rights." The rights accorded to even members of the lower economic classes have the perverse effect of limiting mobility.

7. The U.S. worker turnover rate is 4 percent per month; that in Japan, 3.5 percent per *year*; see Ronald Henkoff and James Rank, "Where Will the Jobs Come From?," *Fortune,* October 19, 1992, p. 58.

8. *Employment Performance* (Washington, D.C.: McKinsey Global In-stitute, November 1994), exhibit 5.

9. Michael Moynihan, "European Attitudes and Jobs," unpublished article, pp. 4–5; see also Richard D. Vine, "Note from the Director General," *Newsletter* (Paris: Atlantic Institute for International Af-fairs, July 1985), p. 1.

10. It is not our domestic production of oil that makes gas cheaper here. Norway produces a higher percentage of its oil needs than the United States does, but the prices of petroleum products are far higher there. Moreover, there is an international market in oil. Gas is cheaper in the United States primarily for political reasons: taxes on petroleum products are far lower here than in other countries.

11. Jaclyn Fierman, "Winning Ideas from Maverick Managers,"

Fortune, February 6, 1995, p. 80. Such treatment is typical of that of the European establishment toward entrepreneurs.

12. Edwin O. Reischauer, *The Japanese* (Tokyo: Tuttle, 1979), p. 165.

13. Wall Street interests did not entirely oppose the creation of the ICC. While price fixing was J. P. Morgan's preferred method of limiting competition, he viewed government regulation as preferable to price wars and excessive competition. See Ron Chernow, *The House of Morgan* (New York: Atlantic Monthly Press, 1990), p. 56.

14. Chinese expatriates, known as China's *nanyang* or nineteenth province, have long played an important role in business throughout Southeast Asia. In Burma, it was common before the nationalization of industry, to refer to going to a moneylender as "going to the turtle," since the Chinese character for a moneylender resembled a turtle.

15. William Echikson, "A New Vision of Europe's Job Woes," *Fortune,* February 6, 1995, p. 15. See also *Employment Performance* (Washington, D.C.: McKinsey Global Institute, November 1994), retailing section.

16. For detailed information on country regulations, see the Economist Intelligence Unit's *Investing, Licensing and Trade* series of publications.

17. *OECD Economic Surveys 1994, United States* (Paris: Organization for Economic Cooperation and Development, 1994), p. 15.

18. Other measures show an even steeper fall. In fiscal year 1994, procurement spending of $45 billion represented a 67 percent reduction in constant dollars, compared with the high-water mark for procurement in 1985; see Keith G. Morrison, "Are Dual Technologies Taking Hold in Industry?," research paper prepared for the Center for Science and International Affairs, John F. Kennedy School of Government, Harvard University, 1994.

19. Robert Eisner, "We Don't Need Balanced Budgets," *The Wall Street Journal,* January 11, 1995, p. A-14.

20. Robert D. Hershey, Jr., "Another Year of Little Rise in Inflation," *The New York Times,* January 12, 1995, p. D-1.

21. Jean-Jacques Servan-Schreiber, *The American Challenge* (New York: Atheneum, 1968), p. 4.

22. Multinational companies still play games with pricing to shift income to low-cost countries.

23. Securities Data Corporation, quoted in "1994 Year-end Review

of Markets and Finance," *The Wall Street Journal,* January 3, 1995, p. R-38.

24. *Investment Dealer's Digest,* telephone interview with the author, February 1996.

25. Robert J. Kunze, *Nothing Ventured: The Perils and Payoffs of the Great American Venture Capital Game* (New York: HarperBusiness, 1990), p. 247.

26. Jagdish Bhagwati and Milind Rao, "Foreign Students Spur U.S. Brain Gain," *The Wall Street Journal,* August 31, 1994, p. A-12.

27. In physics, chemistry, physiology or medicine, and economics, *World Competitiveness Report: 1994* (Lausanne: World Economic Forum and IMD, 1994), p. 545.

28. *OECD Economic Surveys 1994, United States* (Paris: Organization for Economic Cooperation and Development, 1994), p. 136.

29. The act, sponsored by Congressman Justin Morrill of Vermont, gave 30,000 acres of federal land per congressman to states to sell to create or subsidize universities. While a few private colleges such as MIT in Massachusetts received funds, most went to create new state universities. In 1890, Congress gave more federal funds to the state institutions.

30. U.S. Bureau of the Census, 1993 *Census* (Washington, D.C.: U.S. Department of Commerce, 1994), table 234.

31. William Johnson and Arnold Packer, *Workforce 2000* (Indianapolis: Hudson Institute, 1987).

32. "Workforce 2005: The Future of Jobs in the United States and Europe," *OECD Societies in Transition: The Future of Work and Leisure* (Paris: Organization for Economic Cooperation and Development, 1994), p. 52.

33. Thomas Sowell, *Inside American Education* (New York: Macmillan, 1992), p. 303.

34. *Report of the Federal Government on Research 1993,* abridged English version (Bonn, Germany: Federal Ministry for Research and Technology, 1993), p. 44.

35. Ibid., pp. 108–10.

36. *Bundesbericht Forschung 1993* (Bonn, Germany: Bundesministerium für Forschung und Technologie, 1993), p. 608.

37. Michael Moynihan, *The World Market Atlas* (New York: Business International Corporation, 1992), p. 78.

38. Rick Atkinson, "In Germany, Another Wall Is Coming Down; Nation Hopes Sale of State Phone Monopoly Will Open Markets and Profit Opportunities," *The Washington Post,* February 5, 1995, p. H-1.

39. *OECD 1994 Economic Survey of the United States,* p. 13.

40. In 1995, the U.S. government began to report productivity growth using a new "chain-weighted" system that has lowered numbers since 1987, relative to its old system of measurement. While the old system may have overstated productivity growth, critics of the new system such as Stephen Roach of Morgan Stanley argue that the new measure grossly understates productivity growth. For consistency and because I believe the new numbers understate productivity growth, I have used the old numbers throughout the text.

41. David P. Hamilton, "Technology (A Special Report): A New World; Restricted Access; Japan Lacks a Homegrown Version of the Internet," *The Wall Street Journal,* November 15, 1993, p. R-18.

42. Richard L. Hudson, "Europe Lingers in the Wake of US Multimedia Might," *The Wall Street Journal,* November 2, 1993, p. B-4.

43. An Oxford graduate, Tim Berners-Lee, is widely credited with inventing the World Wide Web in 1989 while at CERN.

44. Lester Thurow, *Head to Head* (New York: Morrow, 1992), p. 113.

CHAPTER 3:
The Brave New Workplace

1. Gates did not develop Microsoft's software himself but purchased the "quick and dirty operating system," or QDOS, from a programmer named Tim Paterson for the reported sum of $75,000. When MS-DOS became a hit, Paterson sued and later won a $1 million settlement.

2. During this period, the company's revenues fell by half, but its earnings and stock price soared as the firm fought off bankruptcy; see Tim Smart, "A Lot of the Weaknesses Carbide Had Are Behind It," *Business Week,* January 23, 1995, p. 83.

3. Capital assets are inherently fungible. In contrast, people retain strong ethnic identities and face language and other barriers. Thus, international alliances of unions have proven extremely fragile.

4. By contrast, in recent years, New York has admitted approximately 150,000 legal immigrants annually. See *1994 Statistical Abstract of the United States* (Washington, D.C.: U.S. Government Printing Office, 1994), p. 12.

5. As estimated by Richard D. Rippe, chief economist of Prudential Securities in Michael J. Mandel, "Plumper Profits, Skimpier Paychecks," *Business Week,* January 30, 1995, p. 87.

6. Gene Koretz "Downside to the Jobs Upturn," *Business Week,* November 14, 1995, p. 26.

7. Government statistics, as quoted in "Why the Cry for Tax Relief?," *Business Week,* January 23, 1995, p. 30.

8. American Mover's Conference, telephone interview, January 1996.

9. Labor markets have always been global in a sense. Chinese and Irish workers, for example, were imported to build America's railroads; Turkish workers drive buses in Germany. Electronic networks will simply expedite the process. As with most things electronic, from storefronts to ledgers to calculators, they will advance previously invented practices.

10. Susan Hightower, Associated Press, July 9, 1995.

11. Michael Moynihan, *Global Consumer Demographics* (New York: Business International, 1991), pp. 237–39; U.S. Department of Labor, *Monthly Labor Review,* November 1993, p. 28.

12. *Monthly Labor Review,* U.S. Department of Labor, November 1993, p. 38.

13. To some extent, baby boomers will always face more competition than other people as they make their way up in the workforce, and they may always exert some competitive pressure on one another's wages. Nevertheless, as they age and accumulate skills, their greater level of experience will justify higher wages.

14. Ronald Henkoff and Ann Sample,"Service Is Everybody's Business," *Fortune,* June 27, 1994, p. 56.

15. Steven Pearlstein, "What's the Speed Limit on Economic Growth? Technology, Labor Trends Spur Debate on Whether the Accepted 2.5% Ceiling is Outdated," *The Washington Post,* January 15, 1995, p. H-1.

16. Myron Magnet and Ani Hadjian, "The Productivity Payoff Arrives," *Fortune,* June 27, 1994, p. 80.

17. Ibid., p. 79. See also *1994 Statistical Abstract of the United States,* "Productivity and Related Measures: 1970 to 1993," p. 426.

18. Sylvia Nasar, "The United States Economy: Back in the Driver's Seat," *The New York Times,* February 27, 1994, pp. 3–6.

19. *Manufacturing Productivity* (Washington, D.C.: McKinsey Global Institute, October 1993), synthesis, pp. 3ff.; *Service Sector Productivity* (Washington, D.C.: McKinsey Global Institute, October 1992), synthesis, pp. 1ff.

20. In an op-ed piece discussing the studies, "The Secret to Competitiveness," *The Wall Street Journal,* October 22, 1993, p. A-15.

CHAPTER 4:
A Renaissance in the Production of Goods

1. After leaving this business in 1985, Motorola returned, primarily through the vehicle of a joint venture with Toshiba, located in Japan. Motorola supplied some microprocessor technology in exchange for access to Toshiba's DRAM technology.

2. For a thorough discussion of the global semiconductor business during the 1980s, including an analysis of the effects of the 1986 Semiconductor Trade Agreement, see Laura D'Andrea Tyson and David B. Yoffie, "Semiconductors: From Manipulated to Managed Trade," in *Beyond Free Trade*, David B. Yoffie, ed. (Boston: Harvard Business School Press, 1993), pp. 29–78.

3. Yields at the beginning of manufacture can be considerably less, yields in a mature process somewhat higher, through a process called ramping up.

4. IBM had previously forced Intel to license its CPU design to others to ensure a second source for its PC; however, aggressive licensing also helped Intel to make its chip a standard.

5. Industry lore has it that U.S. executives including Motorola founder Bob Galvin met with Japanese executives before the agreement and demanded that they receive access; otherwise they threatened to bring multiple trade actions. Japanese executives reportedly answered, "You can have Toyota or Nissan, but not both." Motorola reportedly chose Toyota, which began to "design in" Motorola chips in cars, creating a long-term partnership.

6. South Korean chip makers are still well behind in technology, even for DRAMs. In 1994, the top three chip makers, Samsung Electronics, Hyundai, and LG Semiconductor, paid royalties of $422 million, or 4.9 percent of their sales, to other firms, a figure they fear will only increase in subsequent chip generations though Samsung has licensed technology to Intel. See article (in Korean) in *Chonja Sinmum*, February 17, 1994.

7. In a time-honored tradition that dates from the beginning of the silicon industry, U.S. firms remain active in high-volume, older-technology products as a "technology driver" to educate the firm about how to obtain larger yields. Only by honing their manufacturing techniques on high-volume chips can firms hope to transfer this knowledge to the manufacture of more intricate and more expensive logical microprocessors such as CPUs.

8. Although originally blocked from fulfilling orders this way by music companies, which feared for their and their authors' royalties, IBM and Blockbuster have said they will go ahead in specialized segments.

9. One interesting fact about U.S. versus Japanese carmakers: since cars were invented, U.S. production has risen and fallen with the business cycle while Japan's has not. Between 1937 and 1938, U.S. production dropped by a third. It dropped by a quarter between 1979 and 1980. And it dropped by 20 percent between 1988 and 1992. In contrast, Japan's production has never dropped by more than 3 percent during its history. This reflects the U.S. pursuit of profits and the Japanese pursuit of market share. U.S. firms have been far more profitable than Japanese ones.

10. Ford estimate, quoted in Douglas Lavin and Audrey Choi, "A New Export Power in the Auto Industry? It's North America," *The Wall Street Journal*, October 18, 1993, p. A-1.

11. While *Motor Trend* is widely considered an objective source, auto magazines differ as to their conclusions. *Automobile* magazine, for example, called the Aurora "not a contender" in its all-star catalog (February 1995, p. 47). Nevertheless, there is no question that U.S. cars have improved dramatically; in 1994, of twelve all-stars chosen by *Automobile*, six were made by U.S. or U.S.-owned companies (e.g., Jaguar, now owned by Ford), four were Japanese, and two were European.

12. "USA vs. the World," *Motor Trend*, Special Section, February 1995, p. 35.

13. B. J. Killeen and Scott Killeen, "Long Term Update," *Motor Trend*, March 1995, p. 135.

14. Valerie Reitman, "Designer Potholes: Japanese Gladly Pay for a Bumpy Ride," *The Wall Street Journal*, September 5, 1995, p. A-1.

15. Paul Ingrassia, Douglas Lavin, "Neon May Be Bright Light for Chrysler," *The Wall Street Journal*, April 23, 1993, p. B-1.

16. "USA vs. the World," p. 66.

17. Cliff Gromer, "The New Age of the Electric Car," *Popular Mechanics*, February 1994, p. 38.

18. *U.S. Industrial Outlook, 1994: An Almanac of Industry, Technology and Services*, 35th ed. (Washington, D.C.: U.S. Department of Commerce, 1994), p. 35–22.

19. The auto-parts firms don't merely service the U.S. market, of course. The bigger ones sell and manufacture all over the world. In early 1995, Monroe, a division of Tenneco, opened a plant making

shocks and struts in Mexico to service Chrysler, Nissan, and Dina, Mexico's largest maker of trucks and buses. GenCorp believes its greatest opportunities lie in Asia. And even GM's parts subsidiary, Delphi Automotive Systems, a $26 billion enterprise, has begun selling in China and India.

20. Gates denies that this was a factor. In a 1993 interview, he said, "The idea that IBM came to us because it feared the Justice Department didn't have a damned thing to do with it. That's bad history"; Rich Karlgaard, "On the Road with Bill Gates," *Forbes ASAP*, February 28, 1994, p. 77.

21. IBM did hold on to the standard for its BIOS, forcing early clones to steal it or work around it. The introduction of a fully compatible third-party BIOS by Phoenix removed the last major barrier to clones making Taiwanese machines, for example, legal.

22. Adherence to a software standard that software developers will support has emerged as a critical factor in hardware success. The Macintosh almost didn't make it. Computers from Commodore, Atari, Next, and others flopped when customers shied away from their lack of software.

23. Jim Carlton, "Apple Is Launching Improved Version of MessagePad Hand-Held Computer," *The Wall Street Journal*, January 30, 1995, p. B-3.

24. International Data Corporation, company reports, published in "Quantum Makes Great Leaps in Disk-Drive Industry; Once a Second-Tier Player, Company Now Commands 23% Market Share," *The Wall Street Journal*, December 28, 1994, p. B-4.

25. Neil Gross and Peter Coy, "The Technology Paradox," *Business Week*, March 6, 1995, p. 76.

26. Peter Coy and Neil Gross, "Telecom: Can the Old Guard Switch Gear?," *Business Week*, March 6, 1995, p. 76.

27. Author analysis using data supplied by Dataquest.

28. Stephen Kreider Yoder, "How HP Used Tactics of the Japanese to Beat Them at Their Game," *The Wall Street Journal*, September 8, 1994, p. 1.

29. Not including office computers. Including office computers, computer expenditure has long surpassed that on televisions; see Neil Gross and Peter Coy, "The Technology Paradox," *Business Week*, March 6, 1995, p. 76.

30. Donna Rosato, "South Korean Firm Buys Zenith, U.S. TV Maker," *USA Today*, July 18, 1995, p. A-1.

31. Susan Carey, "South Korean Company Seeks Control of Zenith,

Last of the U.S. TV Makers," *The Wall Street Journal,* July 18, 1995, p. A-3.

32. "South Carolina Not Ready to Concede Nucor Inc. Steel Mill to Virginia," *The Virginian-Pilot,* February 20, 1995, downloaded from Knight Ridder/Tribune News Service.

33. *U.S. Industrial Outlook, 1994,* p. 13-2.

34. Daniel Machalaba, "Rail-Car Builders Gather Steam as Train Traffic Booms," *The Wall Street Journal,* May 11, 1994, p. B-4; Daniel Machalaba, "Railroads Face Unfamiliar Problem: Too Little Capacity," *The Wall Street Journal,* May 31, 1994, p. B-4.

35. *US Industrial Outlook, 1994,* p. 40-5.

36. "AMT Industry Estimates, December, 1994"; handout provided to the author by the The Association for Manufacturing Technology, January 1995.

37. As quoted in Rajn Narisetti, "Machine-Tool Orders Jumped 27% in December," *The Wall Street Journal,* January 31, 1995, p. B-6B.

38. Keith G. Morrison, "Are Dual Use Technologies Taking Hold in Industry?," unpublished research paper prepared for the Center for Science and International Affairs, John F. Kennedy School of Government, Harvard University, Boston, May 1994.

39. Stephanie Anderson, "Who's Afraid of J&J and 3M?," *Business Week,* December 5, 1995, p. 66.

CHAPTER 5:
The Continuing Boom in Services

1. Jacqueline M. Graves, "Building a Fortune on Free Data," *Fortune,* February 6, 1995, p. 66.

2. *Manufacturing Productivity* (Washington, D.C.: McKinsey Global Institute, October 1993), synthesis, pp. 3ff., and *Service Sector Productivity* (Washington, D.C.: McKinsey Global Institute, October 1992), synthesis, pp. 1ff.

3. The company chose to give up this guarantee after court judgments against it followed traffic deaths involving Domino's drivers.

4. A large number of employees have, however, gone on to own McDonald's franchises, and McDonald's has proved to be a ladder of mobility for African Americans who now own 12 percent of its franchises. See Jonathan Kaufman, "A Break Today; A McDonald's Owner Becomes a Role Model for Black Teenagers," *The Wall Street Journal,* August 23, 1995, p. A-1.

5. A full treatment of this issue should include a discussion of elasticity. Demand for music and entertainment, for example, is fairly elastic: as prices rise, purchases slow; as prices drop, they increase. In contrast, for obvious reasons, the demand elasticity for doctors is very low. People in need will pay almost anything for a top doctor.

6. After World War II, a large number of jobs teaching English in Japan were given to Japanese Communists.

7. Gabriella Stern, "Major Overhaul: Car Dealerships Seem About to be Combined into Big Retail Chains," *The Wall Street Journal,* February 10, 1995, p. A-1.

8. Steven Brill, "Japan's Latest Import: Retail Culture," *International Herald Tribune,* February 2, 1995.

9. Marcia Berss, " 'We Will Not Be in a National Chain,' " *Forbes,* March 27, 1995, p. 50.

10. Ani Hadjian, "He Wants You to Eat Fish Tacos," *Fortune,* March 20, 1995, p. 31.

11. Howard Rudnitsky, "Leaner Cuisine," *Forbes,* March 27, 1995, p. 43.

12. Leo Troy, "The Rise and Fall of American Trade Unions," in *Unions in Transition: Entering the Second Century,* Seymour Martin Lipset, ed. (San Francisco: ICS Press, 1986), p. 87.

13. Ellen James Martin, column dated January 30, 1994, for the Universal Press Syndicate.

14. Russell Mitchell, "PG&E: One Step Ahead of Future Shock," *Business Week,* November 14, 1995, p. 68.

15. Allanna Sullivan, "Mobil Bets Drivers Pick Cappuccino over Low Prices," *The Wall Street Journal,* January 31, 1995, p. B-1.

CHAPTER 6:
Cyberspace and the Information Superhighway

1. Russell Mitchell, "Safe Passage in Cyberspace," *Business Week,* March 20, 1995, p. 33.

2. Edmund L. Andrews and Joel Brinkley, "The Fight for Digital TV's Future," *The New York Times,* January 22, 1995, sec. 3, p. 1.

3. Jeff Goodell, "The Supreme Court," *Wired,* March 1995, p. 121.

4. Russell Mitchell, "Safe Passage in Cyberspace," *Business Week,* March 20, 1995, p. 33.

5. The fate of Atari and Commodore, both makers of computers as

well as video games, is instructive. Both firms held on to proprietary systems. Despite the high quality of their systems—Atari's Amiga won wide favor among early multimedia devotees—they lost the standards race, could not get third-party developers to write enough software, and eventually left the PC business. In video games, Nintendo and Sega gained market share by selling game players for less, whittling down the U.S. companies' bases until they could no longer get third-party developers to write leading games for their platforms. (Atari remains active in video games.) Apple alone among the early PC companies was able to survive because, with its Macintosh operating system, it reached a critical mass.

6. Joan E. Rigdon, "CyberSource Begins to Offer Software of Symantec and Others on the Internet," *The Wall Street Journal,* January 31, 1995, p. B-6.

7. Industry wags often observe that had Apple licensed out the Macintosh operating system years ago, it might have secured all of Microsoft's current revenues and won the race for computer standards. Indeed, Gates is said to have suggested the idea to Apple. Only when it demurred did he proceed to develop Windows. Apple subsequently sued Microsoft (as well as Hewlett-Packard), claiming it had stolen the look of its program, but lost its suit in early 1995.

8. G. Christian Hill, "Sellers of Unix Systems Adopt Standard in Bid to Fight Off Microsoft's Advance," *The Wall Street Journal,* March 13, 1995, p. B-6.

9. Peter H. Lewis, "Peering Out a 'Real Time' Window," *The New York Times,* February 8, 1995, p. D-1. Information on the Mbone is also available on the Rolling Stones Mbone page on the Web, "http://www.stones.com/mbone/."

10. For example, AT&T is now trying to strike an alliance with France Telecom and Deutsche Telekom. MCI, meanwhile, has formed an alliance with British Telecom. USWest has struck a deal with a British firm to form a network in London.

11. As quoted in David Kline, "Savvy Sassa," *Wired,* March 1995, p. 113.

12. As quoted in Ralph T. King, Jr., "Microsoft Signs Up On-Line Vendors," *The Wall Street Journal,* February 8, 1995, p. B-6.

13. Gregory A. Patterson, "Spiegel and Time Warner to Scale Back Cable Shopping Venture, Use Internet," *The Wall Street Journal,* January 30, 1995, p. B-6.

14. Poll conducted by Frank Luntz for the Hudson Institute, cited

in Gerald F. Seib, "Politics and Policy," *The Wall Street Journal,* August 31, 1994, p. A-14.

CHAPTER 7:
Where the Renaissance Will Occur

1. The biggest question mark in making demographic predictions is migration. While fertility rates may change for any number of reasons, existing age patterns are generally an excellent predictor of new births. In the U.S. context, however, immigration poses a large problem to demographers. For a further discussion of these issues, see U.S. Bureau of the Census, Current Population Reports, *Projections of the Population of States by Age, Sex and Race: 1989 to 2010 (P25/1053)* (Washington, D.C.: U.S. Department of Commerce, 1990), pp. 6–10.

2. While good data on which parts of the country are doing what are available from the Commerce Department's Bureau of Economic Analysis and from the Bureau of the Census, they are not readily accessible to the public. Urban Decision Systems has converted the government data tapes into PC format, matched categories that have changed over time, and projected figures through 2005.

3. Oscar Suris, "Dirty Driving: Clean Air Deadlines Pull Clunker Vehicles into Inspection Line," *The Wall Street Journal,* August 17, 1994, p. A-1.

4. *Population Projections for States by Age, Sex, Race and Hispanic Origin: 1992 to 2020 (P25/1111)* (Washington, D.C.: U.S. Department of Commerce, 1994).

5. Michael Selz, "More Businesses Set Up Shop in Western US," *The Wall Street Journal,* May 23, 1994, p. B-1.

6. "Projections Show More Growth for South and West, Less for Northeast and Midwest," *Census* (Washington, D.C., U.S. Department of Commerce), vol. 29, no. 5 (May 1994), p. 1.

7. A number of economic theories underlie the theory of clusters. Among them: in a crowded cluster, actors throw off "externalities," or goods for free, that benefit their neighbors. And agglomeration economies, as they are called, benefit from the fact that information is a nonconsumable resource that is easily disseminated and able to multiply within a cluster.

8. Orange County is home to the University of North Carolina at Chapel Hill and adjacent to Duke.

9. Tompkins County is home to Cornell University.

10. Eastman, who was childless, gave $100 million, or $1 billion in today's dollars, to the university, other schools, and hospitals. See Milt Freudenheim, "A Doting Uncle Cuts Back and a City Feels the Pain," *The New York Times,* October 8, 1995, p. B-1.

11. While MIT, which is private, is a land-grant college, most of the land-grant schools are public.

12. One of the big myths of conservative ideologues is that hightech businesses flourish in opposition to government regulation. In fact, an astonishingly large percentage of them get their start from government subsidies. These include government subsidies of the original research at universities, of the professors at universities who found firms, and of space in research parks; in addition, they include state and federal grants for high-tech projects, as well as government purchasing arrangements.

13. Annalee Saxenian, "Lessons from Silicon Valley," *Technology Review,* July 1994, p. 44.

14. Kenneth Labich, "The Geography of an Emerging America," *Fortune,* June 27, 1994, p. 94.

15. Jeffrey Young, "Jewel of the Rockies," *Forbes ASAP,* pp. 23–24.

CHAPTER 8:
Looking at the Twenty-first Century

1. The debate on multiculturalism is rich and varied, but a lengthy examination of its history can be found in Michael Lind, *The Next American Nation* (New York: The Free Press, 1995).

2. After the completion of the transcontinental railroad, for example, the Southern Pacific Railroad Company dominated California politics for forty years.

Index

About the Author

Michael Moynihan is a senior policy advisor within the U.S. Department of the Treasury. Previously, he was a consultant to the World Bank in the office of the vice president for environmentally sustainable development and senior technology advisor within the U.S. Department of Commerce, where he provided advice on technology policy and studied capital availability for research and development.

As a senior consultant for the Economist Intelligence Unit, he advised Fortune 500 clients on technology strategy and market trends and authored nine books on such business and management topics as total quality management (TQM), market trends, and managing human resources across borders. While at the Economist Intelligence Unit, he developed the concept of strategic technology leveraging (STL) as a way for companies to manage their portfolio of technology alliances and, in partnership with Arthur D. Little, coauthored the book *Leveraging Technology in the New Global Company*. Mr. Moynihan has written for *Harper's, The Washington Post*, and other publications.

Mr. Moynihan was the Robert C. Seamans Fellow in Technology and Public Policy while at the John F. Kennedy School of Government at Harvard University, and holds degrees from Columbia College and Harvard University.

He lives in Washington, D.C.